Nebraska
Symposium on
Motivation
1985

Volume 33

University of Nebraska Press
Lincoln and London 1986

Nebraska Symposium on Motivation 1985

The Law as a Behavioral Instrument

Richard A. Dienstbier   *Series Editor*

Gary B. Melton   *Volume Editor*

Presenters

Laura Nader   *Professor of Anthropology*
University of California, Berkeley

Stephen J. Morse   *Orrin B. Evans Professor of Law,*
Professor of Psychology, and Professor of
Psychiatry and the Behavioral Sciences
University of Southern California

Jack P. Gibbs   *Centennial Professor of Sociology*
Vanderbilt University

Richard J. Bonnie   *Professor of Law and Director of the*
Institute of Law, Psychiatry and Public
Policy
University of Virginia

Stanley L. Brodsky

Gary B. Melton

Michael J. Saks

Professor of Psychology
University of Alabama
Professor of Psychology and
Law and Director of the
Law/Psychology Program
University of Nebraska–Lincoln
Associate Professor of Psychology and
Adjunct Professor of Law
Boston College

*Nebraska Symposium on
Motivation, 1985,* is Volume 33
in the series on
CURRENT THEORY AND
RESEARCH IN MOTIVATION

Copyright 1986 by the University of Nebraska Press
All rights reserved
Manufactured in the United States of America
International Standard Book Number 0-8032-3100-8 (Clothbound)
International Standard Book Number 0-8032-8132-3 (Paperbound)

The paper in this book meets the minimum requirements of American National Standard for Information Sciences–Permanence of Paper for Printed Library Materials, ANSI Z39.48-1984.

"The Library of Congress has cataloged this serial publication as follows:"
Nebraska Symposium on Motivation.
   Nebraska Symposium on Motivation. [Papers] v. [1]–1953–
   Lincoln, University of Nebraska Press.
      v. illus., diagrs. 22 cm. annual.
   Vol. 1 issued by the symposium under its earlier name: Current Theory and Research in Motivation.
   Symposia sponsored by the Dept. of Psychology of the University of Nebraska.

   1. Motivation (Psychology)

BF683.N4   159.4082   53-11655

Library of Congress

Preface

*T*he topic of the current volume of the *Nebraska Sym-
posium on Motivation* can be
simply stated as how the law affects people. Although the various
facets of such a general topic cannot be fully addressed in a single
volume, the range of answers found herein suggests the diversity
of possible responses and reflects the scope of the area of Law/
Psychology.

It is particularly appropriate that this volume was developed during the tenth anniversary of the founding of our Law/Psychology
Program at the University of Nebraska–Lincoln by the able head of
that program, Professor Gary B. Melton. It has been a pleasure to
work with Professor Melton both in his role as volume editor and as
the leader of our Law/Psychology Program.

The Symposium series is supported largely by funds donated in
the memory of Professor Harry K. Wolfe to the University of Nebraska Foundation by the late Professor Cora L. Friedline. This Symposium volume, like those of the recent past, is dedicated to the
memory of Professor Wolfe, who brought psychology to the University of Nebraska. After studying with Professor Wilhelm Wundt,
Professor Wolfe returned to this, his native state, to establish the
first undergraduate laboratory of psychology in the nation. As a student at Nebraska, Professor Friedline studied psychology under
Professor Wolfe. The editors are grateful to the late Professor Friedline for her bequest and to the officers of the University of Nebraska
Foundation for their continued interest in and support of this series.

RICHARD A. DIENSTBIER
Series Editor

Contents

Foreword

Harvey S. Perlman

Dean, University of Nebraska College of Law

"Interdisciplinary" has become a watchword within universities in the past two decades. It symbolizes the realization that the world is in fact "interdisciplinary"—that persons do not separate out the psychological, economic, moral, or legal aspects of their lives into cubicles resembling the modern university organization. Individuals act or react in response to numerous contemporaneous stimuli, each of which in turn interacts with the others. There is much to be gained by isolating each stimulus for closer examination, but there is much to be said for also looking at them in combination.

This publication of the proceedings of the annual Nebraska Symposium on Motivation celebrates not only the 33rd anniversary of the Symposium but also the 10th anniversary of the University of Nebraska Law/Psychology program. The program at its inception was designed to provide students with the opportunity to obtain both a PhD in psychology and a JD in law through a coordinated curriculum and also to create an environment for faculty of both disciplines to interact to mutual advantage.

Forging two disciplines together is not without its difficulties, given differences in language, methodology, data base, and basic assumptions. That the two faculties are still speaking to each other is some sign at least of acceptance. That this Symposium is devoted to "The Law as a Behavioral Instrument" is some measure that the interaction can be a fruitful one.

The title of the Symposium is, as it should be, a declarative statement and not a question. Law is a behavioral instrument; few think otherwise. But one becomes less certain if one tries to explain the causal relationship between law and behavior or to predict the response to a legal stimulus.

During the past decade the views of economists on the behavioral consequences of legal regulation have had a significant impact on legal analysis. The discipline of psychology has lagged far behind. The "rational utility maximizer," for many legal scholars, has defined the behavioral assumptions of legal engineering. The teachings of psychology have offered some insight relative to a much narrower slice of the legal world.

There may be several explanations for this difference. (It has frequently been observed that economics seems to attract persons who by nature are more aggressive, immodest, and self-assured than those drawn to psychology. I see no personal gain or satisfaction from commenting.) The ability of economists to fall back on a single unifying principle of behavior—utility maximization—gives them an unfettered, if invisible, hand in commenting on a wide range of legal issues. And it may be that the law's dependence for the most part on economic sanctions to enforce its commands makes economics appear more relevant to legal issues.

But economists admit—at least most of them do—that they deal in macrojudgments about human behavior. The predictions of economists describe behavior at the margin. Their sweeping analysis may be accurate in sum—that is, an increase in sanction will reduce the total incidents of the prohibited behavior—but may fail to explain the behavior of a significant percentage of the addressees of the legal command. Psychologists may have much to offer for more individualized inquiries. Their insights here can be applied to individuals to explain, perhaps to predict, their response to legal incentives.

At least one tension that has surfaced in recent legal scholarship is the trade-off between fairness and efficiency. A few psychologists have added to our understanding of perceptions of fairness relative to legal processes, but much more is possible to balance the extraordinary play that efficiency has had in recent times.

The vast bulk of interaction between psychologists and lawyers has been in very natural settings, such as mental health law, where the legal system is dependent on mental health professionals to observe the facts upon which the legal rules are based. This area is much like the issue of antitrust, where everyone expects economists to have something to say regarding rules that directly regulate economic activity.

The impact of law and economics on legal scholarship has been substantially enhanced because economists have sought to provide insight into "nontraditional" areas where the behavior is not explicitly economic, such as in family law or in procedural areas. The surface potential for insight from psychology on legal issues seems hardly to have been scratched.

The papers for this Symposium are headed in the right direction. The diversity of their subject matter only hints at the potential for research and study, which is as broad for law and psychology as it is for law and economics. The legal system will benefit if the literature of law and psychology, as represented by this Symposium, continues to expand its horizons.

Introduction:
The Law and Motivation

Gary B. Melton
University of Nebraska–Lincoln

This year's Nebraska Symposium on Motivation is unusual in at least three ways. First, this Symposium, for the first time on a psycholegal topic, fortuitously coincides with the 10th anniversary of the University of Nebraska–Lincoln's Law/Psychology Program. This coincidence obviously provides an opportunity for self-congratulation. Besides being the pioneer, the UN-L program remains the largest graduate program in psycholegal studies, in terms of number of students, levels of training, and depth and diversity of opportunities for scholarship. More important, the anniversary provides an opportunity for reflection upon the evolution of the field and the directions in which it should go. In that context, it is noteworthy that there are now at least 26 institutions offering programs of training in psychology and law and scores more offering coursework on the topic (Grisso, Sales, & Bayless, 1982; Melton, in press). Psycholegal studies have clearly been an academic growth area in the past decade, although the growth has often taken place more in blotches than organically.

Second, this is doubtless the most interdisciplinary volume in the Symposium's venerable history. Not only is the topic itself cross-disciplinary, but the authors are drawn from anthropology, sociology, law, several subdisciplines of psychology, and various combinations of these disciplines, and their papers draw heavily upon still others (e.g., economics, philosophy). For good measure, this year we even held the Symposium in a theater in an art museum.

Third, unlike some recent volumes of the Nebraska Symposium on Motivation, this one is expressly focused on motivation. Specifically, the authors were charged with examining various aspects of the significance of law as a motivating factor in human behavior. In that regard it may be useful to identify some of the issues underlying the theme "The Law as a Behavioral Instrument."

The State of the Art

The growth of psycholegal studies has been impressive, considering its virtual nonexistence a decade ago. Nonetheless, as Loh (1981) put it, "legal psychology [in its present state] reflects the operation of the 'law of the hammer'; give a child a hammer and it will find that everything needs pounding. It is a natural tendency to frame new problems in ways that require for their analysis those methods and concepts with which one is most familiar" (p. 173). Thus the areas of law in which there has been the most psychological study have been those that appear to fit neatly with existing lines of research—for example, studies of the jury, borrowing from the literature on small-group processes; studies of eyewitness testimony, borrowing from the literature on perception, memory, and decision making. Even in these areas, researchers have often failed to make the most basic accommodations to protect external validity. As Konečni and Ebbeson (1981) noted, "finding oneself in a 2 × 3 × 4 within-subjects simulated-jury experiment and making the guilty/not guilty decision 24 times in a row within 10 minutes on a 100-mm scale is clearly somewhat different from being in a jury once in a lifetime, watching a 7-day trial, and deliberating for 2 days behind closed doors with 11 complete strangers" (p. 488).

Psycholegal studies have also been too dependent on a Perry Mason image of the law. Most work has been in the area of criminal justice, and the trial process has received extensive attention despite the relative rarity of trials in both civil and criminal litigation. As Monahan and Loftus concluded in their *Annual Review* chapter (1982), "the study of 'private law' (e.g., contracts, torts) and of noncriminal public law (e.g., administrative law, tax) is among the most pressing research priorities in the field" (p. 466). As a general matter, substantive assumptions in the law also have been given relatively little attention by psychologists. Sociolegal studies typically have been similarly myopic, as Abel (1980) showed in a review of his work as editor of *Law and Society Review*.

Happily, these gaps are beginning to be closed. The methodological and legal sophistication of research in traditional topic areas has increased substantially (see, e.g., the jury studies reported in Haney, 1984, and Hastie, Penrod, & Pennington, 1983), and there have been at least some forays into nontraditional areas. For example, in the area with which I am most familiar—children's legal status—there is now a core of legally sophisticated psychologists and psychologically sophisticated lawyers who have greatly increased the level of knowledge in the past five years, although there are still many unanswered questions (Melton, 1984; Melton, Koocher, & Saks, 1983). (I should add that there are few signs that judges and legislators are eagerly incorporating this new literature into their decision making.)[1]

The Law as a Behavioral Instrument: A Neglected Topic

One of the most curious remaining gaps has been in the effect of law on behavior. This general topic should be a natural for psycholegal study, in that perhaps the most obvious and pervasive psychological assumption in the law is that the law is effective in controlling behavior. As we shall see, this assumption is important in jurisprudential studies, but the significance for psychology is perhaps even more profound. By systematic examination of the law's effects on behavior, we might gain a better sense of the ways social forces do and do not shape community life and the behavior of individuals. However, social scientists, especially psychologists, have given very little attention to the significance of law in everyday experience and behavior.

IS THERE A QUESTION?

There are at least three broad reasons for this neglect. First, there may be a perception that there is no real question about the extent to which the law affects behavior. As Zimring and Hawkins (1977) noted in a seminal article on the subject, "there seems to be a failure to recognize a distinction between issues relating to the *morality* or *expediency* of prohibiting particular types of behavior and issues relating to the *efficacy* of such prohibitions. There is a tendency for

---

1. A study group sponsored by the Society for Research in Child Development is examining the factors affecting legal policymakers' use—or nonuse—of child development research (Melton, in preparation).

views to vary with the subject from alcohol to firearms to racial discrimination, and to vary according to the speaker's view of the rightness of prohibiting the particular behavior. The conclusion to such discussions is often the comforting one that the law can succeed in doing right but will inevitably fail when authorities attempt to prohibit what should not be prohibited" (p. 61).

Stated somewhat differently, there is a belief that *of course* the law affects behavior; it is *The Law*, and the Supreme Court is the omnipotent Supreme Being that has the last word on how a dispute shall be resolved. If there is substantial noncompliance, it is because the law really is not The Law. For example, in the popular mind, the framers of highway safety laws didn't really mean to set the maximum speed limit at 55 mph; what they *really* meant was 60 or 65 mph.

In fact, however, there are numerous areas of law in which the reality, though not necessarily the perception, is that the law, far from being ominipotent, has no real means of remedying violations. Thus, even if the public perception (and the perception of scholars) is that the answer to the question of the law's effect on behavior is self-evident, there clearly is a need to explore when and how the law does affect behavior, points that I will discuss in some detail later.

CONCEPTUAL PROBLEMS

A second reason for the minimal research on the effect of law is that it is difficult to do. As Gibbs discusses, there are serious conceptual and methodological problems in determining the efficacy of law. If someone is in compliance with the law, we cannot infer that he or she is willfully *obeying* the law. The behavior may be a response to social norms or other contingencies that may or may not be the results of the law. Even time-series designs provide inadequate tests of these competing hypotheses, because changes in the law or its enforcement may reflect coincident social trends.

Analogously, noncompliance cannot be assumed to be direct disobedience of the law. The law is unlikely to be fully disseminated; I would wager that no one in the Symposium audience had memorized the United States Code, the Nebraska Revised Statutes, the Lincoln Municipal Ordinances, or even the Bylaws of the University of Nebraska Board of Regents. When the law is disseminated, its requirements may be unclear, or affected citizens may find it impossible to comply. Even willful disobedience may not be *experienced* as noncompliance. The speeders mentioned earlier may rationalize their behavior as compliant with the spirit of the law. A more noto-rious example was the post-*Brown* massive resistance to school de-segregation. Law-and-order conservatives were able to resolve cognitive dissonance by assuring themselves that the Supreme Court's action was illegitimate, decided according to sociology rather than law (Rosen, 1972).

Much more could be said about the complexity of apparent com-pliance or noncompliance with the law. For now, though, the point has been made that there are substantial difficulties in assessing the influence of law—so much so that research may be deterred.

THE NEGLECT OF SYMBOLISM

The third reason for the paucity of research on the behavioral effects of law is more subtle. That is, the most important effects of law may be *symbolic*, and social scientists have been late to recognize the functions of law that are not directly instrumental or utilitarian. For example, jury research has been overwhelmingly directed to-ward the rationality of juries' decision making; that is, how well do juries process the evidence and decide cases according to the law? This general question is, of course, important in itself. For example, when juries' efforts to follow the law are stymied by incomprehensi-ble instructions (Elwork, Sales, & Alfini, 1982), justice obviously has not been served. However, the jury's accuracy in carrying out the law may not be the most important dependent variable, as illus-trated by the historic debate about the propriety of jury nullification (compare, e.g., Simson, 1976, with Scheflin & Van Dyke, 1980; see *United States v. Dougherty*, 1972) and the recent trend toward explicit delegation of determination of criminal responsibility to jurors acting according to their sense of justice (see, e.g., *State v. Johnson*, 1979). We need to examine the latent, symbolic effects of the jury. What is the meaning of the experience of jury trials to the jurors themselves (see Smolka & Tapp, 1979; Tapp & Keniston, 1976), the parties, and the community? Does a greater sense of justice accrue from judgment by peers? Does the ritual of the jury, as the expres-sion of the community conscience, have socializing effects on the community as a whole? These questions assume special significance in the light of both the relative infrequency of jury trials[2] and the

2. The vast majority of cases—both civil and criminal—are settled out of court. When it is considered that a portion of the cases that do go to trial are heard by judges, it is clear that relatively few cases are ever decided by a jury.

continuing trends toward reduction[3] or elimination[4] of juries in those cases that do go to trial.

The observation that we may not always be asking the right questions about the effects of law is illustrated by a paradox of purpose inherent in contemporary American law. On the one hand, law frequently is intended to change both social norms and individual behavior. In this context, law is conceptualized as clearly *instrumental*, as establishing contingencies resulting in behavior change. Thus legal policies commonly have the purpose of fostering or, more frequently, deterring particular behavior.

On the other hand, in a democratic society law is perceived as consensual, as the reflection of the community will. In that context, law is perceived as having a largely *symbolic* function, as institutionalizing the mores of the society. Even Judge David Bazelon (1982), perhaps the paragon of an activist, social-welfare-oriented judge, has taken such a position. "The law . . . ," he wrote, "is seldom the spearhead of social evolution; it merely conforms to and ratifies changes in society and social perceptions" (p. 6). However, though based on a normative principle, this view of law as inherently conservative and consensual has implicit psychological assumptions. Even if law functions primarily as an expression of the community ethic, we clearly believe that such symbolic statements of what is good have a hortatory effect both on individuals and on the community as a whole.

Conceptualizing such effects in testable terms is no small order. However, in this Symposium there is an attempt to consider both instrumental and symbolic functions, the contribution of law to both social change and social stasis. Although his conclusion is debatable, Abel's (1980, p. 826) critique of the instrumentalist model is worth considering: "knowledge about and attitudes toward law are studied because they are believed to influence compliance or violation, whereas the more significant public perceptions and feelings are likely to focus on law as the object of political, economic, and

3. The Supreme Court has held that six-person juries meet the demands of the Sixth Amendment in criminal cases (*Ballew v. Georgia*, 1978). As of 1980, 12 states used six- to eight-person juries for at least some criminal trials (National Court Statistics Project, 1982).

4. The movement toward alternative forms of dispute resolution will, of course, further reduce the proportion of jury trials. Among cases that do go to trial, there has been an ongoing dispute about whether a jury trial is necessary or desirable in complex civil litigation (see, e.g., Rubin, 1982).

social struggle. Law *is* an instrument, but not for the ends it proclaims."

Is the Law a Toothless Tiger?

In considering the complexity of relationships among law, behavior, and social structure, it may be useful to return to the first reason I suggested for the lack of psychological research and theory on the impact of law on behavior: disbelief that there is a real issue. The disparity between law on the books and law in action (see Pound, 1910) has been a theme in American jurisprudential theory for the past century. I suspect that there is little skepticism among readers of this volume about the realist theory that judicial decisions reflect sociopolitical reality (see, e.g., Llewellyn, 1962) or even the critical legal theory that judges commonly act to advance particular social interests (see, e.g., Unger, 1983; see also Galanter, 1974).[5] These views square with intuition about political action, and judges, after all, either are themselves elected or are appointed by elected officials. Even if there is such a widespread cynicism about the origins of the law in action, substantial lack of compliance with the directives of the legislature and the judiciary may seem far-fetched to those of us who are basically law-abiding (presumably most of the readers of this volume).

However, for some kinds of decisions the ability of the courts to enforce the law is highly questionable. Indeed, winning the case is merely half the battle. A party prevailing on the merits of the case (if it even gets into court) may still be frustrated in its efforts to achieve justice.

Consider the following hypothetical case, which unfortunately bears considerable resemblance to a number of class actions on behalf of institutionalized persons in recent years. Nicholas Smith is a 30-year-old resident of Enormous State Training School (ESTS) for mentally retarded persons. Mr. Smith lives on a ward of 40 severely and profoundly retarded men. At times there is only one attendant on the ward. Mr. Smith receives no habilitation services. Before entering the institution three years ago, he was toilet trained and able to feed himself and to assist in dressing himself. Now he has lost

---

5. By raising this point, I do not intend to imply that law is *only* an accommodation to sociopolitical reality. That the law also includes its own formal analytical properties that are at least partially autonomous seems undeniable.

most of his self-help skills, and he also uses less language. Mr. Smith's self-abusive behavior has increased. He has sustained repeated self-inflicted wounds on his arms and face, and he has lost much of the vision in his left eye. As a result of this behavior, Mr. Smith is kept in restraints much of the time. He is often not fully clothed, and sometimes he goes several days without being bathed. State administrators and legislators are aware of the situation at ESTS, and they find it regrettable but unavoidable in a time of a depressed economy and political pressures to reduce state spending.

That Mr. Smith has been egregiously mistreated by the state is indisputable. Certainly, one might assume, he should be able to achieve vindication of his own and his coresidents' civil rights in the courts. But consider the roadblocks that are likely to arise.

First, Mr. Smith must get access to the courts. Obviously, he is not able to bring such action independently, and he may have no relatives who are able and willing to act in his behalf. Legal aid and protection/advocacy services have been cut back sufficiently that there often is no one actively guarding residents' interests. The United States Justice Department has authority to file suit under the Civil Rights of Institutionalized Persons Act (1981), but it has generally refused to do so (Lampson, 1983). Indeed the Reagan Justice Department has been assiduous in withdrawing from ongoing institutional litigation and even filing amicus briefs *against* institutionalized persons ("Justice Department opposes," 1984).

If the allegation of violation of civil rights is actually filed, the federal courts (which often are most responsive to such claims) will be unable to act while state litigation is pending, even when state officials have violated both state and federal law. In what Justice Stevens called a "voyage into the sea of undisciplined lawmaking" (*Pennhurst State School & Hospital v. Halderman*, 1984, p. 944), in one of a series of cases involving a state facility for mentally retarded persons in Pennsylvania, the Supreme Court rejected pendency jurisdiction and expanded the immunity of state officials in federal courts.

Assume, though, that Mr. Smith is able to achieve access to the courts for potential redress of violation of his civil rights. The Supreme Court has skirted establishment of a broad constitutional right to treatment or habilitation as a corollary to the substantive due process clause of the Fourteenth Amendment. The Court has recognized only that Mr. Smith and others like him are owed safe conditions, freedom from bodily restraint, and whatever habilitation is necessary to enable them to live in safety free of restraints (*Young-*

berg v. Romeo, 1982). This minimal right to habilitation can actually be read rather expansively (cf. Halpern, 1976; Melton, 1983). Regardless, though, it is questionable whether a broad reading really adds anything to the protection accorded Mr. Smith. The standard the Court recognized for determination of liability for deprivation of civil rights was essentially the same as that typically used in professional malpractice actions, "a substantial departure from accepted professional judgment, practice, or standards" (*Youngberg v. Romeo*, 1982, p. 323). Even when such unprofessional conduct can be established, the professional is immune from liability if the deprivation of civil rights resulted from budgetary problems.

It might be argued, though, that monetary damages would be a hollow victory for Mr. Smith. So, too, would be an order for his release. What Mr. Smith really needs is injunctive relief to ensure that he is not subject to continued unnecessary restraints and inhumane living conditions. But how will such an injunction be enforced? Surely the court will not hold the entire state legislature in contempt. (There may be cause, however, to hold state administrative officials in contempt when they fail to act in good faith to secure the appropriations necessary to meet constitutionally adequate standards of care; see *Halderman v. Pennhurst State School & Hospital*, 1982.)

In fact, the evidence is that state agencies often ignore court orders or simply go through the motions of appearing to comply. For example, in a study of the aftermath of several state-court decisions in Pennsylvania (C. A. Johnson, 1979), it was found that agencies often believed that there was so little risk of enforcement that they did not even make an effort to find alternatives to their illegal behavior.

Assume, though, that the state is motivated to comply—that it is a "friendly suit" and that the state enters willingly into a consent decree. As a matter of fact if not necessarily of law, the state is not a unitary actor. Although the relevant administrator may be highly motivated to comply, the legislature or the governor may not. Moreover, given the length of time institutional class actions often stay in the courts (e.g., in the case of *Wyatt v. Stickney*, 1971, for more than a decade), it is probable that the state administration will change over the course of the suit. Thus there still may be political conflicts over implementation of the decree, and the actors with the most power may also be the most resistant.

Even if the principals are compliant, however, line workers may not be. Institutional structures are often well ingrained through civil service laws, union contracts, and social custom. Without attention to change of these structures—which may be rather inflexible—the decree may never be really implemented (Melton, 1983; Reppucci, 1977; see, e.g., *New York State Association for Retarded Children, Inc. v. Carey*, 1978). The community may also be resistant to changes in institutional structure (see, e.g., Frohboese & Sales, 1980; Hafemeister, in preparation), especially when jobs or common social constructs about necessary care for mentally retarded persons (cf. Kiesler, 1982) are affected.

There may be other realities that impede implementation of a decree. For example, the decree in *Wyatt v. Stickney* (1972) called for the employment of more mental health professionals in Alabama institutions than there were in the entire state. Vigorous attempts to recruit nationally, including salary bonuses, were unsuccessful (professionals, not surprisingly, were less than eager to flock to a state hospital in rural Alabama) and irritated existing staff (Stickney, 1976). Moreover, a focus on upgrading institutions may have the negative side effect of diverting funds from community-based services and locking in an archaic and perhaps inherently destructive large-institution model of delivery of care, or simply "transinstitutionalizing" Mr. Smith and others like him to other facilities or systems not subject to the decree (Warren, 1981).

I do not mean to sound like a psycholegal nihilist and imply that legal decisions generally or institutional class actions specifically are inherently hollow victories. In some instances, change may result from a fortuitous blend of an activist judge, highly motivated state officials, and adequate structures for implementation of a decree (Yohalem,1984; see also F. M. Johnson, 1976). It is possible in some cases, for example, that courts can use their authority to impose a special master (Federal Rule of Civil Procedure 53) to facilitate the parties' negotiating and implementing a decree. Also, even if the decree is never fully implemented, the decision on the merits in a class action against one institution and the resulting order may provide guideposts to other facilities motivated to protect residents' rights. The point I do wish to make clear is that law is not self-enforcing. Without changes in the relevant social structures and behavioral demands, judicial decrees (or statutory enactments) aimed at changing institutions are likely to be ineffective.[6]

6. It may be argued that the scenario described in the case of Mr. Smith is not applicable to private parties. Obviously, because of the doctrines of sovereign immunity and separation of powers, there are special problems in ensuring compliance with the

To understand the circumstances in which the law affects behavior—or to use such an understanding to foster change through the law—requires an appreciation of the limitations of reach within the law itself. But it also requires a sophisticated understanding of the social forces shaping the law and the nature of contingencies necessary for changing or maintaining both individual and group or institutional behavior. As already noted, study of the effects of law has the potential to inform both the law and psychology about the forces shaping our collective behavior and experience.

The Contents of This Volume

The papers in this volume present diverse perspectives on the relationships among law, motivation, and social structure in affecting individual and group behavior. These relationships are complex and invite the integration of diverse perspectives—legal, philosophical, sociological, anthropological, economic, and political, as well as psychological. Some have suggested that law and social science should be considered a separate discipline. Clearly, analysis of empirical issues on the law requires facility with both legal and scientific styles of analysis and their integration. It also demands consideration of the relevant behavioral issues within a problem-centered rather than a discipline-centered framework. As Nader notes, criticisms of the law for failing to attend to empirical evidence are a bit arrogant when social scientists do not cross disciplinary boundaries even within the social sciences. The papers in this volume are unusual in their broad law-and-social-science approach to the complex relationships among the law, social structure, and individual behavior.

Each author takes an interdisciplinary approach to a particular aspect of these relationships. In the opening paper, Nader reverses the question of the instrumentality of law. She examines ways the users of law shape the disputing process cross-culturally.

Morse then considers the question of causality in law from a more

---

law by state officials. However, there are many instances in which law directed at private parties is essentially unenforceable (e.g., prohibitions of purchase of cigarettes by minors) or in which no effective remedy is available (e.g., school truancy). Issues about enforcement of child support orders are also illustrative (see, e.g., Mnookin, 1981). Moreover, private parties often lack the resources or motivation to seek legal redress. In that regard, as Nader points out, we may actually be an *under*litigious nation.

philosophical perspective. Does causality imply compulsion? Can moral concepts of agency and responsibility be compatible with determinist views of the motivation of behavior?

In the third paper, Gibbs examines the problem that is probably most commonly raised in discussions of the law's efficacy as a behavioral instrument: Does the law deter criminal behavior? In an elegant theoretical paper, Gibbs identifies the multiple propositions implicit in deterrence doctrine and points out the difficulties inherent in attempting to test the validity of these propositions.

Bonnie considers the efficacy of law in reducing unhealthy and unsafe behavior, whether through deterrence or through incentives. In his analysis, he draws heavily on economic (as well as psychological and sociological) analyses of risk assumption.

Brodsky moves the discussion to levels that are at once broader and more microscopic. Although he considers the role of the law in changing institutional behavior, he does so from a clinical perspective. How might one assess the link between legal requirements and institutional behavior?

In the final paper, Melton and Saks focus on the law's role in maintaining social stasis. They consider ways the law fosters structures that reward desirable behavior and socializes citizens through modeling and cues for good behavior. In the end, they return to a clearly motivational topic—the ways law may be internalized and provide consciousness of a right or a duty and the resulting motivation to act accordingly.

In short, this volume provides a broad interdisciplinary analysis of the instrumentality of law. To oversimplify somewhat, the authors address the effects of individual and group behavior on the law (Nader) and the effects of the law on the behavior of bad or potentially bad actors (Bonnie, Gibbs), good actors (Melton and Saks); mad actors (Morse), and institutions (Brodsky). Taken as a whole, the papers present a vivid picture of both the usefulness and the difficulties of an interdisciplinary approach to understanding the relationships between the law (and other social forces) and human behavior. The authors forge frameworks for analysis of the law as a behavioral instrument and provide a broad new agenda for psycholegal and sociolegal studies.

REFERENCES

Abel, R. (1980). Redirecting social studies of law. *Law and Society Review, 14,* 805–829.

Ballew v. Georgia, 435 U.S. 223 (1978).

Bazelon, D. L. (1982). Introduction [to Mental Health Symposium]. *Law and Contemporary Problems, 45,* 3–6.

Elwork, A., Sales, B. D., & Alfini, J. J. (1982). *Writing understandable jury instructions.* Charlottesville, VA: Michie/Bobbs-Merrill.

Frohboese, R., & Sales, B. D. (1980). Parental opposition to deinstitutionalization: A challenge in need of attention and resolution. *Law and Human Behavior, 4,* 1–87.

Galanter, M. (1974). The future of law and social sciences research. *North Carolina Law Review, 52,* 1060–1067.

Grisso, T., Sales, B. D., & Bayless, S.(1982). Law-related courses and programs in graduate psychology departments. *American Psychologist, 37,* 267–278.

Hafemeister, T. (in preparation). Decision making by policy makers in the course of a controversy over deinstitutionalization.

Halderman v. Pennhurst State School & Hospital, 673 F.2d 628 (3d Cir. 1982), *cert. denied,* 104 S.Ct. 1315 (1984).

Halpern, C. R. (1976). The right to habilitation: Litigation as a strategy for social change. In S. Golann & W. J. Fremouw (Eds.), *The right to treatment for mental patients* (pp. 73–98). New York: Irvington.

Haney, C. (1984). Death qualification [Special issue]. *Law and Human Behavior, 8* (1/2).

Hastie, R., Penrod, S. D., & Pennington, N. (1983). *Inside the jury.* Cambridge, MA: Harvard University Press.

Johnson, C. A. (1979). Judicial decisions and organization change: Some theoretical and empirical notes on state court decisions and state administrative agencies. *Law and Society Review, 14,* 27–56.

Johnson, F. M. (1976). The Constitution and the federal district judge. *Texas Law Review, 54,* 903–916.

Justice Department opposes federal right to community living. (1984). *Mental and Physical Disability Law Reporter, 8,* 296–297.

Kiesler, C. A. (1982). Mental hospitals and alternative care: Noninstitutionalization as potential public policy for mental patients. *American Psychologist, 37,* 349–360.

Konečni, V., & Ebbesen, E. (1981). A critique of theory and method in social-psychological approaches to legal issues. In B. D. Sales (Ed.), *The trial process.* NewYork: Plenum Press.

Lampson, M. (1983). Senate subcommittee reviews Justice Department's enforcement of Section 504 and CRIPA. *Mental Disability Law Reporter, 7,* 492–493.

Llewellyn, K. N. (1962). *Jurisprudence: Realism in theory and practice.* Chicago: University of Chicago Press.

Loh, W. D. (1981). Legal psychology [Review of *The trial process*]. *Science, 214,* 173.

Melton, G. B. (1983). *Child advocacy: Psychological issues and interventions.* New York: Plenum.

Melton, G. B.(1984). Developmental psychology and the law: The state of the art. *Journal of Family Law, 22,* 445–482.

Melton, G. B. (in press). Training in psychology and law. In I. B. Weiner and A. K. Hess (Eds.), *Handbook of forensic psychology.* New York: Wiley.

Melton, G. B. (Ed.). (in preparation). *Reforming the law: Impact of child development research.* New York: Guilford Press.

Melton, G. B., Koocher, G. P., & Saks, M. J. (Eds.). (1983). *Children's competence to consent.* New York: Plenum Press.

Mnookin, R. H. (1981). Using jail for child support enforcement [Review of *Making fathers pay*]. *University of Chicago Law Review, 48,* 338–370.

Monahan, J., & Loftus, E. (1982). The psychology of law. *Annual Review of Psychology, 33,* 441–475.

National Court Statistics Project. (1982). *State court organization 1980.* Washington, DC: Bureau of Justice Statistics, Department of Justice.

New York State Association for Retarded Children, Inc v. Carey, 393 F. Supp. 715 (E.D.N.Y. 1978).

Pennhurst State School & Hospital v. Halderman, 104 S.Ct. 900 (1984).

Pound, R. (1910). Law in books and law in action. *American Law Review, 44,* 30–41.

Reppucci, N. D. (1977). Implementation issues for the behavior modifier as institutional change agent. *Behavior Therapy, 8,* 594–605.

Rosen, P. (1972). *The Supreme Court and social science.* Urbana: University of Illinois Press.

Rubin, A. B. (1982). Trial by jury in complex civil cases: Voice of liberty or verdict by confusion? *Annals of the American Academy, 462,* 86–103.

Scheflin, A., & Van Dyke, J. (1980). Jury nullification: The contours of a controversy. *Law and Contemporary Problems, 43,* 52–115.

Simson, G. (1976). Jury nullification in the American system: A sceptical view. *Texas Law Review, 1976,* 488–506.

Smolka, P., & Tapp, J. L. (1979). *The jury as a socialization experience.* Unpublished manuscript, University of Minnesota.

State v. Johnson, 399 A.2d 469 (R.I. 1979).

Stickney, S. S. (1976). *Wyatt v. Stickney*: Background and postscript. In S. Golann & W. J. Fremouw (Eds.), *The right to treatment for mental patients* (pp. 29–46). New York: Irvington.

Tapp, J. L., & Keniston, A. (1976, September). Wounded Knee—advocate or expert: Recipe for a fair juror? In J. L. Tapp (Chair), *"What is a fair jury?" Psychological and legal issues.* Symposium conducted at the meeting of the American Psychological Association, Washington, DC.

Unger, R. M. (1983). The critical legal studies movement. *Harvard Law Review, 96*, 561–676.

United States v. Dougherty, 473 F.2d 1113 (D.C. Cir. 1972).

Warren, C. A. B. (1981). New forms of social control: The myth of deinstitutionalization. *American Behavioral Scientist, 24*, 724–740.

Wyatt v. Stickney, 324 F. Supp. 781 (M.D.Ala. 1971), *enforced,* 344 F. Supp. 373 (M.D.Ala. 1972) *and* 344 F. Supp. 387 (M.D.Ala. 1972), *modified sub nom.* Wyatt v. Aderholt, 503 F.2d 1305 (5th Cir. 1974).

Yohalem, D. (1984, August). [Discussant] In L. Behar (Chair), *Improving services for children through litigation: Risks and strategies.* Symposium conducted at the meeting of the American Psychological Association, Toronto.

Youngberg v. Romeo, 457 U.S.309 (1982).

Zimring, F., & Hawkins, G. (1977). The legal threat as an instrument of social change. In J. L. Tapp & F. J. Levine (Eds.), *Law, justice, and the individual in society: Psychological and legal issues* (pp. 60–74). New York: Holt, Rinehart & Winston.

A User Theory of Legal Change as Applied to Gender

Laura Nader

University of California, Berkeley

Introduction

*T*he study of law as a behavioral instrument is of course a study in dynamic, not static phenomena, an interest in the forces that produce change or process. The dynamics, however, may center on the actions of individuals or groups, or they may be more historical in nature, with a number of accumulated institutional changes over time effecting a change in the processes of law.

In thinking about legal change I have moved between a more extensive processual form of change that develops over decades and centuries and change of a more limited sort that comes to our attention through ethnographic descriptions of particular people and events in time and space. The latter intensive ethnographic approach focuses on understanding specific triggering mechanisms, whereas the extensive historical method outlines the waves of change that follow the initial triggering.

The approach I have used is contextual and bottom-up and in that way is different from what I might call a linear institutional approach to understanding legal change. The historical institutional approach compares institutions at different points in time and, if there is a difference in the institutions of different time periods, attempts to explain differences in terms of socioeconomic changes such as industrialization or urbanization.

My perspective is actor oriented and consistently underlines the observation that not only does the law change people, but people change the law. In the same vein, my approach is not strictly de-

velopmental, for example implying that political complexity generates change in legal behavior. The theory I have been examining
stems mainly from an assumption (often implicit) that the user, in
particular the plaintiff user—not an abstraction like the courts, or
judicial decision, or even variables like urbanization and industrialization—is the driving force in law as a behavioral instrument.

Although in my recollection Thomas Jefferson wrote about the
law's growing organically by the use people made of it, it was the
anthropological linguist Edward Sapir who set me to thinking about
my materials through a user model. In his writings on linguistic drift
Sapir wrote:

> The drift of a language is constituted by the unconscious selection on
> the part of its speakers of those individual variations that are cumula-
> tive in some special direction. This direction may be inferred, in the
> main, from the past history of the language. . . . As we look about us
> and observe current usage, it is not likely to occur to us that our lan-
> guage has a "slope," that the changes of the next few centuries are in a
> sense prefigured in certain obscure tendencies of the present and that
> these changes, when consummated, will be seen to be but continua-
> tions of changes that have already been effected. We feel rather that our
> language is practically a fixed system. . . . The feeling is fallacious."
> (1921, p. 155)

If we paraphrase this concept of linguistic drift and apply it to thinking about legal change, we have an interesting proposition before
us: "The drift of a legal system is constituted by the unconscious
selection on the part of its users of those variations that are cumulative in some special direction. Our legal system has a 'slope,' and the
changes of the next few years are prefigured in certain tendencies of
the present." To explore the notion of drift and apply it to an understanding of the process of legal change, we must pay a good deal
more attention to the concepts of use and users and to patterns of
access to the system.

In 1978 I published a paper entitled "The Direction of Law and the
Development of Extra-Judicial Processes in Nation State Societies"
(Nader, 1978). The bottom-line argument had to do with the concept
of access and the status of litigants and relationships between them.
The image presented is of people looking for solutions to grievances. Whether they find access to favored conflict-resolving institutions open or closed determines whether they set into motion
changes that reverberate inside and outside the judicial system.
When court systems are part of the nation-state apparatus, court-

use patterns can be manipulated by the state through administrative means. Therefore the direction of law can be controlled to some extent by the state's blocking access to the courts for some people. For example, in nation-state societies the state defines itself as user by becoming the plaintiff in criminal cases, and the "true" plaintiff and his or her family become victims. The change from plaintiff to victim status, from an active to a passive role, must, I argued, have changed the status of the defendant as well. Because anthropologists have observed that the plaintiff role is relatively more active in non-Western societies, it has been more generally argued that change in relationships between litigants is a trend accompanying (but not necessarily caused by) modernization and the increasing movement of people. While I do not dispute the effects of modernization and mobilization on legal change, I argue that we must view these institutional changes through their effects on users of the law.

I further pursued the idea that a change in relationship between litigants could trigger behavioral change in a second paper on legal change, entitled "From Disputing to Complaining" (Nader, 1983). As this title implies, over time in nation-states the plaintiff has moved from a position of relative power, which gave him or her procedural means to dispute, to a relatively powerless role that allows room only for complaining. Furthermore, this change in potential litigant role seems to have come about through the change in relations that resulted from industrialized wage labor:

> As consumers have become distanced from the producer, both informal and social control (community pressures by means of public opinion and alternative consumption options) and formal social control (that is, government law that would include many of the so-called informal justice procedures as well) have escaped their grasp. The result is increased unilateral behavior—complaining or exiting. In state systems of law the plaintiff role atrophies because of use monopoly by the state. The law drifts in the direction of its dominant users. (Nader, 1983, p. 91)

The individual plaintiff was gradually removed from litigation. Exploring the concept of user became the next step. In my article "A User Theory of Law" (Nader, 1984), I attempted to focus further on the plaintiff role in legal change and to outline a user perspective on the judicial process. It was part of my ongoing effort to loosen the grip of the idea of a judge-determined court (as, for example, in the concept of "judicial decision making") and to replace it with an interactive model that gave sociological significance to all the players in the litigating game. This chapter elaborates on some of the ideas in that last paper, paying particular attention to gender and relative rank between males and females as an example of the dynamics of legal change.

Relevant Ideas

A number of ideas have proved useful in the comparative study of how law operates as a behavioral instrument—of how law changes in relation to its environment. The first idea is that the search for justice is both fundamental and universal in human culture and society. The second idea is that law "behaves," that is, that law varies in relation to its social and cultural environment. A related idea is that what goes on when parties dispute in front of or in the company of others depends on the overall interaction between the participating parties; such an idea encourages social scientists to treat all parties as if they were potentially of equal importance for the research agenda. And a final notion that incorporates the previous ideas and elaborates upon them—a user theory of law—involves our thinking about the direction of law as dependent in large measure on who is motivated to use the law and for what.

A background note on the sociology of knowledge in this area of research is in order. Few of these ideas were commonly found in the behavioral science literature on law when I began to write on the subject in the early 1960s. Although by the 1960s there were a number of important anthropological monographs on law in other cultures (see Nader, 1965, and Moore, 1969, for a summary of the work in anthropology to those dates), there was little in the way of general theories of law behavior, and what there was dealt with the economic, relational, procedural, and political aspects of law. In allied fields—in sociology, for example—the situation was not even as good as in anthropology (by the sociologists' own statements); sociological behavioral studies of law were for the most part produced after the 1950s, but they continue to grow unabated. Yet during the 1950s the general absence in both anthropology and sociology of research on law in Western societies led David Riesman (1954) to ask just why this should be so in an article that I used to assign to my social science students as a demystifier.

Since the 1950s and 1960s a good behavioral literature on law in the United States has been accumulating; in spite of such work, however, intellectual stimulation across the behavioral sciences has been uneven. The borrowing of ideas and data for building behavioral science theories of law has been occurring only in the past decade. Actually, for all we might criticize the nation's law schools for the absence of behavioral research, they have perhaps been better at utilizing ideas from the behavioral sciences than the behavioral sciences have been in borrowing from each other. For this reason especially, I am grateful to the Nebraska Symposium on Motivation for providing this opportunity for exchange.

Of the ideas I wish to discuss here, nearly all are now a part of the research literature on law across the behavioral sciences and in legal history. Both psychologists and anthropologists have been interested in universals; the specific idea of the justice motive and how it works was introduced into my thinking through the work on justice theories of social psychologist Melvin Lerner and his associates (Lerner, 1975, 1980; Lerner & Lerner, 1981). The idea that law varies with changes in the social and cultural environment has been with us in anthropology at least since Sir Henry Maine (1861) postulated that with shifts in family structure, the law changes from being based on one's status to being based on contracts between individuals. Maine's idea has been heavily used in anthropology as part of the structural-functional approach to human behavior. This idea has been particularly useful in relation to law and social control research by Africanist anthropologists such as Elizabeth Colson (1953) and in my own work in Mexico, and it has heavily influenced the work of sociologist Donald Black. The specific idea that law moves downward and varies with status has been written about in the social science literature, but it is most successfully elaborated by Black in his book *The Behavior of Law* (1976). The integrative notion that users (that is, individuals in specific roles and ranks) make and change the law is my own elaboration, with which I am working to understand the dynamics of change. My thinking was certainly influenced by Edward Sapir's seminal work on linguistic drift (1921) and later by the work of American legal historians Willard Hurst (1981) and Lawrence Friedman and R. V. Percival (1976). Furthermore, and in this vein, Richard Kagan's (1981) work on Spain analyzes how the number of users expands and contracts with changing conditions of political economy.

In the following pages I will discuss each of these ideas briefly and then show how they have been useful in understanding some things about legal change in the United States and Mexico. I discuss them specifically in relation to data collected from a Zapotec Indian community in Oaxaca, Mexico, because that kind of microdata allows us to posit broader evolutionary change. An examination of case materials from that community, looking at same-sex and cross-sex court cases in particular, is made in an effort to determine whether and where gender (only one variable) makes a difference in courtroom content.

UNIVERSALITY OF THE JUSTICE MOTIVE

In 1953 a world conference of anthropologists published the volume *Anthropology Today*, an encyclopedic inventory that included Clyde Kluckhohn's paper "Universal Categories of Culture." Kluckhohn drew our attention in this article to the problems, interests, and objections of anthropologists studying universals in culture. Although he argued that "biological, psychological, and sociosituational universals afford the possibility of comparison of cultures in terms which are not ethnocentric" (1953, p. 517), his piece is generally discouraging: "There are, admittedly, few genuine uniformities in culture content unless one states the content in extremely general form—e.g., clothing, shelter, incest taboos, and the like" (p. 519). At the same time, he leaves us with the concrete possibility of studying universals because "all cultures constitute . . . distinct answers to essentially the same questions posed by human biology and by the generalities of the human situation" (p. 520).

When in the early 1960s I began to construct a work plan with students who were going to study the disputing process, I argued that they could work anywhere in the world because "in any society there are various remedy agents which may be referred to when a grievance reaches a boiling point" (Nader, p. 23). And in all societies that we know about, people dispute. At the time I merely made this observation; I did not attempt to explore or explain it. What I was attempting to account for was the variety: all societies do not dispute about all the possible things humans could dispute about; all societies choose among a number of modes of disputing, and so on. I only returned to the question of universals, to the ubiquitous drive toward justice, after being introduced to the social psychology literature on justice theories and after the publication of *The Disputing Process: Law in Ten Societies* (Nader & Todd, 1978).

The phrase "justice motive," to which I was introduced by Melvin Lerner, captured for me an important notion. I quote from Lerner:

"the awareness of an injustice elicits corrective activity with such regularity that it appears for all intents and purposes to have the characteristic of a biologically-based reflex of tropism. And this reflex-like action to an injustice is often of sufficient strength that all other considerations are set aside" (Lerner, Ms., p. 1). Lerner could be talking about the many societies that anthropologists have studied. Could it be that in all societies people dispute and develop procedures for doing so because of the presence of a universal justice motive? Although I am aware of conflict and harmony theories that may also shed light on this problem, here I want to stick to the notion of a justice motive. If it *is* universal and universally provided for, we can ask to what degree specific cultures or groups in cultures allow for or constrain the exercise of the justice motive, particularly in the context of government law.

I have thought about the justice motive in two contexts: as differentially distributed through a population, that is, with some people characteristically more motivated by it than others, and as differentially distributed throughout the history of the same population. In relation to the first observation, not much is known. I used to think that some people were justice motivated and others not, but an incident on an airplane led me to reconsider. The same man who would not seek compensation when a stewardess dropped his breakfast in his lap, ruining his clothes, told me he would be outraged with the telephone company's billing errors and that in that context he would exercise the justice motive. It appears that each person has a justice profile, just as do social groups (Sursock, 1983). My book *No Access to Law* (Nader, 1980) is about those consumers who do exercise the justice motive in relation to economic grievances.

If we look at the exercise of the justice motive in relation to a historical dimension, I have more to say. In the West and perhaps in conjunction with the rise of the modern nation-state, the justice motive has atrophied for a variety of reasons, an observation in stark contrast to popular notions that "litigation is increasing at an unprecedented rate."[1] In criminal law, for example, with the evolution

---

1. Donald Black's piece "Jurocracy in America" (1984) explicates the controversy regarding the assertions of "litigation explosion" in the United States. His article was stimulated by Michel Crozier's *The Trouble with America*, in which Crozier describes the American condition as a condition of "legal madness." Black documents what is known and concludes that "the role of law in everyday life remains extremely small," and that "virtually all conflicts are settled *without* litigation" in the United States.

of government law the real plaintiff has become the victim because in criminal cases the state automatically becomes the plaintiff. In civil law potential plaintiffs frequently do not exercise the justice motive because of cost, access, time, and other factors.

In most societies that we anthropologists know anything about, the plaintiff is motivated to secure justice and a certain kind of justice because he or she is the victim as well as the plaintiff; the two roles are one. This observation is generally ignored in the process of transplanting Western law first into colonies and later into the new nations by new nationals, educated abroad, and this has caused major unrest in developing nations around the world. In Zambia, for example, when the state became the plaintiff the courts began to punish defendants convicted of cattle rustling by sentencing them to jail, whereas compensation is what is of interest to the real plaintiffs, as it was under traditional law. In such situations one could say that plaintiff energy is frustrated and then atrophies as plaintiff and victim roles become separated. It is in the role of plaintiff that other societies are so different from ours.

Again, an aside on the sociology of knowledge may be warranted. We do not know much about the plaintiff and the evolution of the plaintiff role.[2] If we look at four of the major behavioral science fields—sociology, political science, psychology, and anthropology—and ask which has focused interest on the evolution of the plaintiff role, the answers are revealing. There are exceptions of course, but generally speaking, when political scientists have looked at courts they have examined the role and hierarchy of judges (as in judicial decision making); when sociologists or criminologists have looked at the justice system their attention has most often been on the defendant. Psychologists and anthropologists who study justice or disputing tend to focus on the plaintiff or at least the victim (see Lerner, 1976; Nader, 1980; Nader & Todd, 1978). For an adequate understanding of government courts as behavioral instruments, we need an interactive model, one that considers the interacting roles of all litigants and third parties.

2. For reference to historical and contemporary analysis of the plaintiffs' access, see Bayley (1983) for the role played by official policing forces and Barnes (1981) for a description of the removal of plaintiffs' access in the interests of the king and state in the history of the Star Chamber; in reference to the contemporary period see Cappelletti (1975) on civil litigation and the public interest.

THE BEHAVIOR OF LAW

Some behavioral scientists have already accepted the notion that law behaves—that at the small group level interaction between litigants and between litigants and third parties forces certain kinds of results in law cases. An early study along these lines was carried out by Duane Metzger (1960) on ethnographic materials from southern Mexico. Metzger used coalition analysis to describe the interactions in court to show how specific kinds of interactions led to different outcomes in Mexican Indian and Ladino courtrooms. He examined the relative balance of power between plaintiff, defendant, and court relative to the variables of ethnicity and community membership in order to show how balance of power affected conflict outcome in court cases, and how the balance between the court and family remedy agents affected cases of family conflict.

At the macro level this notion of behavior has been used to illustrate how law changes with changes in the sociocultural environment. Donald Black uses the ethnographic materials to explain under what conditions "law varies inversely with other social control" (1976, p. 6). "In rural Mexico for instance, one community has more family control than another, and this explains why its marital disputes are less likely to go to court" (p. 107). On the other hand, as Black has put it, "law is stronger when other social control is weaker" (p. 107), which was a major finding of Beatrice Whiting's *Paiute Sorcery* (1950), in which she postulated that sorcery was stronger when political organization was weak or decentralized.

In addition, law changes with relationships. Earlier studies by Gluckman (1955) and others postulated a connection between court procedure (i.e., compromise) and types of relationships. The idea that the nature of relationships sets restraints on the settlement process is usually formulated as follows: Relationships that are multiplex and involve many interests demand certain kinds of settlement, such as compromise, that will allow the relationship to continue. Disputants in simplex relationships will rely on adjudication or arbitration in settlement attempts that will lead to win-or-lose decisions. Later studies (Starr & Yngvesson, 1975) found that in struggles to control scarce resources, individuals may rank the resources higher than the relationships. Thus both the organizational and the social relational dimensions of disputing must inform any dynamic understanding of variety. The research on the behavior of law in a framework of intrasociety comparison is the major contribution of the volume *The Disputing Process* (Nader & Todd, 1978), which

summarizes the contributions of members of the Berkeley Village
Law Project.

A User Theory of Law

An interactive model is imperative for a user theory of law. The interactive model for understanding court users includes all of the immediate participants—the third parties and the litigating parties at a
minimum; others such as witnesses could be included as well. To
reiterate, a user theory of law would be based on the assumption
that law is made and changed by the cumulative efforts of its users
and is pushed forward in a particular direction by the dominant users. Such unconsciously generated cumulative movements may be
considered separate from and yet as important as any consciously
created ones attributable to legal engineering. This position would
argue that over time small claims courts develop a special profile because of the kinds of cases accepted, because lawyers may not be
invited to be users, and because only users who translate their cases
into monetary solutions are accepted. A medical analogy would be a
comparison between a general hospital and a cancer hospital; over
the decades the two hospitals will develop different kinds of expertise, technologies, and philosophies because of the difference in
users.

As I mentioned in "From Disputing to Complaining" (Nader,
1983, pp. 72–73), Willard Hurst (1981) pointed out, in discussing the
historical legal data from the United States, that what people were
litigating about changed from the nineteenth century to the twen-
tieth, as did procedural style, but that in another sense there was no
significant change at all; the users did not change: "Nineteenth-
century litigation involved only limited sectors of the society in any
bulk" (Hurst, 1981, p. 420). There were no more merchants suing
fellow merchants than there were in the twentieth-century dockets,
and people of small means were not often plaintiffs except in torts or
family matters (p. 421). The users of courts themselves did not
change much in the United States even under conditions of rapid
social change, and when they did, as in the 1960s when cases involving minority groups, consumer groups, and women increased in
frequency and success, a movement to develop alternatives to the
judicial system began to take form. In other literature, such as
Kagan (1981) on Spain, there have been documented shifts in the
use of courts over several hundred years. Exactly how use patterns

effect the change in law is not clear in either Hurst's or Kagan's materials beyond their saying that the law has been marginally used in the United States over the period studied, whereas in Spain it was centrally placed at the period of high use, meaning that there was a broadening of the array of litigating parties. I will come back to these points in the next section. The law courts of the Zapotec community I will discuss here might be described as central—in the sense that the courts dealt with a wide range of litigating activity on issues that personally touched the lives of the many members of the society who used the courts.

Gender and the Law in Oaxaca, Mexico

THE HISTORICAL DIMENSION

Oaxaca was one of the most heavily populated Indian areas of Mexico before the conquest. The indigenous village communities were grouped within the context of high cultures having complex division of labor, intensive agricultural production, city-states, warfare—in a word, civilizations. With the arrival of the Spaniards a variety of disasters struck. The native power elites were decimated, and the Indian cities where the elites lived were destroyed. Although the fragmentation of urban native political organization was complete, in the rural areas the political devastation was not so thorough; there the destruction was caused by epidemics and by coercive labor practices, some involving resettlement. The strength of the Indian communities in Oaxaca and particularly in the mountains of the area continued to center on the discrete landholding village, where the strongest allegiances were to the community and to family.

The legal history of Oaxaca from the conquest to the present is sketchy. One work that is of major importance in understanding the present is *Drinking, Homicide, and Rebellion in Colonial Mexican Villages*, by William Taylor (1979). Throughout his analysis Taylor stresses the importance of the free village and the political solidarity found there. In his conclusion Taylor observes that the incidence of homicide was patterned: "The forms and settings of homicides committed by villagers repeat the overt expressions of village solidarity. Lethal violence was concentrated within the nuclear family and in its relations with outsiders [to the village]. There were surprisingly few intracommunity homicides that might have threatened the political peace of the village" (1979, p. 153). One need not romanticize these villages; village solidarity meant village survival. The pattern that Taylor observes for Oaxaca—violent households and relatively peaceful (although not conflict free) communities—is not universal for rural communities but is a product of a particular type of political system. Taylor believes that in much of Indian Mexico at the end of the colonial period the family was mainly a conjugal arrangement— a productive and reproductive unit—rather than the prime focus of allegiance, and he links this attitude with the Indian concept of the individual, which stressed responsibility to the community and the primacy of community.

In discussing gender in relation to litigating parties, Taylor's findings are clear: there are striking differences between Indian men and women both as victims and as offenders (read plaintiffs and defendants) in homicides and aggravated assaults. "Indian women rarely killed—they comprise only three percent of homicide offenders and only seven percent of assault offenders. Female victims were considerably more numerous but still no more than thirty-three percent of homicide or assault victims" (Taylor, 1979, p. 84). Women were rarely defendants, most often victims or plaintiffs. It is not unusual in societies that most assault and homicide cases involve male victims of male assailants. What was unusual in eighteenth-century Oaxaca, according to Taylor, was the high proportion of females as victims of female offenders. Among Indians in general, a high proportion of the victims and/or plaintiffs were wives, sex partners, and sex rivals, a pattern much higher than among non-Indians of the same period. The fundamental conflict that produced serious violence centered on the position of the woman in the nuclear family household. Taylor sees this conflict as functional because violent conflict was restricted to relationships from which it was least likely to spread to factionalism at other levels of the community.

THE ETHNOGRAPHIC PRESENT

In 1957 I went to do fieldwork in a bilingual Zapotec Indian village in the Sierra Madre of Oaxaca, in a relatively remote area called the Rincón (Nader, 1964). Talea, the village I worked in, had a population of slightly over 2,000, and my research spanned a decade (1957–1968). During this period I studied the systems of social control used by these Zapotecs, and in the process I collected 409 cases recorded from the three village courts—the *presidente, sindico,* and *alcalde* courts. In theory, a case moves from the presidente court to the alcalde and the sindico courts. In practice, however, cases may be initiated in any of the three. I have characterized the style of proceedings in these courts as one that attempts to "make the balance." Where power relations are unequal, authorities may alter proceedings to equalize the imbalance in power. Litigants represent themselves and are given ample time to air their grievances. The authorities who hear these cases are respected, elected members of the community who use their knowledge of town affairs to resolve a case. Cases may be adjudicated, arbitrated, or mediated depending on the situation and the relationship between the litigants. In analyzing these case materials I focused on the court from the perspective of the users—the town officials, the defendant, and the plaintiff.

The mountain Zapotec court is a place where resources are gathered and competed for. Generally the plaintiff uses the courts to win compensation or to dispense punishment. The defendant, although often an unwilling participant, uses the courts as an asylum, a safe place to vent anger and rebuild a damaged reputation. The town officials as users see both plaintiff and defendant as potential sources of funds and labor for town projects, since court costs and fines may be levied in cash or work-hours. It was in the active role of plaintiff that these people differed most from the profile of court users in the United States. The Zapotecs are a rights-conscious people who push hard for remedy, and plaintiffs in particular are high on the justice motive. Furthermore, the use of the court reflects both the developmental cycle of its users and the distribution of authority in the town. Men use the courts heavily between the ages of 30 and 55; women are most likely to use the courts if they do not have male relatives to protect them.

I began my analysis of case samples with the aim of presenting those facts about court use and users that could be stated in numbers. I used these samples to reveal the regular and irregular patterns of action by court users, identifying them by sex, age, relationship, and class and indicating what they used the courts for and how sanction was applied. A profile of change and continuity in the status of court users over a period of time should provide an empirical base indicator of change and drift in the legal system, or of nonchange and continuity. Such change did not show up in the decade under study, which was a period before great change—the opening up of the road system and the subsequent flow of out-migration.

What can we learn about gender from counting? Although status and rank vary by sex in this village, both men and women use the courts, and the patterns of court use by sex are fairly clear-cut and consistent across the three courts (see Table 1). I was particularly interested in the number of women plaintiffs because there is widespread agreement that urban Zapotec women claim and exercise their rights with ease (Chinas, 1973; Royce, 1974), and because from a cross-cultural perspective the number of women who contest cases appears to be high. But more on this last point later.

Although men and women use the courts for different purposes, the proportion of males and females who use the courts as plaintiffs is relatively equal, $\chi^2(1)=0.41$, n.s. In the presidente court 45% of the plaintiffs were female and 32% were male; the distribution in the alcalde court is about the same for both sexes (45%). The sindico court is almost the exact opposite of the presidente court, with 45% of the plaintiffs being male and 34% female. The state rarely brings cases in the three village courts, and in all three courts a small percentage of cases are nonadversarial.

If we look at defendants who use the courts, the pattern is also clear: men use the courts as defendants in greater proportion than women (see Table 2 for sex of defendants), $\chi^2(1) = 111.85$, $p < .001$. Males account for 73% of the defendants in both the presidente and the alcalde court and 64% of the defendants in the sindico court. These figures are more in line with figures from the comparative record with the United States.

If we look at the relationships between plaintiffs and defendants across the sample of 409 cases (see Tables 3 and 4), we find there is a tendency for individuals to avoid bringing their consanguineal relatives to court, but affinal relatives (those connected by marriage) frequently appear in the courts. Disputes between both types of kin account for approximately half of the cases brought to the sindico and alcalde courts and one third of the cases in the presidente court. This pattern does not surprise me, and I would expect to find it common in towns like this one that are not factionalized.

When we focus on family cases alone (Table 4), we see that most disputes are between wives and their husbands; if we added the cases of men and women who live together as lovers, the category would become even more swollen. These disputes help to contextualize the pattern of high female court use noted earlier. Husbands rarely bring their wives to court, and children only seldom bring their parents to court. If we look at the residence pattern between plaintiff and defendant by court (Table 5), over twice as many peo-

Table 1
Sex of Plaintiffs by Village-Level Court

User	Presidente		Alcalde		Sindico		Total Cases
	Number of Cases	% of Total	Number of Cases	% of Total	Number of Cases	% of Total	
Male	49	32	84	46	38	45	171
Female	69	45	85	46	29	34	183
State	23	15	5	3	8	10	36
Couple (husband/wife)	1	1	3	2	2	2	6
Nonadversarial female	7	4	2	1	1	1	10
Nonadversarial male	2	1	2	1	5	6	9
Nonadversarial group	1	1	—	—	—	—	1
Adversarial group	1	1	2	1	2	2	5
Total	153	100	183	100	85	100	421
Missing data	327		315		164		
Possible total[a]	480		498		249		

[a] Some cases had as many as three plaintiffs. To accommodate these cases, we included spaces for as many as three plaintiffs for each case. The possible totals are derived from three times the number of cases for each court. The many instances of missing data are cases that had fewer than three plaintiffs.

Table 2
Sex of Defendants by Village-level Court

User	Presidente		Alcalde		Sindico		Total Cases
	Number of Cases	% of Total	Number of Cases	% of Total	Number of Cases	% of Total	
Male	124	73	133	73	62	64	319
Female	36	21	43	23	23	24	102
State	2	1	—	—	2	2	4
Couple (husband/wife)	—	—	—	—	1	1	1
Nonadversarial female	2	1	1	1	1	1	4
Nonadversarial male	6	4	4	2	5	5	15
Nonadversarial group	—	—	—	—	—	—	—
Adversarial group	—	—	2	1	2	2	4
Total	170	100	183	100	96	100	449
Missing data	310		315		152		777
Possible total	480		498		248		1,226

Table 3
Relationship between Plaintiffs and Defendants by Village-Level Court

User	Presidente		Alcalde		Sindico		Total Cases
	Number of Cases	% of Total	Number of Cases	% of Total	Number of Cases	% of Total	
Consanguineal kin	11	10	10	8	6	17	27
Affinal kin	26	24	49	40	12	33	87
Neighbors	5	4	6	5	5	14	16
Lovers	10	9	14	12	2	5	26
Other	58	53	43	35	11	31	112
Total	110	100	122	100	36	100	268
Missing data	50		44		47		141
Possible total	160		166		83		409

Table 4
Type of Family Relationship by Village-Level Court

Plaintiff vs. Defendant	Presidente		Alcalde		Sindico		Total
	Number of Cases	% of Total	Number of Cases	% of Total	Number of Cases	% of Total	Total
Husband vs. wife	1	4	6	17	1	9	8
Wife vs. husband	17	63	22	61	5	45	44
Parent vs. child	3	11	3	8	4	37	10
Child vs. parent	3	11	4	11	1	9	8
Sibling vs. sibling	3	11	1	3	—	—	4
Total	27	100	36	100	11	100	74
Missing data	133		130		72		335
Total cases	160		166		83		409

Table 5
Residence Pattern between Plaintiff and Defendant by Village-Level Court

Plaintiff vs. Defendant	Presidente		Alcalde		Sindico		Total
	Number of Cases	% of Total	Number of Cases	% of Total	Number of Cases	% of Total	Total
Together	27	27	8	30	3	43	38
Separate	71	71	17	63	3	43	91
Transitory	2	2	2	7	1	14	5
Total	100	100	27	100	7	100	134
Missing data	60		139		76		275
Total cases	160		166		83		409

ple litigate who do not live together as who do live together, $\chi^2(1) = 21.78$, $p < .001$.

In sum, it is women who make extensive use of the courts to obtain their domestic rights. Such is not universally true, and certainly not for other parts of Mexico. In another paper (Nader & Metzger, 1963) we described a village in Chiapas, Mexico, where women never take their husbands to court for resolution of a conflict; they use the courts to terminate a relationship. We argued there that to understand why marital disputes go to court one needs to understand the patterns of authority in relation to the distribution of conflict resolution resources. Although the authority of older males could make their full use of the court unnecessary, at present in Talea the older family males have limited authority because of patterns of early inheritance, separate residence for young couples, readily available substitutes for both spouses and parents with respect to sex and substance, and families' refusal to accept responsibility for marriages they have not arranged. In such situations the court then assumes the responsibility lost or abandoned by the family and exercises the authority over marriage vested in it as a representative of the state. But it is not the court that initiates cases. For the most part that is done by women, who use the courts to improve their positions.

It has been said that law varies directly with rank and that the lower ranks have less law than the higher ranks (Black, 1976, pp. 17, 22). It has also been argued that law is inactive between intimates, that "a person is [less] likely to sue a close kinsman than a friend, an acquaintance, a neighbor, a fellow tribesman," and so on (p. 42). However, Talean court cases dealing with male/female relations do not seem to follow the pattern of more downward than upward complaints; the justice motive is exercised by women. In particular, women use the courts against men (upward social control) in order to balance or improve the power differentials between them. And if affinal cases are examples of intimate cases (as I believe them to be), then, contrary to Black's argument, law among intimates is alive and active and indeed may dominate user activity in the courts. In property cases the highest total percentage is between males (presidente court 38%, alcalde court 37%, sindico 33%) although in both presidente and alcalde courts an equally high percentage of cases concerning property (presidente 31%, alcalde 28%) involve male versus female litigants. When we examine violence cases in the three courts, those that involve physical aggression are prepondantly female versus male in the presidente court, although as villagers move toward the use of external law (that is, through the sindico and alcalde courts) more males are involved as court users.

In order to examine the behavioral effect of the sex of users, I isolated five sets of village cases for analysis. All shared the attribute of being cross-sex cases. The first two sets deal with complaints surrounding paternity (which may be brought by males or females) and with cases of physical abuse brought primarily by a woman against the man she is living with, whether husband or lover. The third set of materials deals with a variety of female/male complaints; they were selected as a set because in all the cases extended family members became involved in the dispute. In the fourth set, men bring women to court for abandonment or adultery. And in the final set the court brings to court women who are accused of aborting a pregnancy.

The styles of court procedures generally vary with each set: paternity cases are accusatory, and all demand compensation. In the physical abuse cases the women usually demand divorce or separation but receive conciliatory or remedial action. The families that participate in female/male cases of the sort in the third set increase the demands for action against the abusing male. And in the last two sets which are male/female cases dealing with abandonment, adultery, and abortion, the style is clearly penal, and the intent is to punish. If certain types of cases were dropped from the docket, their associated styles would cease to dominate the character of the court; for example, a schoolteacher presidente once suggested that all family cases, with the exception of the last two sets, should be dropped from the court. Such action would clearly make for a Zapotec court characterized by a penal style. At the moment, however, the users determine the court style, and women plaintiffs play a predominant role in that determination.

Numbers do not tell the whole story about court use, however. To say that women use the courts as plaintiffs about as frequently as men do and for roughly the same matters does not delineate the roles of males and females and the way each sex is valued or devalued by the other and in the society at large. In other words, statements about the degree of court interaction are bound to leave out much of the substance of male/female relations. The case materials themselves contain rich records of how men and women express themselves in court when under interpersonal stress, how they define and fight for justice. In these villages no woman has ever sat as judge, and few women, as I have already indicated, appear as defendants in male/female cases. Nevertheless, we see that the most frequent complainants in cross-sex cases are the women, and it is only the women who complain about physical abuse. The outcome of the litigation is as stereotypical as the complaint itself; both result from the shape of women's lives in the village. Women marry before they are twenty, in arranged marriages or, more recently, by choice free from parental persuasion or admonition. The way she has married affects a woman's complaint pattern. In an arranged marriage, the parents of the woman will take part in ensuring that if problems arise they will be resolved, whereas free-choice marriage stimulates less parental responsibility and possibly more abuse from husbands. Relative rank, as in the wealth of male or female, the presence of extended family in the village, and distance from family are also factors in the shape and outcome of disputes. What does not vary over time is the willingness of women to search for justice in a public forum, even though men dominate that forum and the town officials pursue minimax (that is, give a little, get a little) solutions for women's problems.

Earlier I mentioned that as these villagers move toward the use of external (extravillage) law, there will be more males involved as court users and presumbly a more penal style. In the district court at Villa Alta (six to eight hours' walk from Talea), there is slightly higher use of the court by male plaintiffs than females and an overwhelming presence of males as defendants. Male and female plaintiffs complain about similar problems at nearly the same rates. The major difference between male and female court users comes when they appear as defendants. Women only infrequently appear in the district courts as defendants, and when they do the offense is usually property related. Male defendants usually appear in court for offenses involving injuries to persons. Women usually bring cross-sex cases and men bring same-sex cases; the latter type is relatively rare for women in the district courts.

District court dockets reflect the dramatic events in Indian communities. They are a manifestation of the stress and discontent of people united by community. In addition, the story they tell is not limited to pathological behavior but reveals a power struggle between two levels of law: local and state (Parnell, 1978). District courts have been able to assert their authority in matters where blood is drawn because, according to state law, the village court does not have jurisdiction over certain matters dealing with bodily injury and property. Virtually all villages send such cases to the district courts. The reason property cases now regularly appear in the district courts is more ambiguous; it may reflect the fact that the administration of land sales at the district level gives Villa Altecan officials power over land cases; it may reflect some advantages that accrue to landowners as a result of their greater wealth.

Villagers do not turn to district courts for help in role-related cases involving daily living unless those cases involve abuse of authority. Then a villager will turn to the district level to balance the power in a dispute with a local-level official. Village officials also turn to the district courts to resolve their problems with citizens, but they are less likely to do so than the other villagers.

Overall, the relationship between the Zapotec people of the Rincón and the district court is one in which Rinconeros turn to the district for extraordinary problems. The blood-drawing violent act, the property case, and conflicts with local authorities all push Rinconeros toward the district courts. The ordinary problems of day-to-day life in the village remain under the jurisdiction of local officials. Whether this situation results from the desires of district officials or local people, the effect is the same. District courts will develop in response to the kinds of cases they receive. The district court in Villa Alta has developed a court apparatus to handle extraordinary problems. As long as local courts handle the ordinary problems and the district courts handle extraordinary problems, the two systems work together, albeit unknowingly; neither is the passive object of a state legal process. Should changes occur at the local level, leaving villagers without a forum for their ordinary problems, we could expect a marked increase in extraordinary acts and a serious crime problem. The opposite possibility, that ordinary life problems will revert, for example, to family remedy agents, is less likely because change is bringing with it a spatial fragmentation of family members owing to general migration patterns.

The development of factionalism in a pueblo that is divided over the desires of some for progress and of others for a more traditional way of life, or by disagreements about the intrusion of Protestant missionaries and the resulting conversions, may make local courts unattractive to one faction. The desires of local officials for greater economic reimbursement may leave the poor without a forum for handling their life problems. And changes in economic structure may leave local officials tied up with property cases or product complaint cases so that there is little time for other small injustices. Whatever the reason for change, a failure on the part of local officials to deal with life problems may be crucial for the pattern of order or disorder.

As we examine the other villages of the Rincón, we become aware of the overall diversity of the area. Each Zapotec pueblo has engineered a distinct pattern for relating to the district court and managing conflicts. It appears that informal rules have been worked out so that one village takes only personal injury cases to the district level and another takes only property-related cases.

That the types of cases taken to the courts can be patterned in this way reflects the fact that law not only controls but is controlled. I pointed out earlier that cases can come to the district court as a result of decisions by either local officials or villagers. The patterns that are found to characterize use of the district courts in this region suggest a system of social control within the villages that affects officials and citizens alike. Both officials and citizens seem to share a view of the function of the district courts. This view varies from village to village, but within each village it is consistent. How that view was formed and how it continues or changes over time are subjects for another investigation. That such patterning exists, however, suggests that we must look at law within the matrix of other social control systems, realizing that law is both an agent of social control and subject to social control.

Contact with the law should not be taken to suggest disorder. The village situation exemplifies this well, but the patterns of court use by sex raise some other interesting questions. As we have seen, females are not reluctant to go to the district courts with their problems. They go as plaintiffs almost as frequently as males, but they differ from males in that they appear infrequently as defendants and almost never as defendants in personal injury cases. When they do appear in the courts as defendants they are more likely to have been taken by a male, not by another female. Female versus female conflicts are rarely found in the district courts, which are places for male versus male conflicts or cross-sex conflict (see Table 6).

In many of the Rincón villages the women may have developed their own separate forums for handling female versus female disputes, which are separated even from the local courts. Females view the district court as primarily a place where problems with men are handled. Nation-state law, by being a male-dominated system, could inadvertently strengthen the female dispute-settling forums. If nation-state law contributes to the demise of local-level legal systems by increasing its control over these systems but fails to recognize the existence of female dispute-settling mechanisms, the female dispute-handling processes may carry the last vestiges of norms and values that distinguish one village from the national system.

The analysis of court users in Talea, the particular village under scrutiny, revealed a court system characterized by a very wide range of citizen participants and a court system that had its agenda determined by the needs of the community. The people have evolved a court process that is equated with justice. Local law has been created by citizen use rather than being imposed upon a citizen body by citizen officials. I have described the process as interactive rather than impositional. The use of the Villa Altecan district court is very much in the same mold: people use the court for a wide array of legal complaints, and at least in terms of male/female use the pattern follows in much the same vein as the use of village courts. In other words, it does not appear that villagers change their posture in dealing with the district court—they view the court process as interactional.

The district court docket in Villa Alta reveals another model. On the one hand, it is impositional: the state determines what cases it will accept and also what cases must be appealed to it. The court deals with the extraordinary, not the ordinary, and of course we are not surprised to discover that there is no broad citizen participation

Table 6
Conflict Dyads in the District Court

Dyad	Number	% of Total
Female vs. female	6	4.68
Female vs. male	31	24.22
Male vs. female	12	9.37
Male vs male	51	39.84
Male vs. male and female	3	2.34
Female vs. male and female	6	4.69
Male and female vs. male	3	2.34
Official vs. citizen	5	3.91
Citizen vs. official	8	6.25
Society vs. official	1	0.78
Society vs. female	2	1.56
Total	128	100.00

in it. On the other hand, the district court means something different to each village in the district. In this sense it can be seen as a flexible institution, one that can be used in a variety of ways by the villages in the district. It is because local law is still under local control that this court can also be described as interactive: all the users (the state and the litigating parties) shape the activity of the court. The underlying concept is still a shared-power theory of law, even though the distribution of that power is variable and dynamic.

DISCUSSION

Let me try to pull together the various threads in the development of an understanding of how men and women as users of the court affect the direction and slope of law and how the law limits the pattern of court use. Basically, I am arguing that the interests of the local community vis-à-vis its citizens and that of the wider society vis-à-vis those same citizens are different, and that the powerholders in the community and in the state system will use their power to achieve their respective goals by encouraging free access to the courts at the community level or by permitting only limited access at the state level. In addition, the rank of men relative to women and to each other affects whether and how gender influences user patterns. Throughout the history of Mexico it has been observed that the process of Mexicanization or more generally Westernization has often meant a change in the status of Indian men and women: women lose status relative to their menfolk, and men lose status relative to men of the dominant society.

Among the Zapotecs of the Sierra Madre of Oaxaca the free landholding village organization is important for reasons that I cited from Taylor (1979) earlier: the threat to community solidarity is less if violence is confined predominantly to the family. On the other hand, at least in the contemporary period, village courts are willing to hear any complaints from women in this realm, and that they do and that their preferred method of handling such intimate conflict is reconciliation is important to the making of court culture.

Village law is egalitarian in the plaintiff arena. Use is generated by exercise of the justice motive. Males and females exercise their rights and remedies in proportion to their numbers in the population. Two conditions are likely to cause the number of women plaintiffs to change: (1) female plaintiffs would decrease with the development of a strong and extended family (because senior family members would mediate marital complaints) or with the development of strong state powers (because even now the state makes it difficult to take marital conflict to court); (2) female plaintiffs would increase with a breakdown in family authority (in which case community courts would substitute for family) or with conditions in which high priority was accorded to community loyalty caused by outside threat, as with the competition between a Mexican district court and a Zapotec community court (in which case a strong community court would monopolize the power to resolve family disputes). When female plaintiffs decrease, there is necessarily a proportionate increase in male same-sex cases. More male plaintiffs proportionately means more male defendants associated with the increased violence that accompanies the gender-status shifts for both men and women as described above: Indian males lose status in the larger society. More male plaintiffs means an increase in penal style. It also means more cases appealed to the district court, eventually resulting in loss of community identity because local law is undermined. When the community court loses the power to control its caseload, users from the village level will be increasingly stigmatized. Having been incorporated into the national social structure, they will be placed at the bottom of the national status ladder. The Zapotecs will have turned mestizo, thereby losing their ease of initiating cases in court.

Mexican state law may be said to have a bias against defendants, who are primarily men. Village law has a bias toward plaintiffs, who are both male and female. If a decrease in the number of women plaintiffs means more use of the court styles that men use, which are accusatory and threatening, then law will move from being restitutive and conciliatory to being penal. The drift of the law will then be in the direction of the extraordinary versus the routine case. Under such conditions Donald Black's proposition, mentioned previously in regard to rank and intimacy, will fit: under governmental law, law varies directly with rank, the lower ranks have less law than the higher ranks, and the law becomes inactive between intimates (Black, 1976, p. 42). The Zapotec village courts are characterized by upward social control, the Mexican state courts by downward social control. The state courts fit Black's proposition because the state restricts the plaintiff role and males monopolize the defendant role.

If women wish mainly to bring grievances from the intimate environment, they will be excluded in courts that emphasize the extraordinary unless their intimate environment cases are extraordinary (in which case the state would be the plaintiff). The drift of the law moves with the dominant users. In Zapotec village law, ideology and values emphasize need, and the courts are expected to respond to human needs, to the requests thrust upon them by users. In that context law is not a product but a service available to all adults irrespective of gender. If women have greater need, then their role as users will increase.

The behavior of law courts in the mountain Zapotec villages has drifted and will continue to drift in relation to changes in family structure, population mobility, and state initiative. I would argue that state activity (and thereby downward social control as well) has been kept to a minimum by the high rate of female plaintiffs who present routine cases relating to female/male relations, and that this situation is possible only because of the free landholding village structure. With increasing contact with the state court, village solidarity decreases, the plaintiff role atrophies, the justice motive is frustrated, and the state becomes the plaintiff in criminal matters. As women drop out of the men's world, gender will be most importantly reflected in the fact that males predominate as defendants in criminal matters.

When I say that the justice motive is frustrated by the state, I am emphasizing that particularly in criminal cases it becomes the business of the state to decide for potential users whether the justice motive should be exercised. It is clear that within any population there is differential justice motivation and that in the history of a population there is differential use of the justice motive over time. But with the advent of state law we have something new: the justice motive is controlled and managed from a central station. As I noted before, women leave their mark on the judicial structure by using the courts particularly as plaintiffs. When courts operate in a more proactive fashion that restricts them, the number of male users increases.

General Significance of Gender in Legal Change

This paper places importance on the concept of use in relation to the development of theories of legal change in courts. In particular, I have emphasized the plaintiff user and the gender of that plaintiff, whether male or female. A focus on both male and female plaintiffs is intended to emphasize the way plaintiff users act as behavioral instruments in courtroom settings in a small indigenous community where the claim bringers set the courtroom agenda. The growth of the law in such a setting could be described as organic, growing in response to user need. Zapotec law is responsive to the specific needs of men and women, as well as to their commonly shared needs. But law is not always responsive to individual need; sometimes courts are proactive. In societies where user initiative is determined primarily by the court, not only does the individual user recede into a subordinate position, but the plaintiff hardly enters into theories about courts at all. Instead, the model is one of the court as a behavioral instrument.

In recent publications about courts, as in *Empirical Theories about Courts* (Boyum & Mather, 1983), for example, theories of courts generally ignore the individual plaintiff participants in their discussion. Scholars instead speak of system behavior or court behavior; Lawrence Friedman, for example, introduces his article in the Boyum and Mather volume with the statement: "Our concern is with the behavior of courts. We leave aside any primary focus on the litigants and their lawyers, though of course this comes up incidently" (p. 9). Krislov, in that same volume (p. 171), refers to a statement that indicates that the major participants in the court are the defendant, the lawyer and the judge. There are other articles in the volume that investigate the role of the third party, but the picture that emerges is of courts acting as managers of litigation. Krislov (p.173) refers to the mechanisms of control when he notes that courts can encourage court use by their narrow or broad understanding of who may litigate and can generate activity by creating rewards for lawyers (as with contingency fees) and by their direct control over the supply of lawyers. According to such a model, it is not the individual plaintiff but the court as dominant user and major player that determines whether litigation contracts or expands. In this context the court is a behavioral instrument moving the individual plaintiff users toward explicit or implicit goals. By comparison Zapotec plaintiffs appear powerful indeed.

However, even those who argue that United States judges alter the behavior of litigants and thus the course of the law would not argue that their power is complete. Krislov (Boyum & Mather, 1983, p. 182) notes that litigation is a by-product of transactions: "an increase in social transactions will produce a proportionate increase in litigation." He also suggests that "litigation is the product of social propensities to litigate and the occurrence of trouble-cases is not automatically determined by set-facts in a dispute." Rather, ability and willingness, or the strength of the justice motive vary in the population. Krislov also notes that "opportunity to litigate can be altered (1) by changes in decision system, limiting or expanding opportunities, or raising or lowering costs; and (2) by outside alternative opportunity." Krislov's intent is to counter the popular notion that litigation is *merely* a product of the plaintiff's attitudes. Thus on the one hand we have theories of legal change that remove the plaintiff from discussion, and on the other we have research about caseloads that rejects the popular notion that individual plaintiffs are the major actors in generating litigation. The interactive model, which is implicit in Krislov's work, helps us examine the conditions under which the roles of court, plaintiff, and defendant alternate as behavioral instruments of change.

It is in this context that gender may serve as an opening wedge to examine triggering mechanisms.[3] If courtroom encounters are dominated by males as judges, plaintiffs, and defendants, then male culture will predominate in the courts, and female discourse will not be heard (except perhaps through male lawyers). In the Zapotec court I studied, female discourse and male discourse are part of the encounter, but such a pattern is not universal in the non-Western world. Anthropologist Michael J. Lowy (1984) describes the distribution of men and women claim bringers in the court, in the department of social welfare, and at rent board hearings in Koforidua, Ghana.[4] Male plaintiffs dominate the court 80% to 20%; the women claim bringers dominate the hearings for family cases in the social welfare department 85% to 15%. However, in the rent control board the proportion approximates the proportion of male to female plaintiffs on the court docket, with 84% male and 16% female. Proportionate figures in other court settings are hard to come by because until quite recently the gender variable was not explored relative to the direction of legal change. If Western legal institutions are male-dominated, the direction of courts and of law more generally will be influenced by male and not by female con-

3. A project on the legal issues of female inmates carried out at the Smith College School for Social Work examined why female prisoners do not utilize the courts to the same extent as their male counterparts (Gabel, 1982).

4. Michel J. Lowy (1984) is investigating the role of men and women in court usage over a 36-year period of urbanization from 1915 to 1951. One of his findings was that over this time "women have generally been the plaintiff in more criminal complaints than civil complaints, whereas, the male pattern is just the opposite—men generally bringing a higher rate of civil rather than criminal cases." The meaning of such a finding is unclear but should be clarified by Lowy's full analysis of the data. Publication of such statistics would facilitate a greater understanding of gender and the cultural dimension in court usage.

structs. The implications of such an observation provide legal change theorists with additional challenge.[5]

REFERENCES

Black, D. (1976). *The behavior of law*. New York: Academic Press.

Black, D. (1984). Jurocracy in America. *Tocqueville Review — Revue Tocqueville*, in press.

Barnes, T. G. (1981). *Law 260, English legal history: A coursebook* (Vol. 2). Berkeley: University of California.

Bayley, D. H. (1983). Police: History. In S. H. Kadish (Ed.), *Encyclopedia of crime and justice*, Vol. 3 (pp. 1121–1123). New York: Free Press.

Cappelletti, M. (1975). Governmental and private advocates for the public interest in civil litigation: A comparative study. *Michigan Law Review, 73*, 793–884.

Chinas, B. (1973). *The Isthmus Zapotecs: Women's roles in cultural context*. New York: Holt, Rinehart and Winston.

Colson, E. (1953). Social control and vengeance in Plateau Tonga society. *Africa, 23*, 199–212.

Friedman, L., & Percival, R. V. (1976). A tale of two courts: Litigation in Alameda and San Benito counties. *Law and Society Review, 10*, 267–301.

Gabel, K. (1982). The legal issues of female inmates. Unpublished manuscript, Smith College School for Social Work.

Gluckman, M. (1955). *The judicial process among the Barotse of northern Rhodesia*. Manchester: Manchester University Press.

Hurst, W. (1981). The functions of courts in the United States: 1950–1980. *Law and Society Review, 15*, 401–472.

Kagan, R. (1981). *Lawsuits and litigants in Castile*. Chapel Hill: University of North Carolina Press.

Keller, E. F. (1983). *A feeling for the organism: The life and work of Barbara McClintock*. New York: Freeman.

Keller, E. F. (1985). *Reflections on gender and science*. New Haven: Yale University Press.

Kluckhohn, C. (1953). Universal categories of culture. In A. L. Kroeber

---

5. For imaginative and pioneering work on this subject in the related field of gender and science, see Evelyn Fox Keller (1983, 1985). Although Keller explores the association between masculinity and science, in law and gender study we have yet to fully recognize the degree to which law is genderized before we ask the questions Keller asks: Why this association between masculinity and science, and how does it manifest itself? See also the brief article by Diane Polan (1982) for her observations on the role of law in maintaining patriarchy.

(Ed.), *Anthropology today* (pp. 507–523). Chicago: University of Chicago Press.

Lerner, M. J. (1975). The justice motive in social behavior. *Journal of Social Issues, 31* (3), 151–170.

Lerner, M. J. (1980). *The belief in a just world: A fundamental delusion.* New York: Plenum Press.

Lerner, M. J., & Lerner, S. C. (1981). *The justice motive in social behavior: Adapting to times of scarcity and change.* New York: Plenum Press.

Lowy, M. J. (1984). Urbanization and court usage in Koforidua, Ghana. Paper presented at the First Annual Conference on Law and Anthropology, University of San Diego School of Law, 10–11 March 1984.

Maine, H. S. (1861). *Ancient law: Its connection with the early history of society and its relation to modern ideas.* London: John Murray.

Metzger, D. (1960). Conflict in Chulsanto: A village in Chiapas. *Alpha Kappa Deltan, 30,* 35–48.

Moore, S. F. (1969). Law and anthropology. In B. J. Siegel (Ed.), *Biennial review of anthropology,* Stanford: Stanford University.

Nader, L. (1964). Talea and Juquila: A comparison of Zapotec social organization. *University of California Publications in Archaeology and Ethnology, 48* (3), 195–296.

Nader, L. (1965). The anthropological study of law. *American Anthropologist,* special issue, *The ethnography of law, 67* (6), 3–32.

Nader, L. (1978). The direction of law and the development of extra-judicial processes in nation state societies. In P. Gulliver (Ed.), *Cross-examinations: Essays in memory of Max Gluckman* (pp. 78–95). Leiden: E. J. Brill.

Nader, L. (1980). *No access to law: Alternatives to the American judicial system.* New York: Academic Press.

Nader, L. (1983). From disputing to complaining. In D. Black (Ed.), *Toward a general theory of social control* (pp. 71–94). New York: Academic Press.

Nader, L. (1984). A user theory of law. *Southwestern Law Review, 38* (4), 301–313.

Nader, L., & Metzger, D. (1963). Conflict resolution in two Mexican communities. *American Anthropologist, 65* (3), 584–592.

Nader, L., & Todd, H. (1978). *The disputing process: Law in ten societies.* New York: Columbia University Press.

Parnell, P. (1978). *Conflict and competition in a Mexican judicial district.* Unpublished doctoral dissertation, University of California, Berkeley.

Polan, D. (1982). Toward a theory of law and patriarchy. In D. Kairys, *The politics of law* (pp. 294–303). New York: Pantheon Books.

Riesman, D. (1954). *Individualism reconsidered and other essays.* Glencoe, IL: Free Press.

Royce, A. P. (1974). *Prestige and affiliation in an urban community: Juchitán, Oaxaca.* Unpublished doctoral dissertation, University of California, Berkeley.

Sapir, E. (1921). *Language.* New York: Harcourt, Brace.

Starr, J., & Yngvesson, B. (1975). Scarcity and disputing: Zeroing-in on compromise decisions. *American Ethnologist, 2,* 553–566.

Sursock, A. (1983). *Individualism and political participation in a French community.* Unpublished doctoral dissertation, University of California, Berkeley.

Taylor, W. (1979). *Drinking, homicide, and rebellion in colonial Mexican villages.* Stanford: Stanford University Press.

Whiting, B. (1950). *Paiute sorcery.* Publications in Anthropology (No. 15). New York: Viking Fund.

Psychology, Determinism, and Legal Responsibility[1]

Stephen J. Morse

University of Southern California

Introduction

*B*laming and excusing are uniquely human activities. We engage in them only when a person has behaved badly, when his or her actions have gone wrong or misfired in some fashion (Brandt, 1969). Then we seek an explanation that justifies blaming and punishing the actor or excusing and staying the imposition of the otherwise just punishment. Psychological (and psychiatric) explanations are used routinely in the criminal law to support claims for excuse and mitigation. These explanations are the foundation for excuses such as insanity, intoxication, negation of mens rea, and partial responsibility. They are often central in sentencing decisions, including sentencing for capital crimes, and they are used increasingly to support other defenses or mitigating conditions such as mistake, duress, extreme emotional disturbance, and the provocation/passion formula that reduces the degree of intentional homicide from murder to voluntary manslaughter. Finally, psychological explanations are crucial in the attempt to create new excuses such as brainwashing, premenstrual syndrome, or battered spouse syndrome.

Although popular and legal dissatisfaction with these legal doctrines and practices and with their accompanying psychological ex-

1. I am heavily indebted to my friend and colleague Michael Moore for my understanding of the issues discussed in this paper. His article "Causation and the Excuses," *California Law Review* (1985) is especially illuminating. I should also like to thank Robert Audi, Scott Fraser, and Will T. Jones for their helpful comments.

Portions of the section entitled "The Criteria for Excuse" have been adapted from Morse (1985). Portions of this paper will also appear in substantially revised form in my forthcoming book *The Jurisprudence of Craziness* (Oxford University Press).

planations regularly arises, we tend to accept without serious question the relevance of psychology to determinations of responsibility. The usual premise for this relevance, sometimes expressed but often not, is that psychological explanations vitiate free will, which is allegedly the foundation of moral and legal responsibility. I suggest that the standard understanding of psychology's relevance to responsibility is incorrect. Here I shall attempt to provide the proper standard and shall propose that psychological expertise should have a substantial but altered role in creating, modifying, and adjudicating excuses and mitigating conditions. It is not my goal to provide a definitive analysis of the problem of responsibility. Rather, I seek a level of abstraction and precision that will provide clarification and guidance to lawyers and psychologists concerned with both social and legal policy and the adjudication of actual cases.

First, however, it is necessary to clarify which excuses I shall consider. I shall primarily be concerned with those conditions that negate the criteria for an actor's moral responsibility. In some cases an act may have been reprehensible, but the actor was not morally responsible for it. For example, mental disorder, infancy, a profound grief reaction, involuntary intoxication, or the feelings of compulsion produced by a gun at one's head may all be the predicate for such an excuse. I shall call all these "responsibility excuses."

Responsibility excuses do not encompass all legal defenses. We must therefore distinguish what I shall term the "policy excuses" and justifications. The former are created on grounds of social and legal policy that have nothing to do with the actor's moral responsibility (see Robinson, 1982). For instance, the minority, "objective" theory of the entrapment defense excuses an actor if police conduct was so outrageous that we believe the actor should be acquitted even if he was entirely normal and predisposed to commit the crime anyway (LaFave & Scott, 1972). We excuse in this case to deter the police, not because the actor's responsibility is compromised. The statute of limitations is another bar to conviction that is unrelated to the actor's bad conduct and moral responsibility.

Justifications are the second class of defenses that we must distinguish from the responsibility excuses (Fletcher, 1978; Greenawalt, 1984). A justification exists when the actor's conduct causes an otherwise prohibited evil, but in the case at hand the harm he or she causes is the lesser of two evils. The defenses of self-defense, necessity, and law enforcement fit in this category. Thus, a person who intentionally sets fire to a farm in order to create a firebreak that will prevent an advancing forest fire from consuming a whole town will have a necessity defense to a charge of arson. In this and other cases of justifications, the actor is not culpable because society has decided that he or she did the right thing in the circumstances. By contrast, the actor with a responsibility excuse has done the wrong thing, but there was something amiss with him or her that has negated moral responsibility.

Consideration of the responsibility excuses reveals that they are individuated according to the cause of the actor's problem rather than by the result the problem causes that is relevant to responsibility. The names of these defenses—insanity, involuntary intoxication, duress, infancy—all refer to the cause of what is amiss with the actor. As new defenses are proposed—for example, brainwashing, premenstrual syndrome, battered spouse syndrome—they too are based on causes. When the law has not accepted a new defense, the hapless advocate is forced to argue that the relevant condition is "really" part of a preexisting excuse. Thus, for example, the battered spouse who has harmed the batterer often must argue that he or she was temporarily insane or some such thing. I believe that individuating excuses by causes is a historical accident that has had a confusing and unfortunate effect on the law of excuses. I shall attempt to show what all the responsibility excuses have in common and to present a unified approach to them that will make sense of what psychology has to offer conceptually and practically to their understanding and adjudication. (For brevity, I shall refer to the responsibility excuses simply as excuses unless I need to distinguish them from other excusing conditions.) I shall conclude by demonstrating the good, practical policy consequences that follow from the analyses presented.

Introductory Cases

Let us begin with true case studies that illustrate the issues. I provide these case studies not to substitute anecdote for analysis but to provide inductively rich material that will demonstrate the legal and human relevance of the abstract and theoretical discussion that will follow.

On the morning of June 18, 1976, Patricia Tempest killed her six-year-old son Gregory by drowning him in a bathtub. She described the event in a confession given two hours after she was taken into custody on the afternoon of the homicide (*Commonwealth v. Tempest*, 1981; all the following material is taken from the official report of the case).

> I got up quarter to eleven or something like that. My husband had already left to go to work. I gave Gregory his breakfast. He was already up watching T.V. It was the last day for kindergarten. I was packing him a lunch for his picnic. I gave him juice with vitamin E. I told him he had to get a bath. He didn't want to go right away. He wanted to finish watching his program so I told him to come up after he did. I went upstairs and filled the tub. I filled it more than normal. When he came upstairs he noticed and said it was kind of deep. He got in the tub himself. I washed the front of his body, then I told him to turn around on his stomach. He told me I didn't wash his face yet. So, I washed his face. I told him to turn on his stomach. When he did I pushed his face down. He struggled and cried, "Mommy you're drowning me." He kept fighting for a couple of minutes—it could have been longer. He still tried to move a little but I kept his head under until he stopped. He didn't move any more so I got out of the tub, I had gotten into the tub to hold him down. I didn't know how long it would take to drown, so I left him there in the tub. He was on his back. His face was sideways. I sat there and told him, "I had to kill you. I'm sorry." I went into the bedroom, put the television on and watched the movie. I went downstairs and got a banana and ate it, and also took my medicine. I came back upstairs and watched another program—$20,000 pyramid [*sic*]. My husband came home at 25 of 4. I told him I killed Greg. I'd drowned him. He went upstairs and came back and looked very sad. (p. 953)

Mrs. Tempest also told her husband Ronald that she had planned the killing three days in advance and had also pondered "bumping off her husband." She told one of the examining psychiatrists, Dr. Glass, that she had considered using poison, drowning, or firearms on her child and husband. The confession contained, in addition, the following exchange:

> Q. When you went upstairs to fill the tub for Greg's bath, had you planned on drowning Greg?
> A. Yes.
> Q. How much water did you put in the tub?
> A. About 3 or 4 inches—I don't know.
> Q. Is this more than normal?
> A. No, but I filled it up more after he got in the tub. (p. 955)

Mrs. Tempest's confession also described her motive for killing Gregory.

Q. Why did you drown Greg?

A. My husband made friends down the street. Greg played with Joey, the little boy down the street. I didn't have any friends. I'm afraid of everybody. I don't really know why I did it. I just did—I didn't want Ronnie and Greg in my life any more.

Q. Why didn't you want them in your life any more?

A. Greg was too demanding. He got on my nerves. Just having to do things for him. I didn't want the responsibility. I didn't want him to go into 1st grade because I would have to talk to other people. I didn't want to be a housekeeper and have people come to my house. My husband did most of the work. (pp. 953–954)

She repeated essentially the same statement of her motive to the arresting officer, her husband, and a psychiatrist. In response to the interrogating officer's question about whether she knew the difference between right and wrong, Mrs. Tempest replied, "Yes, I know killing Greg was wrong." The rest of the confession was "coherent" and evinced "appellant's lucidity."

Mrs. Tempest had been emotionally disturbed since adolescence, suffering from depression and low self-esteem. She perceived herself as unattractive and a loner. Before the homicide, beginning at age fifteen, she had been hospitalized for mental disorder seven or eight times, twice following suicide attempts. She married Ronald Tempest and bore and brought up Gregory despite her problems. A psychiatrist who counseled the Tempest family described them as "intact and affectionate." Mrs. Tempest was examined after the homicide by a psychiatrist, who diagnosed her as suffering from chronic schizophrenia, acute type.

Faced with this horrifying tale, most people will assume there is something wrong with Mrs. Tempest. Although she was neither delusional nor hallucinating when she drowned Gregory, her deed nonetheless seems inexplicable. We can understand filicide in some cases, but her reasons appear crazy. On the other hand, Mrs. Tempest seems otherwise rational, and her behavior meets the requirements of a logical practical syllogism, though it is extreme. Still, *normal* people simply do not do that sort of thing. Hence it is a classic case for the use of psychology to solve the puzzle or at least to help clarify it. Consideration of a responsibility excuse is a certainty in such an instance. But what kind of theory of excuse do law and psychology provide?

Now let us consider the recent case of Arthur Martin Boyd, Jr. (*State v. Boyd*, 1984; all the material following is from the official report of the case). Boyd had lived with Wanda Phillips Hartman for some time, but they had been separated for several months, during which Boyd returned to his wife and children while also trying to reconcile with Hartman. On the day of the killing Boyd bought a lock-blade knife, the murder weapon, and followed Hartman to a bank where a church group was conducting a car wash. Although Boyd had been drinking, he was apparently not intoxicated. Boyd and Hartman talked for a time, and then Hartman started to leave. When Boyd tried to prevent her from doing so, Hartman said she had nothing further to discuss and that if he were going to kill her, "he should hurry up and get it over with." Boyd pulled out the knife and stabbed Hartman 37 times, killing her.

Boyd was convicted of first-degree murder. At the sentencing phase of his trial, he offered testimony about his distressing childhood. His father abandoned him when he was a child and his grandfather, to whom he looked as a father figure, died. Boyd had a history of alcohol and drug abuse; before the murder he was on an "antiabuse" program, which he voluntarily discontinued the day before the murder. Since the age of 14 he had been either in prison, on probation, or on parole for numerous offenses including nonsupport, larceny, assault with intent to rape a 14-year-old girl, assault on a police officer, and others. He loved Hartman, who he knew was seeing another man, and Boyd was trying his best to effect a reconciliation.

To support his claim for mitigation, Boyd attempted to introduce the testimony of a criminologist, Dr. Jack Humphrey, who had studied the background of homicide offenders and had interviewed Boyd. Humphrey's research found that homicide offenders experience more stress in their lives before the homicide than nonoffenders. Those who kill persons close to them have experienced more loss than those who kill strangers. Humphrey wrote, "The more loss in someone's life, the more likely they are to become self-destructive. And it seems that killing a family member or killing a close friend is an act of self-destruction." Humphrey interviewed Boyd and concluded that Boyd's conduct conformed to the pattern exhibited by the study group of killers who killed persons close to them: Boyd's father had abandoned him and his grandfather had died; he could not keep a job and was often incarcerated; he had few friends and kept losing them. Humphrey attempted to testify that "what was true of the people who had killed someone close to them was especially true of Mr. Boyd."

The defense theory for admitting the expert testimony was that it would "link together all of the defendant's mitigating evidence into a unified whole which explained the apparent contradiction of killing the person the defendant loved the most" and that it would show that the killing was "primarily a depression caused self-destructive act, closely related to the impulse that leads to suicide, resulting from a life history of an inordinate number of losses . . . and culminating with the threatened loss of Wanda Hartman" (p. 197). The defense concluded that: "Without the glue, the entire structure of the defendant's theory of mitigation was shattered into little pieces. Presented only as broken bits, there was virtually no hope that the defendant could convince the sentencing jury that his was a case arising out of the 'frailties of human kind' which called for compassion and mitigation of the ultimate penalty of death" (p. 197).

In short, the defendant's theory of mitigation was that the homicide was caused in large part by an admittedly unfortunate childhood history that produced particular personality dynamics in Boyd. Again, we must ask, why should this relatively typical kind of psychological explanation have excusing or mitigating force? What is the theory of excuse that it suggests?

The Determinist Theories of Excuse

Examination of practice, theory, and judicial opinions discloses three categories of theoretical relationship between psychology and legal excuse: the pure product theory, the causal determinist theory, and the irrationality and compulsion theory. It is the major burden of this paper to show that the first two theories are wrong despite their popularity and that the third theory is conceptually correct and the basis for the optimum development of excuses and use of psychological expertise in individual cases. Although one could use examples from any of the responsibility excuses to address the contention, the insanity defense has produced the richest jurisprudence and analytical writing. It will therefore furnish the vast majority of the instances discussed.

THE PURE PRODUCT THEORY

The pure product theory of excuse is the simplest and most simple-minded, holding that the actor is excused if his or her act is the product of mental disorder or some other psychological (or other) cause. It has scarcely been adopted by the law; the first notable instance is the New Hampshire insanity defense test, announced in *State v. Pike*, (1870), which reads as follows: "if the [crime] was the offspring or product of mental disease in the defendant, he was not guilty by reason of insanity." It was also adopted in the short-lived but widely noted *Durham* test for insanity in the District of Columbia. This test provided that "an accused is not criminally responsible if his unlawful act was the product of mental disease or defect" (*Durham v. United States*, 1954). The Boyd case, for example, is an instance where the defense implicitly used the pure product theory at the sentencing phase of trial in order to support a claim for mitigation. Stripped to its essentials, the claim was that the homicide was the product of an unfortunate and abnormal life history and psychological constellation.

Even in those jurisdictions that employ one of the more popular and extensive insanity defense tests such as the *M'Naghten* (1843) or American Law Institute (1962) rules, my impression is that experts operate at the trial level as if they were functioning under the pure product theory. That is, they offer their conclusions in the language of the applicable test, but their underlying reasoning is simply that the person should be excused because the act was a product of mental disorder (*United States v. Byers*, 1984, Bazelon dissenting). Too often, experts of a rather Kraepelinian sort simply diagnose the defendant, assert that he suffered from the disorder at the time of the offense and conclude that he was therefore not criminally responsible. Rarely do the experts or the law provide a reasonably precise meaning of "product," and even more rarely do they provide a normative theory linking the concept of "product," whatever it may mean, to excuse. To be sure, experts testifying under even a pure product test should offer an explanation linking mental disorder to some theory of excusing; the pure product theory might then resemble the other theories in practice, but this seldom occurs. Indeed, dissatisfaction with the productivity requirement and the conclusory nature of the mental health testimony it produced were fundamental reasons the United States Court of Appeals for the District of Columbia ultimately abandoned *Durham* in the famous *Brawner* case (*United States v. Brawner*, 1972). As Judge Bazelon recently lamented, however, the experts still offer conclusory opinions—opinions that I believe are based implicitly upon the pure product theory.

The pure product theory is simple-minded because it assumes precisely what needs to be demonstrated—that acts produced by mental disorder or other psychological causes *should* be excused. For instance, in cases like *Tempest*, the expert diagnoses the defendant as suffering from an affective or schizophrenic disorder and opines that she was thus not responsible for killing the victim. The conclusion is often put in the language of the applicable insanity defense test, but it takes little insight to discern the pure product theory. In *Tempest*, for example, one of the experts testified that although Mrs. Tempest could tell right from wrong "on the surface," she *really* could not do so as a result of her psychosis. In other words, Mrs. Tempest was legally insane because she was psychotic.

There is of course an underlying theory of excuse lurking beneath the unadorned conclusions the pure product theory produces, but it is often difficult to elicit it. Sometimes the bold conclusion stands alone: experts and others take it for granted that a mental disorder or other psychological explanation (usually involving alleged abnormality) does and should excuse, but this is egregious question begging. More often, however, one discovers that a variety of the determinist theory is the link between mental disorder and nonresponsibility. This is often expressed in vague terms of lack of free will. It is said, for example, that the defendant whose conduct is the product of disorder or some other psychological cause is not responsible because he or she lacked free will or free choice (used as a synonym for free will). Thus, to the extent that the pure product theory is a theory of excuse at all, it tends to be an unarticulated version of the dominant, causal deterministic theory, to which we shall now turn.

THE CAUSAL DETERMINIST THEORY

It is a commonplace that the dominant psychological images of persons are all deterministic. The various images are derived from sometimes competing and sometimes complementary causal models, but all subscribe to the view that human behavior is a species of natural phenomenon that is causally necessitated by preceding events according to invariant, lawlike generalizations. Biological causal theories posit that behavior can be explained primarily by the workings of the brain, nervous system, and endocrine system, which in turn can be explained according to basic laws of biology, chemistry, and physics. Psychological theories posit, for example, that psychodynamic laws or cognitive and noncognitive laws of learning can explain behavior. Sociological theories explain mental abnormality in terms of the usual laws governing the interaction of individuals with social groups. But all believe that behaviors, like the movements of planets and billiard balls or the physiology of plant cells, are simply phenomena that can be explained according to universally valid laws. Of course, therapies based on some of these theories insist that the patient or client exercise the freedom to take responsibility for himself or herself, but in principle the entire therapeutic interaction is itself explicable according to the laws that produce behavior. Many philosophers distinguish the claim that all events have causes from the claim that all events are determined, but for various reasons few mental health professionals make this distinction. I shall therefore use the terms "causation" and "determinism" interchangeably unless otherwise indicated.

The further assumption that determinism and responsibility are incompatible—what is called the incompatibilist position (van Inwagen, 1983)—is as commonplace as the assumption that psychology is deterministic. Positing incompatibility again assumes what needs to be proved, however: Why does causal determinism negate responsibility? Although many philosophers have provided richly argued answers to these questions, the usual answer at the junction of psychology and law is framed simply in terms of free will. The determined person supposedly lacks this attribute. The meanings of determinism and free will in most legal-psychological discourses are usually and unfortunately vague, however (Fingarette, 1972). I especially have no idea what is typically meant by free will, or its opposite. Nor do I understand the relationship of this ill-defined term to determinism. Most often, I believe, the conclusion that a person lacks free choice is simply that—a conclusion about responsibility that is meant to achieve a legal or moral result. It appears to sound like an argument or a reason, but it is neither.

A more specific argument for the incompatibility of determinism and free will would include the following type of syllogistic reasoning. If every action is causally necessitated by *prior* events, no one could ever have acted otherwise. Because free will implies the ability to act otherwise than one did, then if determinism is true, no one has free will. If free will is a precondition of responsibility, then no one can be responsible (Watson, 1982). Let us examine this "determinism/nonresponsibility" syllogism.

"Causal necessity" is the least problematic term, usually referring to the view that all phenomena, including behaviors, are in principle explicable and predictable (at least probabilistically) according to the impersonal, causal laws of nature. In simplest form, it implies that everything that occurs was always going to occur (or was probably going to do so at a particular probability level) and that if we had perfect information we could predict accurately what would occur (or the correct probability that it would do so). Although it is conceptually impossible ever to prove that this is an accurate series of assumptions about the material world (Mackie, 1977), it is not an implausible view of the physical phenomena of the universe. Indeed, it is a fundamental working hypothesis of social and natural scientists. Philosophers of science and other cognoscenti could of course quibble or object vociferously to the precision of my depiction of determinism, but it does comport with the average lawyer's and psychologist's understanding, and it is precise enough to work with at the level of analysis I am pursuing. It is also the definition adopted by virtually all those lawyers and psychologists who adhere to the causal determinist theory of excuses. So far, so good, then.

The difficulty with the determinist syllogism is the assumption that determinism entails nonresponsibility. Why is caused behavior incompatible with responsibility? Most writers are unclear about this, but they appear to believe that if behavior is caused, it is somehow unfree and not the actor's responsibility. For instance, a recent paper argued that there are mountains of data to disprove free will. What could this possibly mean? If it means that there are many data to demonstrate that behavior, like all other phenomena, is caused, it is trivially true; few would argue otherwise. But what does this have to do with responsibility? Does it mean that all behavior is compelled or irrational? Does it mean that all actors lack the ability and opportunity to behave differently when they act? It is apparent that the argument does not mean these latter things, but if not, why should we worry about whether we have free will (Dennett, 1984)? For another example, a law professor has written in a well-known article,

An intentionalist interpretation of an incident gives moral weight to autonomous choice and expresses the indeterminacy of future actions. . . . A determinist interpretation considers behavior by looking backward and it expresses no moral respect or condemnation of these predetermined acts. Most basic issues of the criminal law are issues of the applicability of an intentionalist model. Notions of blameworthiness and deterrence are both based on the assumption that criminal actors make intentional choices. . . . It is quite apparent, however, that standard criminal law doctrine often interprets facts in determinist modes. For example, duress, insanity and provocation are determinist excuses for otherwise criminal conduct. (Kelman, 1981, pp. 597–598)

But in what way is the crazy person or the person subject to duress more or less caused than anyone else? And in what way is the act of the actor subject to duress not intentional?

Put another way, the argument seems to be that if the behavior was predictable according to the deterministic laws that allegedly shape the universe, then the actor was not a free moral agent who may justly be held responsible. The determinist premise of the argument is admittedly plausible, but the conclusion—that causation is somehow an excuse per se—is, I believe, a non sequitur. The argument that causation is the predicate for a responsibility excuse, though obscure, appears to be based on two separate theories: first, that caused behavior is compelled behavior, and second, that caused behavior is excused simply because it is caused. I believe that both theories are confused.

Causation is not compulsion. Let us first consider the notion that compulsion is the root of the deterministic theory of excuse. If a person is compelled to perform an action and was not responsible for placing himself in the position where the compulsion was foreseeable, then he should not be held responsible for the action. It is generally held that persons who were compelled to act could not have been expected to act otherwise and that it would therefore be unjust to hold them responsible and to blame and punish them for that action. The important task, then, is to clarify the meaning of compulsion.

There are two ordinary linguistic and behavioral varieties of compulsion: physical and psychological. The former exists when an irresistible force moves one's body although one does not will the movement and may even be trying to the utmost not to perform it. In these cases a person literally has no choice and has not acted. If a much stronger person pushes you into a pond, you have been compelled to get wet and are not responsible for falling into the pond or for getting wet. If the police forcibly carry a drunk person into a public place, the drunkard has been physically compelled to be in public and cannot be convicted of public drunkenness (*Martin v. State*, 1944). In standard criminal law terms, these are cases of no actus reus; the person would be acquitted because the prosecution failed to prove its prima facie case, not because an affirmative defense was proved. Although it would be outrageous to blame and punish in such cases, quite obviously such cases are not what the determinist has in mind, because few actual instances of behavior are of this type.

Psychological compulsion exists when the actor is not physically forced to act, but circumstances produce a dreadfully hard choice that leaves no acceptable alternative. Even though the person has a choice—no force is physically coercing bodily movements—he or she believes there is no alternative. For example, a person is psychologically compelled to provide information when an interrogator threatens to torture a loved one if the person is silent. The compelling circumstances may also be primarily of intrapsychic origin, as in the case of pedophilia. Not that in either case the actor has a physical choice whether to act, and if he does act he does so intentionally. If the threatened person talks or if the pedophile has sexual contact with a child, he does so intentionally. We may nonetheless absolve the actor for talking or molestation if the threat or the impulse were strong enough. In standard criminal law terms, psychological compulsion is encompassed by the affirmative defenses of duress and, in some tests, insanity. Again, however, psychological compulsion is not what the determinist has in mind, because few behaviors are performed in response to hard choices of this type. In most cases of action, as we all know from everyday experience, the actor is not compelled by a hard choice that precludes acceptable alternatives. All of us are presumably caused by something to do what we do, but in very few instances are we compelled to act according to any coherent, morally relevant sense of compulsion. All behavior is caused, but not all behavior is compelled; causation is not compulsion.

Cases of legal insanity provide an important application of this analysis. Most cases of legal insanity do *not* involve psychological or physical compulsion. Crazy actors may act on the basis of delusional reasons, but these actions are usually no more compelled than the behaviors of normal actors who act for intelligible, rational reasons. Acting in accord with one's beliefs—desires and beliefs that are themselves caused—is not psychological compulsion (unless one delusionally believes that he or she is in a hard-choice situation; but such an actor is also irrational). In almost all cases, neither crazy nor normal actors face hard choices. Aleksandr Solzhenitsyn taking his stand and a crazy person who commits an act because he believes it will magically bring peace on earth are both caused to act as they do, but neither is compelled. We would not hold Solzhenitsyn nonresponsible for his stand. And we might excuse the crazy person, but not because his behavior was more caused or compelled. Thus, when we say that the person who acted in accord with his or her crazy beliefs was compelled, we are really talking very loosely. What is usually meant is simply that we believe the actor should be excused. The locution "compulsion" is just a loose shorthand, albeit a confusing one, for that conclusion.

Compulsion cannot be the basis of excuse in the causal determinist theory because all behavior is causally determined, but, clearly, not all behavior is compelled according to any sensible meaning of the term "compulsion." Something surely caused Mrs. Tempest to kill Gregory, but she was not compelled to do so. Some behaviors, all of which are caused, are compelled and therefore excused, but they are excused because they are compelled, not because they are deterministically caused.

Causes are not excuses. The second causal, deterministic theory of excuse is that causation itself is an excuse. But conceptual and practical difficulties beset this theory too. In brief, because all behavior is caused but not all behavior is excused in a system where moral concepts have meaning, causation ifself cannot be an excuse.

Consider the following examples, which demonstrate the implausibility of the simple causal theory (and the implausibility of the theory that caused behavior is excused because it is compelled). Assume that a writer is working at her desk by a window as sunset approaches. When the natural light becomes insufficient to continue working, she turns on the desk lamp. According to any coherent account of causation, her turning on the light was caused primarily by her perception of the increasing darkness. Now take an example of an internal, physiological cause for behavior. Suppose the same writer works straight through the usual dinner hour. Later that evening she notices she is very hungry and eats something. Her eating is çlearly caused. The writer is caused to turn on the lights and caused to eat, but there seems no reason to excuse her from responsibility for her acts in either case. Remember that the determinist syllogism holds that if all actions are causally necessitated, no one could act otherwise and therefore no one is responsible. What does it mean, however, to say that one could not act otherwise?

In both of our examples the writer was not physically or psychologically compelled to act as she did, and she had the potential or ability and the opportunity to act otherwise if she had so decided. She might have remained in the dark or fasted until morning. Moreover, in both cases the action seems entirely rational. The same is true of Solzhenitsyn when he took his stand. Although his actions surely had causes, he was neither compelled nor irrational. According to the determinist theory, Solzhenitsyn should not be held responsible or morally applauded because his profession of belief, too, was caused. At this point the determinist theory seems incoherent because our generally shared view is to hold both the writer and Solzhenitsyn very much responsible. In most instances of behavior it appears that the person is not irrational or compelled and had the ability and opportunity to act otherwise but did not do so. The determinist answer is that even if the person had the ability and opportunity to behave otherwise, he or she could not have done so. But even if one believes that every event in the universe had to occur as it did and was always going to do so, this still seems to have little to do with the responsibility of persons for their conduct.

Moral and legal analysis and the causal determinist theory of excuse have little in common because each interprets "could not have done otherwise" according to a different conception of human action. The causal theorist treats persons as impersonal, mechanical phenomena, whereas moral theories treat persons as self-conscious beings who act for reasons. According to the causal account, the person's goals, desires, beliefs, and reasons for action are irrelevant. Looked at purely causally, these are simply the outputs of a particular sort of biophysical contraption. The phrase "could not have done otherwise" therefore does not refer to the self-reflective abilities and actions of a *person*. It refers only to the predictability of behavior in conformity with lawlike generalizations. Thus, since the actions of the writer and Solzhenitsyn were predictable, they allegedly could not have done otherwise. This is a confused form of fatalism (Dennett, 1984).

By contrast, goals, desires, beliefs,and reasons for actions have everything to do with moral and legal responsibility. As we shall see in greater detail below, a moral and legal analysis of action holds responsible an actor who seems to act for rational reasons and is not compelled. In other words, human actions are morally and legally distinguishable from the movements of machines. The concepts of morality and responsibility apply to *persons* acting according to goals, beliefs, desires, and reasons. They most assuredly do not apply to impersonal, mechanical, nonhuman phenomena. It makes no sense to hold nonhuman causes such as the winds or the tides morally responsible for the effects they produce. The causal theory has little to do with ordinary notions of morality and responsibility, and indeed moral notions are irrelevant to them. If people are to be praised and blamed, it must be on grounds other than causation.

The most important objection to the causal, determinist theory of excuse, even if it is coherent and relevant to moral evaluation, is that it should in principle excuse everyone for all behaviors. Because all behavior, normal and abnormal alike, is caused according to the determinist theory, every act of every actor is performed without responsibility. No matter which theory of causation the determinist subscribes to, he or she endorses the view that all behavior is causally determined. We are all products of our biology; we all have learning histories; a profound and deep psychodynamic formulation can be constructed for all behaviors; we are all products of our culture or the inevitable forces of historical materialism. Or whatever. No one should be praised and no one should be blamed on moral grounds. The practices of praising and blaming make no sense if the causal determinist theory is justified. Perhaps the determinist is willing to praise or blame on solely instrumental grounds to make the machines work "better," but then what is the normative source of the goal "better"? There is no way out: if causation excuses, all must be excused for everything, and no one should be praised or blamed. The causal determinist theory of excuse is thus an incoherent *moral* theory, because if everyone were excused, the deepest premises about human conduct and the social, moral, political, and legal culture based upon these premises would be meaningless.

Selective determinism is false. To avoid the unhappy but inevitable reductio of the causal, determinist theory, some have adopted the position that only some behavior is causally determined, a viewpoint that has been aptly termed "selective determinism" (Hollander, 1973). Selective determinists are not always clear about their position, but we can identify a variety of examples. Norval Morris, for example, writes that "what is at issue is the degree of freedom of choice on a continuum from the hypothetically entirely rational to the hypothetically pathologically determined. . . . Certainly it is true that in a situation of total absence of choice it is outrageous to inflict punishment" (Morris, 1982, p. 61). The meaning of this quotation is obscure, but Morris appears to equate the degree of free choice (free will?) and responsibility a person has with the degree to which the behavior is not determined or is uncaused. He implies that there are degrees of causation, from an uncaused event to a fully caused event. Other selective determinists seem to believe that causation is dependent on the present possession of scientifically valid information about causes. Yet other selective determinists hold that only if some abnormal variable is part of the causal chain can it be claimed that the actor is determined and unfree (Bonnie & Slobogin, 1980). Others believe that if certain human behaviors are governed by laws that are irreducibly statistical or probabilistic rather than by laws that yield certain predictions, then these behaviors are uncaused or undetermined. Other selective determinists, finally, simply have favored classes of persons whom they choose to believe are caused—in contradistinction, evidently, to themselves.

Selective determinism appears attractive, for it seems to retain the moral consequences of the determinism/nonresponsibility syllogism while simultaneously offering a practical solution to the dilemma the total determinist account presents. But the selective determinist theory fares no better than the nonselective determinist theory.

If one treats behaviors, as scientists do, as empirical phenomena that, like all other phenomena, are subject to the causal laws of the universe, then it is incoherent to claim that only some behavior is caused and that other behavior occurs without being caused. As a thought experiment, simply try to construct a determinist theory that posits that only some phenomena are determined. Let me suggest that you will not be able to construct such a theory.

We know a great deal more about the causes of some behaviors than of others, but this does not mean that the latter are uncaused. It means only that we are ignorant of those causes. For instance, there is extremely good evidence that poverty is a predisposing cause of crime (Cantwell, 1983). By contrast, we know far less about the predisposing causes of criminal behavior among the rich, but the crimes of the wealthy are as surely caused as those of the poor. People are not "free" and "unfree" in proportion to the degree to which their behavior is caused, because causation is not a matter of degree. A particular cause may contribute to a behavioral effect with varying strength under different conditions, but all behavior is fully caused by the sufficient set of factors that produces it.

In Norval Morris's recent widely noticed and influential book

Madness and the Criminal Law (1982), Professor Morris provides a clear example of the error of selective determinism. To support his claim that it is morally just to abolish the insanity defense, Morris notes that we do not excuse the poor although poverty is far more statistically criminogenic than mental disorder. Although his premise is correct, the conclusion does not follow. That poverty is, in general, a stronger predisposing cause of crime than mental disorder does not entail the conclusion that the crimes of the mentally disordered are less caused than the crimes of the poor. The crimes of both are equally caused. Morris's statistical observation means only that *in the absence of other information,* including the laws of crime causation, we can predict criminal behavior among the poor with fewer false positives than when we make similar predictions about the mentally disordered. The relative predictive success with the poor does not imply that their crimes are more caused, however. To repeat: it demonstrates only our present state of information about causation. For another example, the far greater statistical incidence of Tay-Sachs disease among Jewish people of Eastern European background does not mean that when they have this terrible disorder it is "more caused" than when it is found among other groups. Mental disorder may not in general be a strong cause of the crimes of the mentally disordered, but their crimes are caused by something.

The argument that only behavior caused by an abnormality is determined also fails. For example, a psychodynamicist might argue that only persons whose behavior was caused by abnormal intrapsychic conflict should be excused because only such persons lack free choice. But, we may ask, are not normal intrapsychic conflicts also causes of behavior? Assuming arguendo that we had a coherent theory of what counts as abnormal intrapsychic conflict and could reliably identify it, it is still true that all intrapsychic contents are causes of behavior according to the psychodynamic model of behavior. Thus, if we wish to excuse those with unconscious abnormal conflict, it must be because we have a normative theory linking abnormality to nonresponsibility; it will not be because abnormal conflict is a cause whereas normal conflict is not. In short, if abnormality is morally relevant, it is not because it is a cause but for some other normative reason.

The possibly irreducible statisticality of certain laws of behavior also fails to provide conceptual support to the selective determinist. The claim of the selective determinist assumes that if an event cannot be predicted with certainty, it is somehow uncaused and free. The argument begins with some observations from particle physics. Quantum physicists appear to have established that it is impossible to predict with certainty the placement of microparticles at a given time; the best we can do is discover the probability that a particle will be in a particular place at a particular moment. Furthermore, the inability to predict with certainty is not the product of lack of information; it appears to be an irreducible uncertainty that can be expressed only statistically.

To move from the discovery of such subatomic irreducible statisticality to the truth of selective determinism—that is, to the argument that some behavior is not causally determined—is a great leap. In the first place, the selective determinist must assume that the irreducible statisticality of some laws of the microcosm of quantum physics suggests that similar irreducibility will apply to macroscopic phenomena, including human behavior. For instance, if the subatomic particles in an object falling through a vacuum are indeterminately situated, must we assume that the velocity and motion of the object itself are indeterminate? This appears to be a very strong assumption (Dennett, 1984). Even if we make it, however, as the eminent philosopher of science Adolf Grünbaum has persuasively shown (1972), it does not follow that members of a reference group whose behavior is irreducibly statistical are therefore uncaused.

In brief, Grünbaum's argument is this. A statistical law allows us to say of an individual who committed a crime, for example, only that he might have been one of those in the group who would not commit a crime. We would not be entitled to say that the criminal behavior of the actor was uncaused by the laws governing human behavior. The statisticality of the law permits us only to declare that we cannot predict beforehand which individuals will offend. This does not lead to the conclusion that all those members of a group subject to statistical laws are somehow part of an acausal subuniverse. In the long run, the accuracy of the statistical law demonstrates that the causal laws of the universe are quite on the job. Indeed, selective determinists often have their argument backward here. If the moral argument based on selective determinism were accepted, all the persons in a group subject to a statistical law would be held responsible, whereas the selective determinist is usually looking for an excuse. Remember, finally, that if the statisticality is reducible through more information, then there is no assault possible on pandeterminism.

A final form of selective determinism is implicitly or explicitly re-sult oriented. For social or political reasons, it wishes to excuse fa-vored actors by claiming that this group was especially caused and therefore should be excused (Hollander, 1973). Because such a posi-tion advances no real argument for the truth of selective determin-ism or for why causes of behavior create excuses, we can pay little attention to this form of special pleading.

If all behavior is caused and selective determinism is false, the causal determinist theory of excuses might try to recoup by claiming that conceptual generalities are irrelevant and that it is the degree of free choice in an individual case that counts. For example, the deter-minist would propose that although mental disorder is not a strong cause of crime in general, in Mrs. Tempest's individual case it robbed her of her free will and thus she should be excused. Note, however, that this account does not treat free will as the absence of causation or determinism. In fact, free will as used in such an argu-ment seems to have little to do with determinism or causation. The assertion that Mrs. Tempest lacked free will is not a claim that her behavior was determined or caused whereas the behavior of other persons is undetermined or uncaused; rather, it appears merely to be a shorthand for the conclusion that Mrs. Tempest should not be held responsible. The causal theorist must therefore give indepen-dent normative meaning to the concept or capacity "free will." We have seen that because free choice is not the absence of determinism or causation, it must be something else. It is the task of those who wish to excuse on the basis of any psychological explanation to say what free will is, how and why it is relevant to responsibility, and what is the relevance to it of the psychological explanation.

I do not like the language of free will. It is confusing. Herbert Fing-arette has argued (1972), and I fully agree, that all discussion of re-sponsibility and excuse would be improved enormously if all talk of free will or free choice (when used as equivalent to or dependent upon free will) were exorcised. As a convenient shorthand for those attributes of a person that are relevant to responsibility, free will is decidedly *not* the equivalent of "undetermined" or "uncaused." Trying to explain the individual case in the way suggested does not save selective determinism; it abandons the determinist theory en-tirely. Mrs. Tempest is not excused because she is caused and others are not, but because there are reasons to be found in the narrative of her life that are normatively relevant to responsibility. For instance, one may decide to excuse her because we conclude that she was nonculpably irrational when she killed her son. Of course the irrationality was caused by something—as is all behavior—but we would excuse her because she was irrational, not because there was a cause for her behavior.

"AS IF" RESPONSIBILITY

Causal determinists might also try, finally, to argue that although determinism is true, we lack the information and technology to ensure a harmonious, productive world. In the meantime, therefore, we must behave "as if" indeterminism were true and treat persons as responsible. But which ones? If determinists try to hold everyone responsible in the "as if" world, they must confront the powerful belief that at least some persons deserve to be excused. They will then need a theory of excuses that is divorced from causal determinism. If they try instead to adopt the selective determinist view, it will be subject to the same objections already raised, and again they will be forced to construct a theory of excuses that does not depend on notions of causal determinism. Indeed, we shall see presently that the perceptive "as if" determinist must accept the moral view of human behavior I described above and consequently will become a compatibilist—one who believes that determinism and free will/responsibility can happily coexist. In any case, I believe indeterminism has as little to do with responsibility as does determinism. Even if no one's behavior were caused, we should still excuse at least some people.

The most profound objection to "as if" responsibility, however, is that it is morally and legally outrageous. If a person truly believes that no one is responsible, then it is reprehensible to hold persons responsible and to blame and punish them on that basis. Doing so fails to take oneself or one's fellow human beings seriously. I believe such behavior is the product of intellectual confusion, intellectual laziness, or cynical posturing. To mount the full objection to this position would go far beyond the purposes of this paper. It is sufficient to declare that I believe this is a position we need not take seriously because those who espouse it do not truly take it seriously.

The agenda so far has been largely negative—to demonstrate that the standard psychological deterministic account of excusing fails conceptually and practically. It is nevertheless possible to construct a coherent account of excusing that is compatible with various psychological theories of behavior and with justifiable assumptions of ordinary morality. The remainder of the paper provides this account and demonstrates the good practical consequences that it produces.

The Compatibilist Theory of Excuse: Irrationality and Compulsion

This section presents a conceptual, empirical, and normative justification of the compatibilist theory of excuse—the claim that determinism and responsibility are compatible. Again, it is not my intention to provide a definitive resolution to a dispute that has divided professional philosophers for millennia. I do wish, however, to offer a theoretical account that will be corrective and useful to psychologists and lawyers who must work at the juncture of the two disciplines in the real world. Although the argument is written from a nonconsequentialist vantage point and thus directly supports retributive justifications for punishment, the argument is also entirely compatible with consequentialist justifications for punishment.

PERSONS AND MACHINES

Morality is concerned with persons who characteristically act with consciousness that they are doing so for reasons and are accountable; it is not concerned with inanimate objects such as machines or electrons that function according to the impersonal laws that explain their workings. It makes no sense whatever to speak of the responsibility or moral and legal accountability of a machine. All aspects of human existence can of course be described and explained impersonally and mechanically. The functioning of the heart, for example, can be described coherently in the language of chemistry, phsyics, and other natural scientific disciplines. Indeed, all physical phenomena can probably be reduced to the operations of their most minute particles. Nonetheless, the language and conceptual apparatus of morality cannot be reduced to that of the natural scientific world without losing its moral meaning.

Consider a person suffering from hypertension and heart disorder who is the sole support of an aged, helpless parent. Her physician tells her that if she stops smoking, exercises moderately, eats properly, and takes her prescribed medicine regularly, she will be able to lead a full life and hence will be able to continue to care for her parent. Now suppose the person weighs this advice and decides that the balanced life prescribed is not worth the loss in pleasure, and, besides, she is tired of supporting her parent. She continues to behave as before and her condition deteriorates, causing her death. Consequently her parent becomes impoverished and leads a life of great suffering. It is certainly possible to describe impersonally and scientifically the reasons her heart stopped beating, but we would not say that her heart is morally accountable for its disease and her death. On the other hand, it would make perfectly good sense to say that the person was morally responsible for her death and the subsequent deterioration of her parent's life. One can plausibly imagine a legal system that would prevent this person from so acting or that would punish her for doing so in the circumstances.

We could describe her behavior in the language of neurophysiology, treating her as a machine that underwent the breakdown of a crucial component. Indeed, with sufficient information we might be able to specify the neurophysiological events that correlate with the human decision making that was occurring. But once again, morality would be irrelevant to such a description. Moral evaluation makes sense only if we view this person as an agent who consciously, rationally, and without compulsion behaved in a manner that caused her heart to fail and her parent to suffer. We can blame her as a person, but not as a machine. There were causes for her intentions, reasons, and consequent actions, but we blame her nonetheless because she acted intentionally, rationally, and without compulsion.

Once we understand the distinction between moral and causal analysis and are aware of the different conceptions of human action embedded in it, there is no conflict: the language and conceptual apparatus of morality and responsibility occupy a domain distinct from the language and concepts of causation and determinism. And this line of reasoning is not based on a form of linguistic or other dualism; there is no doubt in my mind that we live in a causal universe wherein biological, psychological, and other causes produce behavior. But causation is not an excuse, and one can consistently and happily believe conceptually that even if causal determinism is true, most persons can be held morally and legally accountable for their deeds.

In his famous article "Freedom and Resentment," the eminent British philosopher Sir Peter Strawson (1962) argues that our concept of what it means to be a person includes the presupposition that people are responsible. Because we all recognize that we interact with, influence, and react to our fellow human beings, we attach profound significance to the intentions and attitude of others toward us and ours toward them. When others injure us, we resent it and blame them unless there is a good reason not to. All these reactions, which are embedded in the very nature of personhood and human interaction, would be irrelevant to the incompatibilist. There would be no resentment, no blame; all persons would be viewed entirely objectively. For Strawson, such an approach is logically possible but probably humanly impossible. Let me quote at some length:

> The human commitment to participation in inter-personal relationships is . . . too thoroughgoing and deeply rooted for us to take seriously the thought that a general theoretical conviction [i.e., strict determinism] might so change our world that, in it, there were no longer any such things as inter-personal relationships as we normally understand them; and being involved in inter-personal relationships as we normally understand them precisely is being exposed to the range of reactive attitudes and feelings that is in question. . . . A sustained objectivity of inter-personal attitudes, and the human isolation which that would entail, does not seem to be something of which human beings would be capable, even if some general truth were a theoretical ground for it. . . . we cannot, as we are, seriously envisage ourselves adopting a thoroughgoing objectivity of attitude to others as a result of the theoretical truth of determinism; and . . . when we do in fact adopt such an attitude in a particular case, our doing so is not the consequence of a theoretical conviction which might be expressed as "Determinism in this case," but is a consequence of abandoning, for different reasons in different cases, the ordinary inter-personal attitudes. (1962, pp. 68–69)

In other words determinism not only is compatible with responsibility, with resenting and blaming, it is in fundamental ways irrelevant to these human, interpersonal activities. Strawson's point, of course, is neither conceptual nor normative; it is based on empirical observations and assumptions. Still, I think it so obviously correct that it would be folly to try to create and impose a normative, moral and legal system that contradicts it. Such a system would not work, whereas a compatibilist system does work.

Finally, let me assert an article of faith, a fundamental value I hold. I believe we ought to treat persons as persons. To provide the argument for this assertion would require a paper in itself and go far beyond the purposes of the present endeavor. I offer this assertion baldly, however, in the belief that it is widely shared among almost all persons in Western cultures and that it would be impossible to understand their behavior unless they did share this value. Intellectual posturing aside, human interaction worth having is almost inconceivable unless people do have this value. In sum, for conceptual, empirical, and normative reasons, I believe that compatibilism is the soundest approach for law and psychology to adopt when assessing blame and excuse.

THE CRITERIA FOR EXCUSE

The remaining task is to construct the criteria for deciding when persons are and are not responsible for their actions—for deciding, in Strawson's terms, when we can properly not resent and blame because the person lacks the fundamental moral attributes of personhood. Since blaming and excusing are interpersonal, social activities, developing the criteria for moral responsibility requires that we begin by examining our social practices and implicit theories about responsibility. In other words, we must ask what criteria for blaming and excusing are applied by ordinary people in everyday life and by social institutions including, preeminently, the law. I believe that this examination discloses a deep consensus that there are two criteria for moral and legal responsibility: the actor must be reasonably capable of rational behavior and reasonably uncompelled. All persons in all contexts might not use exactly these terms, but if one considers any situation in which an actor is excused, it seems clear that the actor's nonculpable irrationality or compulsion is the basis for the excuse.

The law and common morality are consistent with this analysis. All legal responsibility excuses fit the described pattern. For example, infancy and some forms of legal insanity are rationality excuses, whereas duress and other forms of insanity are compulsion excuses. To be more specific, the insanity defense standards that Anglo-American jurisdictions employ accurately map the moral criteria for responsibility. Inspection of the tests discloses that they address rationality problems (e.g., *M'Naghten*, 1843, the first prong of the American Law Institute [ALI] test [1962]) or compulsion problems (e.g., so-called irresistible impulse tests, the second prong of the ALI test). The language of the standard may vary from jurisdiction to jurisdiction, but all are concerned with irrationality, compulsion, or both. In everyday life, too, we excuse our fellows if they "couldn't help themselves" or of they "weren't themselves" or were "out of their minds" for nonculpable reasons. A friend who is irascible and cruel will be forgiven more easily if he is under great and unavoidable stress that compromises his rationality and self-control; in contrast, he will be blamed if neither is compromised.

In sum, the criteria for autonomy and moral and legal responsibility are rationality and self-control, whereas the criteria for excuse are that the actor is nonculpably irrational or compelled. Thus a psychological (or any other) causal explanation of behavior is just that—an explanation; it is not an excuse.

The discussion so far has been premeditatedly vague about two issues that must now be clarified: the meanings of rationality and compulsion and the extent to which these factors affect responsibility. Rationality is notoriously hard to define (Brandt, 1983; Macklin, 1983), but a reasonable working definition would include reference both to the sensibleness of the actor's goals and the logic of the means chosen to achieve them. It is of course difficult to say that the preferences or goals of another are irrational or not sensible, but there is no alternative to making these judgments within the social context in which those preferences are held. In a rough and ready fashion we may ask whether, given the social context, any sense can be made of the actor's goals, whether any reasonable person could hold them, whether they are logically or empirically intelligible. Thus, in our society it is generally considered not irrational to be a member of a "fringe" religion because our society approves of and encourages diverse religious beliefs. In contrast, it does not make sense to want (truly) to be a Martian. These judgments about the intelligibility or rationality of goals can be made as long as we recognize that few goals are rational or irrational in an ultimate sense and make a general presumption in favor of rationality.

The rationality of means an actor chooses to achieve goals is easier to assess, because it involves factual beliefs about the world or logical relationships. The inquiry becomes whether instrumental behavior is rationally connected to achieving identified goals. In Aristotelian terms, is the actor a good "practical reasoner"? As my colleague Scott Bice has shown so helpfully (1980), an actor may be irrational about means/ends relationships in many respects. First, an actor may believe that certain means will not achieve the preferred goal but may employ those means nevertheless. If the actor's beliefs accurately reflect the preferred goals, this choice of means is a clear instance of irrationality. Second, it may be that the actor believes the means will achieve the preferred goals, but the belief is empirically unjustifiable. For example, a law student who wishes to succeed in law school but tries to do so by minimizing class attendance or failing to complete assignments and maximizing recreational reading instead has an irrational belief about the means chosen. A third and related form of irrationality arises when the goal of the action conflicts with a goal the actor considers superior. Suppose we ask our law student how getting a degree ranks compared with other goals. The response is that graduation is far superior to most other goals, including being well-read. The student's behavior is then irrational because recreational reading is inconsistent with and inferior to the higher-ranked goal of graduating. A fourth type of irrationality about means exists when the actor believes the means chosen are a less efficient method to achieve a particular goal but cannot give an independent and superior goal that the less effective means serve. This form of irrationality is well known to economists. Finally, the actor may believe the means chosen are the most efficient to achieve a goal, but the belief may be empirically implausible.

This list of types of means/ends irrationality is surely not exhaustive or the only way to individuate the types of irrationality, but it does provide a framework for thinking about instrumental irrationality. If one tests this framework with cognitive craziness, say a delusional belief system, it works very well indeed. For instance, the person who gouges his eye out because he believes he is the Lord's prophet and that mutilating himself will produce peace on earth (see *Mayock v. Martin*, 1968) surely has an intelligible, rational goal, but the means chosen violate instrumental rationality in a number of ways. If the actor has beliefs that are simply not justifiable on any reasonable view of the world and seems incapable of correcting the errors by logic or evidence, then it is fair to conclude that the actor is irrational with respect to the behavior in question.

Now let us turn to a discussion of the criteria for compulsion, a discussion that owes much to Robert Audi's influential conceptualization (1974). Although it is a vague concept at best, we may define psychological compulsion generally as hard choices that society cannot ask defendants to make at their peril. But what are the criteria of choices so hard that a defendant's "wrong" choice should be excused? First, it must be that the defendant experiences substantially greater physical or psychological pain if he or she behaves lawfully/rightly than if he or she behaves unlawfully/wrongly (Audi, 1974). In other words, the pain produced by performing the lawful/right act must outweigh the pain produced by performing the unlawful/wrong act, which is usually a strong counter to wrongdoing (Goldman, 1970). Let us consider a range of examples. The typical case of duress fits this criterion: the defendant will suffer greater pain if he or she does not perform the commanded, wrongful deed than if he or she does. Now consider the drug-dependent person (DDP) who is physically addicted to the drug. The DDP who does not take the drug will undergo the psychological and physical pain of withdrawal. This pain may very well be greater than the pain produced by fear of violating the law or by other psychological factors such as the loss of self-respect. Finally, take the hypothetical case of a driver who rounds a turn on a mountain road and sees two children lying in the road. If the driver runs over the children, surely killing both of them, he himself lives; if the driver swerves to avoid them, he will go over the edge of a cliff, plunging to certain death (the hypothetical case is taken from Kadish, Schulhofer, & Paulsen, 1983, p. 798). Although theoretically all lives are equal, the immediate pain of losing one's own life is greater than the pain produced by the possibility that the law may punish one in the future. In all these cases, the actor's logic is intact, but the actor faces a very hard choice.

The second criterion of a hard choice is that the actor's primary motivation for choosing the wrong alternative must be fear of the anticipated pain from choosing the right alternative (including pain to cherished persons). Even when the right choice would produce more pain than the wrong choice, if the person chooses wrong for personal gain rather than for fear of pain, the choice is not hard because the action chosen is what the actor positively *wants* to do. Consider the example of Aleksandr Solzhenitsyn. Failing to profess his political beliefs (the "right" choice from the Soviet viewpoint) would have caused greater pain than professing them, but his profession was hardly compelled. It was not the fear of pain from failure to profess that motivated him; it was instead an affirmative, easy choice. By comparison, the person subject to duress acts out of fear of the consequences of not following the command. The DDP may take drugs for fear of the pain abstinence will produce. By contrast, the person who takes drugs primarily for the pleasure they produce and not for fear of the pain of withdrawal is not compelled. The fear of pain often creates the driven, or pressured, quality typically associated with cases of compulsion: the feeling that the actor "had no choice."

The last criterion of compulsion is that the actor should be excused only if the wrong action was the one reasonable alternative (this is perhaps another way of saying that the person must be non-culpable for the compulsion). For example, the duress excuse would not apply if the actor could overcome the threatener or escape without undue danger. The DDP would have no compulsion excuse to the crimes of possession and use, nor would the kleptomaniac have a defense to theft, if treatment programs or other alternatives were available but had not been tried in good faith. In most pure cases of inner compulsion, where the actor's rationality is unimpaired, reasonable alternatives will be available. If a reasonable alternative is available, it is fair to conclude that the choice was not too hard and that the actor may fairly be blamed and punished for wrongdoing.

Assessing the difficulty of a particular choice requires a quantitative and qualitative evaluation of the three criteria outlined above. In general, the degree of compulsion increases in proportion to (1) the increase in the differential in pain between acting lawfully/rightly and unlawfully/wrongly; (2) the increase in fear and decrease in personal gain as the motive for acting unlawfully/wrongly; and (3) the decrease in availability of and ease of using the alternatives. These evaluations are difficult to make, especially in cases of inner compulsions, where there are fewer objective indicators, but these guides to assessing the hardness of a choice should furnish some benchmarks. Weighing the pain balance and assessing motivation will be problematic processes requiring impressionistic judgments based on the actor's psychological and physical makeup (Audi, 1974). There is no substitute for such judgments, however, that will be less impressionistic, or less so than many other legal judgments. Nor does the difficulty in making these judgments necessitate the conclusion that the law will need expert opinions on this issue. Experts can provide behavioral data, but weighing the pain balance and assessing motivation are normative judgments that require only commonsense inferences from the behavioral data.

The criteria I have offered for compulsion comport with our moral theory and practice. If a choice is too hard, it is *unfair* to blame and punish the actor who has no reasonable alternative. This is not to say that the actor has no choice. Indeed, the French distinguish between physical compulsion and moral compulsion to capture precisely this difference (Fletcher, 1978). Saintly persons might be willing to undergo any pain rather than harm another, but morality and the criminal law cannot expect such saintly behavior from ordinary persons. In addition, the possible future punishment of the criminal law will have little deterrent effect on a person faced with the immediate and severe pain of making the "right" choice in a hard-choice situation.

A particularly thorny issue for lawyers and psychologists is whether compulsion can be produced by internal states as well as external threats. I have been assuming so far that it can, but the question now needs further analysis. Mental disorder provides a good example of the theoretical problem. Many persons believe that disordered behavior or other behavior produced by disorder is particularly compelled, and consequently, that there is some special relation between mental disorder and compulsion. By contrast, I believe the relation of mental disorder to compulsion is frustratingly vague and that there is no such special or necessary relationship. To begin with, movements performed under the influence of mental disorder do not fit the model of involuntary action adopted by the law or common sense. Consider the Model Penal Code (MPC), for example, which generally considers an action involuntary if the bodily movement is "not a product of the effort or determination of the actor, either conscious or habitual" (American Law Institute, 1962, § 2.01). Acts influenced by mental disorder are not reflexive, unconscious, or the like; crazy persons may have crazy reasons for their actions, but their acts are clearly products of conscious efforts or determination. Thus the MPC insanity test that absolves an actor who "lacks substantial capacity to conform his conduct to the requirements of law" (§4.01) excuses the actor for a reason other than because the criminal conduct was involuntary.

Are disordered persons excused because their acts, though voluntary, involve hard-choice situations? Again, the answer appears to be no. Crazy persons may act on the basis of hallucinations, delusions, or other misperceptions of reality, but they usually act without the pressure of a hard choice, albeit for crazy reasons. Moreover, just because the crimes of crazy people are *caused* does not mean they are compelled. All actions are caused, but not all are the product of facing a hard choice. Much of the argument that the acts of crazy persons are compelled, or could not be helped, or are involuntary is simply a form of loose talk meant to justify the conclusion that crazy persons are not responsible. Very few crazy persons face hard choices because of craziness, however, and very few are therefore compelled.

Consider the example of a person who acts on the basis of a religious delusion. Such a person is not compelled simply because he or she acts on the basis of a strongly held, albeit crazy, belief. Nor is the person compelled because craziness influenced the behavior. In the absence of hard choice, action pursuant to a crazy belief or desire is no more compelled than action based on a sane belief or desire. The proper reason to excuse, of course, is that the person was irrational even though narrowly aware of right and wrong, not that the person was compelled. A person grossly out of touch with reality, all mixed up about the world, finds it harder to behave appropriately, including lawfully/rightly. "Harder" in this case does not imply compelled in the volitional sense, however. It simply means that it is *more difficult* to act appropriately if crazy thoughts and feelings interfere. Again, the law should treat such cases as instances of irrationality, not compulsion.

Are there any cases of crazy persons in which a pure, internal compulsion excuse seems proper? The only appropriate instances appear to be the so-called impulse disorders, where the actor is cognitively rational but has an inner craving to do a prohibited act—for example, the kleptomaniac's impulse to steal, the DDP's desire for drugs, or the pedophile's desire for sexual contact with children. Are these hard-choice situations, however, and further, are they distinguishable from other "normal" predispositions such as "moneyphilia" (the greedy person's love of money) that may lead to illegal behavior?

Although impossible to prove because there are no valid tests of the strength of pure inner cravings, it seems likely that inner cravings can sometimes produce hard-choice situations. If the inner craving is strong enough that it produces fear of the pain caused by refusing the craving and no alternative courses of action are available, then perhaps an excuse should obtain. But why should the law excuse the kleptomaniac or DDP but not the moneyphile? One could argue, of course, that the moneyphile does not suffer from a disease whereas the kleptomaniac or DDP does, but this would allow the tail to wag the dog. Medical categories should not dictate legal excuses. If a particular moneyphile meets the hard-choice moral/legal criteria for excuse, why should it matter whether the condition is considered a mental disorder (Feinberg, 1970)? Both normal and abnormal cravers will sometimes face true pain caused by factors for which they are not responsible. People who suffer from abnormal cravings may have fewer alternatives than people who suffer from normal cravings, but it is surely true that normal cravers are sometimes in situations where there are no reasonable alternatives. The upshot of this analysis is that there may be a few cases of inner craving that fit the hard-choice criteria for compulsion, but it will be difficult to decide which inner compulsions should count. For example, should an excuse for inner compulsion be limited to abnormal cravings?

Perhaps the dilemma created by the fuzzy distinction between normal and abnormal cravings can be resolved in the following definitional manner: we might wish to redefine as abnormal any craving that *compels* illegal behavior because the law cannot expect unusually difficult self-restraint. Thus, such strong inner cravings must be abnormal by definition. It is of course possible to classify these extreme conditions as mental disorders; such conditions fit the American Psychiatric Association's generic definition of mental disorder (1980, p. 6). But such redefinition simply begs the hard conceptual questions of what behavior should be considered mental disorder and whether mental disorder should be a necessary criterion for a compulsion excuse. As a practical matter, few persons might try to raise such a defense for fear of facing lifelong restraint, even if they are not responsible for their inner cravings.

The consideration of the distinction between normal and abnormal cravings also helps clarify the law's treatment of various strong desires to offend. For example, in a recent case the court rejected the defendant's claim that "pathological gambling" should support an insanity defense in part on the ground that a very strong desire does not amount to a compulsion (*United States v. Lyons*, 1984). Was the court's analysis correct? Any strong desire to offend will certainly cause pain if the person forgoes offending, and one can argue that the desire must have been very strong indeed if fear of the law was not strong enough to inhibit the offense. Thus a defendant could claim that forgoing gambling, raping, burning, or whatever, produced substantially more pain than offending, and that fear of the former motivated the offense.

The problem with such claims is that they simply are not credible, except perhaps in extreme cases. We do not believe that it is fear of the pain of not raping, burning, or gambling that drives the actor. Instead, we are quite sure in most cases that it is the pleasure offending will produce—a personal gain—that drives the person. In a given case, however, the defendant may be able to convince us that the desire or craving was so intense that fear of the pain of not satisfying it was the true motive for offending. Indeed, the actor might claim that he hated the impulse and loathed himself for having it. Perhaps these situations are what is meant by "pathological" impulses of any type, and an excuse should obtain in such extreme cases. Note, however, that compulsion causes us to classify the impulse as "pathological"; the label "pathological" does not cause us to classify the case as one of compulsion.

Finally, one might argue that there is no volitional problem at all in the case of inner cravings. Herbert Fingarette and Anne Hasse, for example, have argued that the person who acts "compulsively" or under the influence of some irresistible impulse, mood, or passion is a person absolutely intent on acting. By what independent criteria, they ask, could one classify such conduct as involuntary? "On the face of it, one would see 'compulsive' conduct as an expression of (stubborn) 'will' *par excellence*" (Fingarette & Hasse, 1979, p. 61). They conclude that something ought to excuse in cases of such extraordinary "persistence," but the ground of the excuse is that the person's behavior is irrational rather than that it is involuntary.

Fingarette and Hasse are surely right that psychologically compelled behavior is intentional and that notions of the will being overwhelmed are metaphysical. The hard-choice criteria are hardly metaphysical, however, and the difficulty of assessing them in cases of inner cravings is primarily a practical ground for distinguishing cases of external compulsion such as duress. If obstinate single-mindedness is a criterion for irrationality, why are not all single-minded persons, such as Aleksandr Solzhenitsyn, irrational? One could distinguish the cases of inner cravings on the basis of the rationality of the goal obstinately pursued, but it is extraordinarily difficult to assess the rationality of goals. For instance, one could reasonably classify the goal of the kleptomaniac as rational—the relief of psychic tension produced by the desire to steal. If the goal is classified as "stealing without reason" it appears irrational, but on what ground, independent of the result we wish to achieve, should we prefer that characterization of the goal? In the case of the DDP or the pedophile, the irrationality analysis is even more problematic. Sexual pleasure or enjoyable drug-induced feelings are quite rational goals, and the means chosen to achieve them, though illegal, are rationally adapted to succeed. Of course if we classify such cravings, especially if they are strong, as irrational in themselves, the cravings and the behaviors they produce can be treated as cases of irrationality, negating the need for compulsion criteria. But are all strong cravings that may lead to inappropriate or illegal behavior evidence of irrationality or abnormality? Would the craving become more normal if its satisfaction were more socially approved?

A final argument for treating some cases of inner cravings as rationality problems would be this: Suppose the actor does not accept such impulses; they do not feel like part of the actor, who is ashamed of them, hates them, disowns them, or whatever. The actor may be able to choose means rationally suited to achieve the ends dictated by the disowned and unaccepted cravings, but one might argue that such a person, whose desires are in such conflict, is not rational. Intense and uncomfortable ambivalence or conflict about one's desires would then become a touchstone of irrationality. In these cases the criteria for irrationality collapse into those for hard choice (or vice versa) because the person suffering from intense conflict arguably faces a hard choice. But does rationality require that persons be the (comfortable) masters of their own houses? These persons' goals are intelligible, and nothing is amiss with their practical reasoning. There is no cognitive misfiring if such persons feel intensely competing desires, even ones that may be deemed unacceptable. Although considering ambivalent persons irrational may be an appealing practical solution to the problem of defining hard choices in some cases of inner cravings, doing so appears to be a conclusory use of an unusual definition. I believe our ordinary intuition in such cases is that the problem is hard choice and not irrationality. Ambivalence is not a criterion for irrationality. Finally, not all persons are ambivalent about their impulses, and some of these persons may yet face hard choices.

Many persons have a strong intuition that compulsion (or hard choice) not tied to irrationality should be an independent basis of excuse, but it is difficult to provide adequate criteria for compulsion that morally justify excusing. I have just tried to do so, but many persons sympathetic to the compulsion ground for excuse will find those criteria unsatisfactory. On the other hand, I have been unable to devise better ones, especially for inner compulsion. This does not mean, of course, that such criteria do not exist. If theoretically satisfactory criteria cannot be provided, however, it is conceivable that inner compulsion independent of irrationality can not provide a moral ground for excuse.

The criteria for lack of responsibility also include the requirement that the irrationality or compulsion must be nonculpable. In other words, the actor should not be excused if the irrationality or compulsion was the result of the person's rational, uncompelled act. If the irrationality is produced by the voluntary and knowing ingestion of a hallucinogen, for example, the actor will not be excused (see Model Penal Code; American Law Institute, 1962, § 2.08). Similarly, if a mentally disordered person is able to control his disorder or its effects, he will not be excused if he fails to do so by neglecting to take his medicine, by not exercising his willpower, or whatever. Note, however, that in these latter cases the actor's culpability may be affected although an excuse based on irrationality or lack of self-control does not obtain. For instance, a hypothetical actor who is delusional because of controllable mental disorder or the voluntary ingestion of a hallucinogen, and consequently does not realize the victim he kills is a person, cannot be guilty of intentional homicide because he lacks the requisite mens rea—he did not intend to kill a person. The actor may be guilty of negligent or even reckless homicide, however, because a reasonable person should have been aware—or the actor may in fact have been aware—that the homicidal behavior was foreseeable. Again, the lack of culpability in this case is based on the absence of a requisite mens rea, not on the presence of the excusing condition of irrationality.

How much irrationality and compulsion are necessary for moral and legal excuse? The degree of rationality or self-control that may be involved in a specific act is rarely an all-or-none matter, and these factors may vary over one's lifetime. Similarly, the degree of rationality or self-control that society and the law require for responsibility may vary over time within a society and among societies. One need not totally lack rationality or be entirely compelled to be excused, but at various times and in various places more or less may generally be expected from people.

The most important point to recognize is that mental health science cannot set the legal standard for irrationality or compulsion in the context of legal accountability, because setting it is not a scientific issue. The standard is a moral and social standard, to be set by those legal institutions empowered by a society to make individual moral and social decisions. In our society, for example, the substantive standards for legal insanity should be set largely by the legislature and interpreted by the courts, and individual cases should be decided by juries and judges.

To conclude this section on the foundations of and criteria for responsibility, let me quote from Daniel Dennett's recent analysis of the "free will" problem.

> What we want when we want free will is the power to decide our courses of action and to decide them wisely, in the light of our expectations and desires. We want to be in control of ourselves, and not under the control of others. We want to be agents, capable of initiating, and taking responsibility for, projects and deeds. (1984, p. 169)

Dennett's advice on how to respond to challenges to free will is this:

> First, inquire closely about just what variety of free will is supposedly jeopardized by the argument. Is it, in fact, a variety worth caring about? Ask yourself whether you have any clearly statable reason to hope you have that variety, any reason to fear that you might not. Would lacking this freedom really be like being in prison, or like being a puppet? For perhaps the conclusion of the new argument is only that no one could have some metaphysical property that is of academic interest at best. (1984, p. 172)

I believe the view I have outlined meets Dennett's tests. Persons are treated as persons who decide and are responsible for their actions unless there are good reasons why, as persons, they should not be held responsible. The version of moral agency I have presented is worth caring about because no one acting under it feels like either a puppet or a prisoner. When one is in the grip of irrationality or compulsion one is excused because the attributes of moral personhood are lacking, not because such persons are caused puppets whereas the rest of us are free puppeteers. All of us are persons equally subject to the causal determinist universe, but this is not the morally relevant issue. Dennett is once again helpful:

> Yes, if we try hard, we can imagine a being that listens to the voice of reason and yet is not exempted from the causal milieu. Yes, we can imagine a being whose every decision is caused by the interaction of features of its current state and features of its environment over which it has no control—and yet which is itself *in control* and not being controlled by that omnipresent and omnicausal environment. Yes, we can imagine a process of self-creation that starts with a non-responsible agent and builds, gradually, to an agent responsible for its own character. Yes, we can imagine a rational *and deterministic* being who is not deluded when it views its future as open and "up to" it. Yes, we can imagine a responsible free agent of whom it is true that whenever it has acted in the past, it could not have acted otherwise. (1984, p. 170)

It is just such beings, all of us, that I have tried to address.

I have also tried to provide criteria for when persons should be excused. These criteria do not provide easily adjudicated, "bright-line" tests. But that would be too much to ask of most legal tests that concern fundamental moral questions whose answers are rarely clear. On the other hand, I do not mean to suggest that my criteria are the best imaginable, though they are the best I can do at the moment. I confess especially to considerable ambivalence about excusing in cases of inner compulsion. In principle, why should the law distinguish between the compulsion produced by a gun at one's head and the compulsion produced by inner variables? Distinguishing between resistible and irresistible inner states is terrifically difficult, however. If we cannot at present develop reasonable criteria for inner compulsion, then perhaps we cannot afford to follow our intuition about such states. Perhaps there really are no such states that should be the predicates for an independent and morally necessary criterion for excuse. In sum, I cannot finally resolve here the question of what the proper criteria of excuse should be. If you wish to substitute others, however, remember that causation or determinism cannot be the criterion. That move is barred.

Policy Implications

IRRATIONALITY, COMPULSION, AND THE EXCUSES

In this section I shall consider a range of present and possible excuses in light of the analysis of the preceding sections and conclude by offering a unitary view of the excuses that does not individuate them by causes.

In the preceding section I elucidated the reasons mental disorder is relevant to responsibility and supported the moral soundness of the insanity defense as it has been developed in Anglo-American law. We excuse some mentally disordered persons because they lack essential rationality or are compelled, not simply because they are disordered. That is, the problems with affect, cognition, and impulses that mental disorder creates can in some cases sufficiently compromise rationality and self-control so as to vitiate moral accountability. Note again that the mentally disordered actor will be excused not because the behavior is caused, but because he or she lacked the fundmental attributes of responsibility at the time of the act. Thus many disordered persons, including those who suffer from severe problems, may nonetheless be held accountable because in the act in question their rationality was not sufficiently compromised or they were not compelled (Morse, 1978, 1984). Again, the degree of irrationality or compulsion necessary to excuse will vary from place to place and time to time.

The preceding discussion of the proper basis for excuse should finally clarify why factors such as poverty that are apparently more powerful causes of crime than mental disorder do not excuse the actor. The reason is that the average poor criminal, despite the undoubted hardships of his or her life, is neither an irrational nor an involuntary actor. If the stresses of social deprivation were to drive a person crazy, then he or she may be entitled to an insanity defense. Again, however, the excuse will obtain because the person lacks the preconditions for responsibility, not because his or her behavior is caused. Presumably, all behavior is caused.

How does the analysis respond to an actor who faced constraining opportunities in life but is neither irrational nor compelled? Let us take the classic case of the socially disadvantaged person who, through little or no fault of his own, is the product of an environment that has provided him with few advantages and even fewer skills. All his efforts to obtain training or assistance are met with indifference by impersonal welfare bureaucracies. In despair, realizing that he will probably never be able to partake of the American dream by legitimate means and will have to undergo degrading conditions even to obtain the minimal requirements for life, he turns to crime—say, burglary. I have, of course, constructed the hypothetical case most sympathetically to the defense. The first thing to note about our hypothetical actor is that his career as a burglar is no more caused than the career of a middle-class burglar. We understand the causes of the poor person's criminal career more easily, but in a causal universe the crimes of both are entirely caused. The possible moral difference between them is not one of causality; rather, it is the difference in the range of opportunities reasonably available. The questions, then, are whether constrained opportunity of this sort should be the basis for a responsibility excuse or for any other kind of excuse.

If "constrained opportunity" is to be a defense, it must be a policy excuse and not a responsibility excuse (compare Bazelon, 1976). There is nothing wrong with the actor; he or she is simply a victim of the inevitably unequal distribution of life's goods. The actor is neither irrational nor compelled (except in extreme cases where a necessity justification might already obtain), because there is almost always some alternative to wrongdoing. Consequently, the basis for the defense would be this: When society has unduly cabined the actor through no fault of his or her own, then society should excuse the actor's bad deeds by way of recompense. This corrective justice approach is surely politically impossible and practically unworkable, however. What should be done with acquitted actors who are rational, voluntary, and dangerous? If they are excused, we cannot lock them up for committing a crime, and because they are normal people they cannot be civilly committed. The defense could be constructed so that it acquits very few people—only those whose opportunities are extraordinarily constrained. Moreover, it would rarely work for crimes of violence or passion. Perhaps, then, not too much danger would be created by some acquittals. Nonetheless, I think even such a minimalist proposal would be politically unacceptable because most people would take the position that life's hardships require firmer exercise of good character and are not proper motivations or excuses for antisocial conduct.

Mercy killing provides another example of the value of the analysis. The true mercy killer does not deserve a responsibility excuse because the person acts entirely rationally and voluntarily. If we wish to acquit mercy killers, it must be either because the act is justified—true mercy killing is right—or perhaps because the strain of watching a loved one suffer created a severe state of irrationality. I assume, of course, that the latter would be a highly unusual case and that the appropriate way to assess the morality of mercy killing is to determine if it is justified rather than to argue that the mercy killer is not responsible. The latter deprives the action of the allegedly loving, caring, respectful intention with which, I assume, a true mercy killing is performed.

If proposed new defenses were considered in light of the criteria for responsibility offered rather than according to confused causal theories, they would be considered far more rationally. Let us take some recent examples: the XYY defense, brainwashing, premenstrual syndrome, and battered spouse syndrome. The XYY defense enjoyed a short vogue when it appeared that men with an extra Y chromosome were more likely to commit crimes than men who lacked the chromosome; that is, the XYY genetic configuration appeared to be a predisposing cause of crime. Immediately, because the cause was genetic, claims were made to excuse the XYY criminals on the grounds that they lacked free choice because their criminality was the product of their (abnormal) biology. Although the empirical assumptions underlying the claim for an XYY excuse are now rejected, the situation furnishes an instructive example. As I hope this paper has demonstrated, this claim was based on the confusion of causation with excuse and the loose use of the term "free choice." XYY criminals are no more caused than other criminals: all are caused. It is simply that a biologically predisposing cause had

allegedly been discovered in this case. But unless biologically predisposed criminals commit their crimes under the sway of nonculpable irrationality or compulsion, there is no moral reason to excuse
them. If it should be objected that the XYY configuration predis-
poses these men to being aggressive, for example, again this is of no
moral relevance. Many persons are aggressive for a wide range of
causes, but being an aggressive type is not, nor should it be, an excuse.

Now consider the so-called case of brainwashing, wherein those
with superior power systematically apply to a person under their
control techniques of cognitive, affective, and behavior change that
produce in the victim a new series of cognitions, attitudes, reactions, hopes, fears, and even a new identity. The transformed person then behaves in an unacceptable way consistent with his or her
new psychology or identity. Patty Hearst's criminal behavior as
Tanya—robbing banks, covering a robbery at a sporting goods store
with a machine gun—is the classic modern example. Let us concede
for the purpose of argument that but for the systematic alteration of
her personality by her Symbionese Liberation Army (SLA) captors,
Hearst would not have become Tanya or have engaged in the criminal behavior. Let us assume, also, that she really became Tanya;
in other words, she was no longer Patty Hearst who was simply
"going along" for fear of being killed. Should Tanya be excused?

Tanya was clearly a rational and voluntary agent who acted
voluntarily for perfectly rational reasons and in a manner rationally
calculated to further her revolutionary goals. Of course she was responsible. It may be objected, however, that she was nonculpably
caused to have the values she did and so on. But so are many children nonculpably caused to have their values by the child-rearing
techniques of their families, the influence of the culture, and a host
of other factors. Indeed, most of us are nonculpably caused to hold
the values and attitudes we do. Suppose, for example, that Tanya
was the child of an SLA couple who brought her up from earliest
infancy to be Tanya. We would not excuse the hypothetical Tanya,
although the only difference between her and the real Tanya is that
she had a consistent identity whereas the real Tanya had a changed
identity. Some might argue that one should not be held accountable
until the actor has spent a substantial amount of time within the new
identity or set of values, thus firmly integrating the identity or
values. But why should this be so? A person who has an instan-
taneous religious conversion is certainly properly praised for his or

her good acts immediately thereafter, and there seems little reason why a person who converts to antisocial values should be treated asymmetrically. Both the hypothetical and the real Tanya were caused, and both were rational at the time of the offense. If we wish to excuse the real Tanya, it should not be because she is not responsible. Instead, if she is to be excused at all, we ought to construct a policy excuse on the ground that it is unfair to punish those who have undergone such ordeals. Construction of such a defense would of course require a normative justification, but that is a task beyond our purposes here.

Premenstrual syndrome (PMS) and battered spouse syndrome are conceptually alike. In both cases the claim is that a cause—in one instance biological, in the other psychological—has deprived the defendant of free will. Like the XYY claim, however, this argument uses loose talk. If PMS and battered spouse syndrome merit a defense, it is not because they are causes of crime. Once again, all crime is caused. If in an individual case, however, premenstrual syndrome or the stress of being battered causes nonculpable irrationality at the time of the offense, then an excuse should perhaps obtain on the ground that the defendant was irrational. Because there is no general irrationality defense, however, defendants must try to shoehorn their claims into a preexisting defense such as insanity or face the unenviable task of convincing a court to adopt a new defense. Neither approach makes sense. Either the defense has to make a spurious analogy—for example, that PMS is a mental disorder—or it must promote the folly of individuating excuses by cause.

What does make sense is to recognize that nonculpable irrationality can have many causes, such as mental disorder, involuntary intoxication, perhaps PMS, and who knows what else. What sound policy reason supports the existence of specific excuses such as insanity or duress rather than two generic excuses for nonculpable irrationality and compulsion? After all, it is not mental disorder or duress per se that excuses; it is the actor's irrationality or compulsion. Thus, any nonculpable cause of these problems ought to excuse. If the law had generic defenses, the causes that now give defenses their names would simply become evidence to support the claim for the generic excuse. For example, mental disorder should be treated as nothing more than evidence to support the plausibility of the actor's more general irrationality claim. Similarly, why should duress be a separate excuse rather than simply a matter of evidence supporting an excuse based on volitional difficulties? Despite the logic of this argument, there are specific excuses and no general excuse for irrationality or compulsion (see *United States v. Moore*, 1973). Speculating about why this state of affairs has arisen in the law would go far beyond the scope of this paper, but it will be sufficient to note that it is primarily a function of the peculiar mode by which the common law evolves.

Although the discussion so far has treated the issues of rationality and compulsion equally, the law does not give them equal weight. A primary focus of insanity defense reform after the Hinckley verdict, for example, has been to abolish volitional tests for legal insanity, leaving only an excuse for irrationality. Even before Hinckley, internal compulsion tests were less popular and, unlike rationality tests, were never the sole test for legal insanity in any jurisdiction (Goldstein, 1967). The reasons for this interesting disparity are both moral and practical. The law has been reluctant to concede that any otherwise rational person's self-control may be so compromised by mental disorder or any other internal cause that an excuse is deserved (Hart, 1968). Before the adoption of the ALI standard, those jurisdictions that adopted a volitional test (in addition to a rationality test) typically used language requiring that the mental disorder totally deprive the defendant of self-control before an excuse would obtain. As is well known, the recently popular ALI test includes a volitional prong, and the excuse is available if the defendant lacked only "substantial capacity"—as opposed to total capacity—to conform (American Law Institute, 1962, §4.01). Nonetheless, substantial doubts about the sufficiency of self-control difficulties remain and are increasing, even among mental health professionals (American Psychiatric Association, 1982).

Further, it is widely believed that internal compulsion tests are more indeterminate and difficult to adjudicate than rationality tests. It is by now a commonplace observation that it is impossible to distinguish between an irresistible impulse and one simply not resisted. No one has the ability to measure internal compulsion. And because factual and normative evaluation of compulsion is so imprecise and necessarily subjective, adjudication of volitional tests elicits the most scientifically suspect sort of expert testimony that brings disrepute to both psychology and the law. Thus, for a variety of reasons, the law does not treat compulsion and rationality tests equally, but for the remainder of this paper I shall continue to do so unless otherwise noted.

RESPONSIBILITY AND EXPERTISE

The final policy issue I shall address is how the psychologist or other mental health professional can be of help when the law assesses a defendant's lack of moral accountability on the basis of irrationality and compulsion. Although my views on responsibility have altered over the years, my conclusions about the proper role of mental health expertise in assessing and adjudicating responsibility have remained stable. In brief, my position is that experts should be entirely barred from offering the following types of testimony: first, diagnoses, no matter how reliable they may be; second, causal speculations, no matter how much theory or even data support them, *if* they are used as the equivalent of an excuse; third, the result of virtually any psychological test, no matter how reliable and valid it may be for clinical purposes; and fourth, conclusions about the ultimate legal issue, no matter how reasonable the conclusions might be or how much they are supported by sensible reasoning on the expert's part. My reasons for proposing these exclusions are simple: this information is not relevant to the moral and legal assessment of responsibility, or it is not a matter of expert, scientific knowledge. Experts should be allowed to offer, first, the most complete clinical observations of thoughts, feelings, and actions they can muster based on their own examination of the defendant and sometimes, perhaps in rare cases, based on information they have obtained directly from other witnesses to the defendant's behavior. Second, they should be allowed to offer hard data in those rare cases where such data are both relevant and available. My reasons for permitting this testimony are as simple as those for prohibiting the other types of testimony: observations and relevant hard data will be legally relevant and are matters of expert clinical and scientific skill and knowledge.

I have already, in other articles (Morse, 1978, 1982, 1984), written scores of pages arguing for the validity of my proposals. Instead of rehashing all the arguments here—which would hardly be an original contribution—let me try anew to justify these proposals briefly in light of the analysis offered in the preceding sections of this paper.

If legally and morally sufficient irrationality or compulsion is the touchstone of nonresponsibility, the relevant evidence necessary to adjudicate the question will be that which describes the defendant's behavior in as much detail as possible. I contend that a diagnosis is irrelevant because it provides no further information on this issue beyond the clinical observations upon which it is based. To take a simple, familiar example, whether John Hinckley, Jr., was schizophrenic, schizoid, or schizotypal does not answer the question whether he was sufficiently out of touch with reality, sufficiently irrational, to deserve an excuse for attempting to assassinate the president. To decide this we do not need a diagnosis, no matter how precise; we need the fullest possible history and description of his beliefs, feelings, and actions. Then the finder of fact, the judge or jury, which is the moral representative of society, can decide the moral and legal question whether Hinckley or any other defendant is sufficiently irrational.

Causes are likewise irrelevant when they are used as the equivalent of an excuse. If the defendant is neither sufficiently irrational nor compelled, there is no reason whatever to inquire into the causes of his or her criminal behavior, because there is no moral or legal ground for excuse or mitigation. But if a defendant did seem to be irrational or compelled, the clinical observations or hard data showing why he or she was irrational would be relevant to showing that the defendant was not faking and that the irrationality was nonculpable. Again, however, before the issue of causation is ever approached it must be determined that the defendant was consciously irrational or met the criteria for compulsion.

For those of the psychodynamic persuasion, I may have just seemed either to miss an important point or to pull a fast one by focusing on conscious irrationality and compulsion. After all, psychodynamic psychology teaches that much behavior that *seems* rational and uncompelled is in fact the product of deep irrationality or unconscious compulsion. I have answered such claims in detail in another article (Morse, 1982), and to repeat the arguments in any detail here would be cruel and unusual punishment to the reader. Let me therefore simply state the conclusions of that argument. First, as a general theory, psychodynamic psychology is not sufficiently confirmed to be the basis of expert testimony in courts of law. Second, even if it is a valid theory, reliable formulations cannot be given in individual cases. Third, even if it is a valid theory that produces reliable formulations, no coherent normative theory links dynamic unconscious psychological processes or contents to a lack of responsibility. The law must therefore focus on conscious cognitive and affective experience. Fourth, even if psychodynamic psychology is valid, reliably formulated in individual cases, and morally relevant, it cannot be the basis of practical legal decision making. Nothing I have read or heard in the four years since that article appeared has caused me to alter those conclusions, and I refer you to the original article for the full argument and scholarly support.

The results of psychological tests, even the best of them, should also be excluded, because test results are almost always irrelevant to legal questions about mental state at the time of the offense (Gass, 1979). They have not been developed or validated to answer legally relevant questions about irrationality or compulsion, and they do not do so. Whether tests yield diagnoses, personality profiles, cognitive or affective profiles, or whatever, such information adds little to the decision about whether the person was sufficiently irrational or compelled at the time of the act in question. Again, we need the fullest picture of the actor's behavior at that time.

But, it may be objected, is not the result of a test relevant if it is either consistent or inconsistent with the conclusion drawn from the actor's actual behavior? The answer to this, logically, is possibly yes; practically, however, the answer is almost certainly no. First, the tests will rarely be given close enough to the time in question to permit the inference that the defendant's mental state was sufficiently similar at both times. Second, tests do not test legal irrationality, and there is no test for compulsion. Moreover, the degree of irrationality necessary to support a legal excuse is typically so great that it is behaviorally obvious and needs no confirmation from psychological tests. If a test is needed for confirmation, this is prima facie evidence that the person was not irrational enough at the time in question to deserve an excuse. Third, I know of no strong evidence that tests are valid indicators of malingering about irrationality, though some may have some discriminatory power concerning malingering about a diagnosis.

Another objection to my near blanket exclusion of tests concerns the use of neuropsychological tests, which afficionados claim are as valid as physical tests for identifying neurological damage and perhaps are even more accurate in many cases. Would not such tests be useful to prove that the actor's irrationality or compulsion was really nonculpable? First, of course, the actor's behavior would have to be sufficiently irrational or compelled. Then the conclusion that the problem was nonculpable would depend on there being hard data linking the type of neurological damage the test discloses to the type of irrationality demonstrated by this actor. If such data existed, I would permit their introduction in the form of statistical statements but would not allow the expert to opine that the defendant was not malingering or could not do anything about his or her irrationality or compulsion.

A final objection to my test ban concerns the burgeoning construction and use of tests that are meant to determine specifically whether a legal criterion is satisfied. For example, there are now tests of competence to stand trial (Harvard Laboratory of Community Psychiatry, 1973) and of criminal responsibility (Rogers, Wasyliw, & Cavanaugh, 1984). The standard development strategy is to validate the instrument on a reference group of persons who have already been found to meet the legal criteria. Then, if a subject is found to achieve the criterial score of the reference group, the investigator concludes that this subject too meets the legal criteria in question. The major difficulty here is that the law does not accept, in Tribe's apt phrase, "trial by mathematics" (Tribe, 1971). The essence of retrospective legal decision making is individualized justice, wherein the finder of fact considers the facts of the individual case in light of the applicable legal criteria. It is irrelevant that the actor in a given case is statistically just like those actors who have been blamed or excused by other juries or judges in prior cases. Finally, moreover, the test does not provide any additional relevant information that is not provided by the fullest picture of the actor's behavior at the time in question.

The expert's conclusion on the ultimate legal issue should be prohibited because it is not a matter of scientific expertise. The ultimate legal conclusion—whether the actor deserves an excuse because he or she is nonculpably irrational or compelled—is just that, a legal conclusion. It must be derived from the facts, but it is nonetheless a legal and moral judgment. The mental health professional has no particular expertise in legal and moral matters, however. On such issues, he or she is simply another lay member of society. When offering a legal conclusion, the expert doffs the white coat of expertise and dons the hat of a thirteenth juror. Twelve persons good and true are quite sufficient; we do not need a thirteenth moral and legal opinion disguised as a matter of scientific expertise.

In short, there are no quick scientific fixes to the problems of assessing and adjudicating irrationality and compulsion. These are commonsense moral and legal judgments that must be based on the actor's behavior at the time of the event in question. If psychologists and other mental health professionals will simply provide their detailed observations and hard data, where relevant and available, then we can trust judges and juries to make the hard legal decisions.

Conclusion: Tempest and Boyd Revisited

Let us now return to the real and horrifying case of Mrs. Tempest to consider in light of the proper criteria her responsibility for killing her son. Neither her mental disorder per se nor its allegedly causal role in her crime is the issue. I assume that some set of causal variables caused her to kill Gregory. The real question, as always, is whether Mrs. Tempest was sufficiently irrational or compelled when she drowned Gregory to justify excusing her for this horrendous deed. It is perfectly understandable that she found motherhood and domestic life confining, anxiety-provoking, and angering, but killing her son hardly seems the means best calculated to cast off the burdens of her life. She could have achieved the same result with much less cost by simply leaving home. Thus the means chosen, though effective, simply do not make much sense in connection with any rational goal she might have been pursuing. On the other hand, despite her history of mental disorder, Mrs. Tempest was not delusional, hallucinating, or otherwise identifiably out of touch with reality at the time. She planned her deed, chose her quite effective means carefully, and carried out her plan successfully. I assume, of course, that sophisticated persons will not conclude that Mrs. Tempest is irrational simply because she killed. Those who believe all criminals must be disordered, thus equating badness with madness, miss the moral point. Should Mrs. Tempest be excused because she was irrational? I do not know, but this *is* the right question.

Whether compulsion existed is harder to assess because there is little evidence concerning it. Mrs. Tempest said she desired to avoid the problems of motherhood and family life, but she did not indicate that she experienced this desire as an overwhelming hard choice. Moreover, the calm, premeditated manner in which she carried out the deed appears to belie such subjective feelings. It is certainly not the case that she felt compelled solely because she was mentally disordered. In light of the evidence available from the appellate decision, I would conclude that she does not deserve to be excused for volitional reasons.

For those who need an ending to our story, I should add that at a bench trial the judge rejected Mrs. Tempest's insanity defense and convicted her of first-degree intentional and premeditated murder.

The Boyd case appears to be a classic attempt to use causation as an excuse. There is a flavor of causation as compulsion in the theory of psychological dynamics—he killed to avoid killing himself—but the basic approach seems to be simply that causation itself is an excuse. Assuming that the history of loss and stress and the consequent personality dynamics were the primary causes of Boyd's killing Hartman, the existence of a causal story does not per se provide a ground for excuse or mitigation of punishment. We do not have as many facts about the killing itself as we did in Tempest, but it appears that Boyd was neither irrational nor subject to compulsion. Multiple stabbings are as consistent with anger as with craziness. Indeed, the jury verdict of first-degree murder suggests that the jurors concluded the killing was premeditated and uncompelled. A sad history or an unfortunate personality is not an excuse or mitigating factor in itself.

If, however, Boyd was nonculpably irrational or subject to compulsion at the time of the killing, then mitigation of punishment might be justified in an indeterminate sentencing scheme or to avoid capital punishment. The question is whether his irrationality or compulsion was nonculpable. Once again, everything is caused, so causation is not the issue. What we must do, therefore, is look to the circumstances and to his description of his mental state at the time of the crime and beforehand. Then we must make the judgment whether circumstance or character is most to blame. If the former is the case, mitigation is far more justified than if the latter is true. Of course, how much as a moral and legal matter we can expect people to bear up under stresses of various sorts, and in the face of contemplated harm of varying severity, is a normative judgment. Because I take the position that people can and should avoid homicide under almost all conceivable conditions, I would probably not mitigate Boyd's sentence at all.

To ensure proper closure again, I should tell you that the trial judge refused to admit Dr. Humphrey's testimony on the grounds that it was irrelevant to mitigation. On appeal, the Supreme Court of North Carolina ruled that the testimony was properly excluded because it did not offer information that bore on Boyd's moral culpability; it only suggested that the killing was predictable. The jury had sentenced Boyd to death.

Assessing responsibility on the basis of rationality and compulsion is harder than doing so according to the causal determinist theory that seems to imply the answer as a logical corollary of the person's diagnosis or the psychological explanation for behavior. There is no alternative, however: the causal determinist theory is conceptually unsound and practically unworkable. Persons must be treated as persons, and criteria of excuse appropriate to persons must be formulated and applied, hard though this task may be.

REFERENCES

American Law Institute. (1962). *Model Penal Code* (Proposed official draft). Philadelphia: Author.

American Psychiatric Association. (1980). *Diagnostic and statistical manual of mental disorders* (3rd ed.). Washington, DC: Author.

American Psychiatric Association. (1982). *Statement on the insanity defense.* Washington, DC: Author.

Audi, R. (1974). Moral responsibility, freedom and compulsion. *American Philosophical Quarterly, 11*, 1–14.

Bazelon, D. (176). The morality of the criminal law. *Southern California Law Review, 49*, 385–405.

Bice, S. (1980). Rationality analysis in constitutional law. *Minnesota Law Review, 65*, 1–62.

Bonnie, R. J., & Slobogin, C. (1980). The role of mental health professionals in the criminal process: The case for informed speculation. *Virginia Law Review, 66*, 427–522.

Brandt, R. (1969). A utilitarian theory of excuses. *Philosophical Review, 78*, 337–361.

Brandt, R. (1983). The concept of rational action. *Social Theory and Practice, 9*, 143–164.

Cantwell, D. (1983). The offender. In U.S. Department of Justice, *Report to the nation on crime and justice.* Washington, DC: U.S. Government Printing Office.

Commonwealth v. Tempest, 496 Pa. 436, 437 A.2d 952 (1981).

Dennett, D. (1984). *Elbow room: The varieties of free will worth wanting.* Cambridge, MA: MIT Press.

Durham v. United States, 214 F.2d 262 (D.C. Cir. 1954).

Feinberg, J. (1970). *Doing and deserving: Essays in the theory of responsibility.* Princeton: Princeton University Press.

Fingarette, H. (1972). *The meaning of criminal insanity.* Berkeley: University of California Press.

Fingarette, H., & Hasse, A. (1979). *Mental disabilities and criminal responsibility.* Berkeley: University of California Press.

Fletcher, G. (1978). *Rethinking criminal law.* Boston: Little, Brown.

Gass, R. (1979). The psychologist as expert witness: Science in the courtroom. *Maryland Law Review, 38*, 539–621.

Goldman, A. (1970). *A theory of human action*. Princeton, NJ: Princeton University Press.

Goldstein, A. (1967). *The insanity defense*. New Haven: Yale University Press.

Greenawalt, K. (1984). The perplexing borders of justification and excuse. *Columbia Law Review, 84*, 1897–1927.

Grünbaum, A. (1972). Free will and laws of human behavior. In H. Feigl, W. Sellars, & K. Lehrer (Eds.), *New readings in philosophical analysis*. New York: Appleton-Century-Crofts.

Hart, H. L. A. (1968). *Punishment and responsibility: Essays in the philosophy of law*. New York: Oxford University Press.

Harvard Laboratory of Community Psychiatry. (1973). *Competency to stand trial and mental illness*. Rockville, MD: National Institute of Mental Health.

Hollander, P. (1973). Sociology, selective determinism, and the rise of expectations. *American Sociologist, 8*, 147–153.

Kadish, S., Schulhofer, S., & Paulsen, M. (1983). *Criminal law and its processes* (4th ed.). Boston: Little, Brown.

Kelman, M. (1981). Interpretive construction in the substantive criminal law. *Stanford Law Review, 33*, 591–673.

LaFave, W., & Scott, A., Jr. (1972). *Criminal Law*. Minneapolis: West.

Mackie, J. L. (1977). *Ethics: Inventing right and wrong*. Harmondsworth, England: Penguin Books.

Macklin, R. (1983). Philosophical conceptions of rationality and psychiatric notions of competency. *Synthese, 57*, 205–224.

Martin v. State, 31 Ala. App. 334, 17 So.2d 427 (Ala. Ct. App. 1944).

Mayock v. Martin, 157 Conn. 56, 245 A.2d 574 (1968).

M'Naghten's case, 4 St. Tr. N.S. 847, 8 Eng. Rep. 71 (H.L. 1843).

Moore, M. (1985). Causation and the excuses. *California Law Review, 73*, 1091–1149.

Morris, N. (1982). *Madness and the criminal law*. Chicago: University of Chicago Press.

Morse, S. J. (1978). Crazy behavior, morals and science: An analysis of mental health law. *Southern California Law Review, 51*, 527–654.

Morse, S. J. (1982). Failed explanations and criminal responsibility: Experts and the unconscious. *Virginia Law Review, 68*, 971–1084.

Morse, S. J. (1984). Undiminished confusion in diminished capacity. *Journal of Criminal Law & Criminology, 75*, 1–55.

Morse, S. J. (1985). Excusing the crazy: The insanity defense reconsidered. *Southern California Law Review, 58*, 777–837.

Robinson, P. (1982). Criminal law defenses: A systematic analysis. *Columbia Law Review, 82*, 199–291.

Rogers, R., Wasyliw, O., & Cavanaugh, J., Jr. (1984). Evaluating insanity: A study of construct validity. *Law and Human Behavior, 8,* 293–304.

State v. Boyd, 319 S.E.2d 189 (N.C. 1984).

State v. Pike, 49 N.H. 339 (1870).

Strawson, P. (1982). Freedom and resentment. In G. Watson (Ed.), *Free will.* New York: Oxford University Press.

Tribe, L. (1971). Trial by mathematics. *Harvard Law Review, 84,* 1329–1393.

United States v. Brawner, 471 F.2d 969 (D.C. Cir. 1972).

United States v. Byers, 746 F.2d 1104 (D.C. Cir. 1984).

United States v. Lyons, 731 F.2d 243 (5th Cir. 1984).

United States v. Moore, 486 F.2d 1139 (D.C. Cir. 1973).

van Inwagen, P. (1983). *An essay on free will.* Oxford: Clarendon Press.

Watson, G. (Ed.). (1982). *Free will.* New York: Oxford University Press.

Deterrence Theory and Research

Jack P. Gibbs
Vanderbilt University

*A*fter nearly two centuries, the deterrence doctrine remains far from a systematic theory. The formulation of a systematic theory is beyond the present work, but steps in that direction are needed if only to facilitate an assessment of deterrence research. However, the first subject must be a conceptualization of deterrence.

Definitions and Types of Deterrence

The term *deterrence* applies to any act and any punishment, but traditionally the deterrence doctrine is associated with criminal justice. Accordingly, the term will be defined as though limited to crime and legal punishments.

Definitions commonly fail to distinguish deterrence from other mechanisms through which legal punishments may prevent crimes. For the moment it must suffice to say that such mechanisms do not involve the threat of punishment and fear. Unless threat and fear are stressed, deterrence is a hodgepodge notion.

Deterrence occurs when a potential offender refrains from or curtails criminal activity because he or she perceives some threat of a legal punishment for contrary behavior and fears that punishment. Space limitations preclude clarifying more than one term. A legal punishment is a legal action by a legal official that is perceived by at least one potential offender as causing pain or discomfort. That terminology is a tacit rejection of the traditional operant conception of punishment (see van Houten, 1983, pp. 13–19), because that conception would make the deterrence doctrine unfalsifiable. Note also that the definition goes beyond statutory penalties and even actual sentences to procedural steps in criminal justice, such as arrest or trial. Those actions presumably are perceived by potential offenders as painful.

TWO CONVENTIONAL TYPES OF DETERRENCE

With few exceptions (e.g., Blumstein, Cohen, & Nagin, 1978, pp. 1–49), writers on deterrence distinguish general deterrence and what is called specific, special, or individual deterrence. Full appreciation of the distinction's significance requires explicit definitions.

General deterrence refers to the deterrence of potential offenders who have not been legally punished. To illustrate, suppose that a student *with no arrest history* reads of someone's receiving a six-month sentence for marijuana possession. Insofar as that experience deters the student, each time that he or she refrains from or curtails possession of marijuana constitutes general deterrence. The crucial consideration is not whether the student had possessed marijuana before reading about the punishment, nor is it the nature of that particular experience. All manner of experiences short of actually being punished, even coming to know of statutory penalties, could further general deterrence.

Specific deterrence refers to the deterrence of potential offenders who have been legally punished. The notion does not deny that vicarious experience of punishment can deter; rather, being punished supposedly furthers deterrence beyond any vicarious experience. Reconsider the individual who was sentenced to six months in jail for marijuana possession. If the incarceration prompts that individual to refrain from or curtail marijuana possession, each instance would be specific deterrence. But contemplate this question: To what extent does punishment for one type of crime deter the offender from other types? Researchers have yet to treat the "generalization" question seriously (see Moffitt, 1983, p. 134), and research is needed to realize a more defensible definition of specific deterrence.

Significance of the distinction. The importance of the general/specific distinction is most obvious when stipulating evidence of deterrence. Assume this finding: ex-convicts commit more crimes per unit of time after incarceration than before. That finding would indicate no specific deterrence, but it would have little bearing on general deterrence.

To appreciate the policy relevance of the general/specific distinction, consider the argument that legislators are preoccupied with general deterrence because it offers cheap crime prevention. What could be cheaper than simply threatening potential offenders? But if recidivists contribute substantially to the crime rate and can be deterred only by serving long prison terms, then crime prevention through deterrence becomes very expensive. Moreover, a strategy for promoting one type of deterrence may not be necessary for the other type. Thus, neither actual punishments nor statutory penalties need be publicized to promote specific deterrence.

A LESS CONVENTIONAL DISTINCTION

The difference between entirely refraining from a criminal act and curtailing commissions is so important that two additional types of deterrence should be distinguished. In the case of *absolute deterrence*, a potential offender has contemplated a crime at least once and has been deterred totally each instance. That an individual has never committed the crime is only a necessary condition for inferring absolute deterrence, because no individual can be deterred without contemplating a crime. To be sure, the term "contemplating" creates difficulties; but if social and behavioral scientists are unwilling to consider covert behavior, they should leave the deterrence doctrine alone.

The idea of partial crime prevention enters into the notion of *restrictive deterrence*. It occurs when, to diminish the risk or severity of a legal punishment, a potential offender engages in some action that has the effect of reducing his or her commissions of a crime. Briefly illustrating, suppose that a bad-check artist follows this rule: Never hang more than one piece of paper in any town. Such rules are indicative of restrictive deterrence because they have the effect of reducing the number of offenses. Driving behavior often illustrates restrictive deterrence, as when drivers exceed the speed limit by only five miles per hour to reduce the risk or severity of a legal punishment.

Significance of the distinction. Contemplate something improbable—evidence that every professional football player has snorted cocaine at least once. The evidence would fuel allegations that the legal control of narcotics is ineffectual, but it would reveal nothing about restrictive deterrence. Similarly, no crime rate is ever so great as to demonstrate negligible absolute deterrence. So although most writers and researchers ignore the distinction, evidence that bears on either type of deterrence—absolute or restrictive—has little bearing on the other type.

The distinction gives rise to a possible paradox; it may well be that so-called professional criminals are deterred the most. Given such an offender, the most commonly overlooked question is this: How many crimes would the offender have committed had there been no threat of legal punishment? Granted the question is unanswerable, it is relevant in debating penal policy. Critics who assert that legal punishments do not deter may never have thought of restrictive deterrence.

Toward a Theory of General Deterrence

Given the general/specific distinction and the absolute/restrictive distinction, there are four types of deterrence. That number alone precludes stating the deterrence doctrine as a simple proposition (e.g., Carroll, 1978, p. 1512), such as: Certain, swift, and severe punishments deter crime. Any such proposition would be a gross oversimplification even if types of deterrence could be ignored. It is not clear whether the proposition refers to statutory penalties, to actual punishments, or to both. Even if general deterrence requires some actual punishments, potential offenders may perceive statutory penalties as a threat.

Attempts to reduce the deterrence doctrine to a simple proposition conceal the doctrine's most significant feature; it is first and foremost a perceptual theory. Whether a punishment threat deters depends not on the certainty, celerity, or severity of punishment in any objective sense but on the potential offender's perception. Therefore, in stating the deterrence doctrine as a theory, a theorist should recognize two classes of punishment properties—the objective and the perceptual. The two can be distinguished roughly in terms of procedures for gathering data. The only systematic way to gather data on perceptual properties is to solicit answers from potential offenders to questions about punishments, but objective properties can be studied without such solicitation.

THE STRUCTURE OF A THEORY OF GENERAL DETERRENCE

Figure 1 is only a step toward a theory of general deterrence. Though more elaborate than the typical formulation, the diagram oversimplifies. For one thing, the distinction between absolute and restrictive deterrence is relegated to tests of the theory. Another oversimplification is more complicated. Six objective properties of punishments and six perceptual properties should be recognized as possibly relevant, but full recognition would require several diagrams. So some of the roman numerals in the diagram actually denote a *set* of postulates or theorems; and if several diagrams were presented, each postulate or theorem would be identified by a capital letter. For example, Postulate IA would assert a direct relation between objective certainty and perceived certainty, while Theorem IIA would assert an inverse relation between objective certainty and the crime rate.

Some social scientists may regard Figure 1 as too complicated. In particular, economists engaging in deterrence research make no attempt to measure perceptual properties, nor do they emphasize those properties in their theoretical statements about deterrence. Indeed, those statements scarcely go beyond the general assumptions or principles of economics (see Cook, 1980, and the literature cited there).

The question of testability. Any formulation of a general deterrence theory should be guided in part by research findings, but current findings are inadequate. There are even doubts as to which variables in a deterrence theory can be taken as mensurable. In that connection, Postulates II and III in Figure 1 are not considered directly testable, because there is no defensible procedure for measuring deterrence.

The point is not that enormous resources would be required to measure deterrence at the aggregate level. Even in comparing individuals, deterrence should not be regarded as directly measurable. The experience of being deterred is real but forever private, and deterrence is not "observed" when asking potential offenders why they have or have not committed a crime.

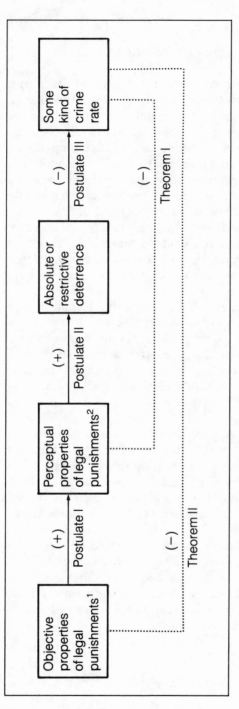

FIGURE 1. Suggested structure of a theory of general deterrence

Note: (Cause or antecedent correlate) → (effect or postcedent correlate); (+) signifies that an increase causes or is correlated with a subsequent increase; (−) signifies that an increase causes or is correlated with a subsequent decrease.

[1] Six properties: (1) objective certainty of actual legal punishments; (2) presumptive severity of statutory or prescribed legal punishments; (3) presumptive severity of actual legal punishments; (4) objective celerity of actual legal punishments; (5) normative scope of statutory or prescribed legal punishments; (6) actual scope of statutory or prescribed legal punishments.

[2] Six properties: (1) perceived certainty of actual legal punishments; (2) perceived severity of statutory or prescribed legal punishments; (3) perceived severity of actual legal punishments; (4) perceived celerity or swiftness of actual legal punishments; (5) beliefs as to statutory or prescribed legal punishments; (6) beliefs as to actual legal punishments.

TWELVE PROPERTIES OF LEGAL PUNISHMENTS

Each property is defined in Table 1. That arrangement permits a focus on requisite data and measurement procedures; but only a few *illustrative* comments can be made, and they ignore numerous problems and issues.

Although the goal is a general explication of the measurement of each punishment property, the reader should have some sense of how those measures would be used in tests of a general deterrence theory. Tests differ primarily in three respects: first, the punishment properties considered; second, the components of Figure 1 that are tested (Postulate I, Theorem I, or Theorem II); and, third, the kinds of comparisons undertaken. The immediate concern is the third contrast. Most early tests entailed a comparison of political units— cities, counties, provinces, states, or countries; but comparisons of the *same* political unit over time and comparisons of types of crimes in the same political unit have been all too rare. Since about 1975 comparisons of individuals have become the most common, but the following explications consider only comparisons of political units.

Objective certainty of an actual legal punishment. Suppose police statistics indicate that 120 robberies occurred in a particular city during 1983, and by the end of 1984 12 of the 120 cases had resulted in the conviction and imprisonment of a suspect. If so, the 1983 *objective* certainty of imprisonment for robbery would be 0.10, or 10%.

In deterrence research any punishment property value pertains to a particular type of crime, but there are several relevant values for each type. Thus, general deterrence research on robbery would be incomplete without measures of the objective certainty for each of the following: arrest, trial, conviction, probation, fine, and incarceration. What has been said of objective certainty applies also to all other punishment properties.

There are several problems in measuring objective certainty. Any particular time period is arbitrary; and because researchers rarely have the resources to trace all cases through the criminal justice process, they consider sentences received, not those actually served. Moreover, researchers commonly resort to an estimate. To illustrate, if 1983 police statistics indicate that 1,600 robberies took place in a particular state and prison records indicate that over 1983–1984 the average annual number of admissions to prison on robbery sentences was 160, then the estimated 1983 objective certainty of im-

Table 1

Twelve Properties of Legal Punishments and Their Definitions

Objective Properties and Definitions	Perceptual Properties and Definitions
Objective certainty of an actual legal punishment: The proportion of instances of some type of crime that resulted in the imposition of the type of legal punishment in question.	*Perceived certainty of an actual legal punishment:* Estimates by potential offenders of the probability that their commission of the type of crime in question would result in the imposition of the type of legal punishment in question.
Presumptive severity of a statutory or prescribed legal punishment: The magnitude of the statutory or prescribed legal punishment.	*Perceived severity of a statutory or prescribed legal punishment:* Estimates by potential offenders as to the amount of pain or discomfort they would experience if subjected to the statutory or prescribed legal punishment.
Presumptive severity of an actual legal punishment: The magnitude of the actual legal punishment.	*Perceived severity of an actual legal punishment:* Estimates of potential offenders as to the amount of pain or discomfort they would experience if subjected to the type of actual legal punishment in question.

prisonment for robbery would be 0.10. Such estimates are questionable because of doubts about the most appropriate time lag and because the procedure precludes taking charge reductions into account.

Whatever the method of estimation, the use of official statistics on the incidence of crime creates doubts. Figures on self-reported or victim-reported crimes suggest that objective certainty values are grossly inflated if based on official statistics. Worse, the infla-

Table 1 *continued*

Objective Properties and Definitions	Perceptual Properties and Definitions
Objective celerity of an actual legal punishment: The amount of time between a criminal offense and the imposition of the legal punishment on the alleged offender.	*Perceived celerity of an actual legal punishment:* Estimates by potential offenders as to the amount of time between a criminal offense of the type in question and the imposition of the type of legal punishment in question.
Normative scope of a statutory or prescribed legal punishment: The types of crimes to which the type of punishment in question applies by statute or some other prescription.	*Perceived normative scope of a statutory or prescribed legal punishment:* Beliefs by potential offenders as to the types of crimes to which the type of punishment in question applies by statute or some other prescription.
Actual scope of a statutory or prescribed legal punishment: The types of crimes to which the type of legal punishment in question has been imposed during some stipulated period.	*Perceived actual scope of a statutory or prescribed legal punishment:* Beliefs by potential offenders as to the types of crimes to which the type of punishment in question has actually been applied during some stipulated period.

tion does not appear even approximately constant among types of crimes or political units.

Objective certainty values for a given type of punishment should vary inversely with the crime rate among political units, and the measure of statistical association would be a test of Theorem II in Figure 1. A separate test is necessary for each type of punishment, because there is no justification for combining the objective certainty values of different punishments.

Perceived certainty of an actual legal punishment. Reconsider the illustrative value of 0.10 as representing the objective certainty of imprisonment for robbery in a particular city. Even if that value is absolutely reliable, lifelong city residents may be totally ignorant of it. Nonetheless, insofar as the certainty of punishment deters anyone, it does so only through perception.

Suppose that each city resident in a supposedly representative sample is asked this question: How many times do you think you could commit robbery in this city before being imprisoned? The reciprocal of the answer would be the respondent's perceived certainty of imprisonment for robbery.

Regardless of the punishment property, the major issue is this argument: Most citizens are law-abiding independent of fear of legal punishment; hence, to combine their perceptions with those of hard-core offenders is indefensible. Although the argument has merit, its advocates never stipulate how hard-core offenders can be identified without arbitrary criteria. Indeed, uniform criteria do not appear feasible; and there are types of crimes, such as shoplifting and traffic violations, where only age and opportunity appear relevant. Moreover, the astonishing suggestion is that researchers should ignore the possibility of absolute deterrence.

Mean or median perceived certainty values would enter into tests of Theorem I in Figure 1. Both kinds of certainty values, objective and perceived, would enter several series of tests of Postulate I, with the tests in *each series* pertaining to the same type of crime and the same political units but different types of punishment (e.g., the objective and perceived certainty of arrest in one test but imprisonment in another). If the measure of statistical association is negligible in all tests, the finding would indicate that successful efforts to increase the objective certainty of punishment are unlikely to increase perceived certainty.

Presumptive severity of a statutory or prescribed legal punishment. This property is illustrated by any statute that stipulates the magnitude of some punishment, such as the maximum fine for armed robbery. However, judicial discretion and indefinite or indeterminate sentences complicate matters, as do special penalties for recidivists. Consider these illustrative statutory phrases: a term of imprisonment not less than two nor more than five years, a fine of not more than $10,000, or both such imprisonment and such a fine. When there are multiple or alternative statutory penalties, all are relevant; but only the minimum and maximum presumptive severity of each penalty need be considered. Unfortunately, expediency is the only rationale for the exclusive consideration of statutory penalties that apply to first offenders.

The word "presumptive" suggests that researchers can justifiably compare the severity or intensity of punishments that differ only in magnitude. Moreover, there is evidence that potential offenders perceive, say, 15 years of imprisonment as less than three times as severe as, say, 5 years.

Perceived severity of statutory or prescribed legal punishments. The severity of qualitatively different punishments can be compared only by reference to the perceptions of potential offenders; and the notion of presumptive severity does not even apply to some punishments, such as arrest or execution. However, there are some horrendous difficulties in eliciting perceptions of severity.

Most individuals evidently regard even one year of incarceration as very painful; hence, when they judge the severity of diverse legal punishments by reference to a five-point interpreted scale (e.g., not painful . . . very painful) they may assign the maximum value to most punishments. An uninterpreted scale ranging from, say, 1 to 100 evidently permits sufficient discrimination; but some respondents seem to judge punishments in an absolute sense, while others tend to distribute them over the scale. Still another alternative is to direct the respondent's attention to some standard punishment, such as one year in jail, and then to pose something like this question about each of all other punishments: If 100 represents how painful you think it would be to serve one year in jail, what number would you say represents the amount of pain that (designation of other punishment) would cause? Respondents answer readily; but it is difficult to deny the possibility that the difference between 100 and, say, 500 is much greater from some individuals than others. For that matter, any choice of a standard punishment is debatable; and whatever the standard, some respondents will perceive it as more severe than other respondents do.

The only solution may be a mechanical device, such as one that registers hand strength, to establish a maximum value for each respondent and then a proportionate value to represent the respondent's judgment of the severity of each type of punishment. Granted doubts about the feasibility of mechanical devices in survey research, some work along that line is needed if only to justify a non-mechanical procedure. To be sure, the problem may be less difficult than suggested; in any case, deterrence researchers need the expertise of psychologists who work on psychophysical scaling techniques in the tradition of S. S. Stevens.

Still another measurement problem arises when combining the perceived severity values of the punishments prescribed for the type of crime in question. Suppose that a statute stipulates only two alternative penalties for burglary—prison or a fine but not both, with a maximum and a minimum for each. The perceptual questions would be such that the following four mean or median *perceived* severity values could be computed for burglary: *MaP*, that for the maximum prescribed prison term; *MiP*, that for the minimum term; *MaF*, that for the maximum prescribed fine: and *MiF*, that for the minimum fine. Given the four values, a total perceived severity value could be computed for burglary in each political unit by this formula: $(MaP + MiP + MaF + MiF)/Nv$, where Nv is the number of values in the numerator (four in the illustrative case). The formula applies regardless of the number or kinds of penalties, including possible maximum and minimum probation terms. However, if the penalties are multiples rather than alternatives, the more appropriate formula is $(MaP + MiP + MaF + MiF)/(Nv/2)$. Finally, when the penalties are of the "and/or" type, the more appropriate formula is $(MaP + MiP + MaF + MiF)/(Nv/1.5)$.

Regardless of the formula, total perceived severity values should vary inversely with crime rates among the political units, and the measures of statistical association would be a test of Theorem I in Figure 1. However, those values would enter into a test of Postulate I only if all of the punishments have additive objective magnitudes.

Presumptive severity of an actual legal punishment. Because of discretionary sentencing and parole, there is no assurance of even a substantial positive correlation between the magnitudes of statutory penalties and the magnitudes of actual punishments. The choice of values to represent the presumptive severity of actual legal punishments is difficult. Since the actual time that convicts will serve may not be known for several years, there is a rationale for considering sentences received rather than those fully imposed. However, a potential offender's beliefs about sentences may stem from experiences pertaining to individuals recently released. So the most relevant data for 1984 might be the average time served by convicts released in 1983 or 1984 rather than sentences received during 1984. What has been said of prison sentences applies also to probation and jail terms but less so for fines.

Now consider the values that would represent the presumptive severity of all actual legal punishments for some type of crime in some political unit during some stipulated period. Suppose there are three statutory penalties for burglary—imprisonment, fine, or probation. The simplest values would be the mean or median for each of the following over a particular year: (1) length of prison sentences received or length of time served on burglary sentences, (2) fines actually levied, and (3) length of probation terms imposed or completed. A more complex measure would express both magnitude and relative frequency of application. Consider prison sentences received for burglary. The formula would be: $\Sigma(APn)$, where A is the length of the prison sentence received by one or more individuals over a particular year and Pn is the proportion of all individuals punished for burglary who received that particular prison sentence. The same formula would also apply to fines or probation.

In the illustrative case, the values would represent the presumptive severity of actual punishments of burglary—one value for imprisonment, one for fines, and one for probation. Those three values could not be combined, nor would there be any presumptive severity value for actual punishments that have no magnitude, such as executions or arrests. So although simple or complex presumptive severity values of actual legal punishments could be used to test Theorem II (Figure 1), no test can be based on a composite value that represents actual punishments of more than one type.

Perceived severity of an actual punishment. The values that represent a potential offender's perception of the severity of various statutory penalties can be used to express his or her perception of actual punishments. Suppose that the maximum statutory term of imprisonment for robbery is 15 years and the minimum 5 years. Now suppose that for prison releases in 1983 the average time served for robbery was 6.5 years. Finally, suppose that a particular potential offender has judged the severity of 5 years in prison as 0.55 and serving 15 years as 0.75, with 1.0 representing maximum perceived severity. Given those values, it would not be necessary to ask the potential offender to judge the severity of actually serving 6.5 years. Approximate though it is, the *interpolated* perceived severity value would be 0.58.

Perceived severity is not limited to objective magnitudes, such as the length of incarceration or fines in dollars. One can speak of the perceived severity of any punishment; and the severity of nonquantitative punishments, such as arrest or execution, can be described only in perceptual terms.

Given a perceived severity value for each type of actual legal punishment, it is a simple matter to compute a total perceived severity value for *all* actual punishments (*TPSVA*) of the crime in question, and that composite value can be such as to express the relative frequency with which each type of punishment has been applied. The formula is $TPSVA = \Sigma(MPn)$, where M is the mean or median perceived severity value for a particular type of actual punishment and Pn is the proportion of all actual punishments of that type. The product of M and Pn is summed over all types of actual punishments, some of which may differ quantitatively and others qualitatively. In the case of procedural punishments, such as trial, the denominator in computing Pn is the number of individuals arrested for the crime in question; otherwise, it is the number convicted. In either case, the *TPSVA* values would enter into a test of Theorem I.

Objective celerity of an actual legal punishment. In research on general deterrence the objective celerity value is the reciprocal of the mean or median time for a particular type of crime and a particular type of punishment in a particular political unit over a particular period. The celerity values could be used for several tests of Theorem II, one test for each type of punishment.

Objective celerity may well be totally irrelevant in connection with general deterrence (see commentary by Bedau, 1982, p.97, on Bailey's research). That argument is best explicated when considering *perceived* celerity, but note that the argument does not deny the possibility of a close direct relation between objective celerity and objective certainty.

Perceived celerity of an actual legal punishment. Although the wording of perceptual questions would depend on the crime and the punishment, this question illustrates the form: If you were to commit burglary and be sentenced to prison, what is your guess as to the amount of time between the burglary and your incarceration? Now suppose that one potential offender answers "eight months" and another "four months." It is difficult to see how either answer could be indicative of a propensity to commit burglary. Even if perceptions of celerity reflect knowledge acquired through criminal experience, there would be no *direct* connection between perceived celerity and criminality.

Consider the matter another way. Suppose that you read of someone's receiving a one-year jail sentence for having possessed marijuana five months previously. The information about the kind of punishment might prompt you to refrain from or curtail smoking pot, but how could knowledge of the five-month delay be relevant?

Normative scope of statutory or prescribed legal punishments. This property is simply the types of punishment recognized in a criminal law code as applicable to the type of crime in question. The notion of normative scope permits recognition of punishments that cannot be described in terms of presumptive severity; but the ultimate question really pertains to perceived normative scope: To what extent do potential offenders know which types of punishments are prescribed for which types of crimes?

Normative scope enters into tests of Theorem II (Figure 1) when investigators use numbers nominally to describe statutory penalties for the type of crime in question. Thus, the number 1 might signify that a prison sentence is mandatory, 2 that imprisonment is one of multiple punishments along with a fine, 3 that imprisonment is one alternative punishment and a fine another alternative, and so forth. The numbers could be dummy variables in an equation where the crime rate is the dependent variable; but the research could be simpler, as when comparing the homicide rates of political units where murder is a capital crime in some units but not in others. Whatever the comparison, the direction and magnitude of the association between a particular statutory penalty and the crime rate is contingent on all other properties of that penalty, in particular its certainty and severity.

Perceived normative scope. The amount of deterrence may well depend largely on what potential offenders believe the punishment for a crime *could be*. Such beliefs are expressed in answers to perceptual questions about normative scope, such as: Can you be fined for burglary? If so, what is the maximum fine? If so, what is the minimum fine?

Deterrence does not require accurate beliefs by potential offenders about the normative scope of statutory penalties. Moreover, beliefs about kinds of punishment could be highly accurate but beliefs as to the magnitude or presumptive severity of each kind of punishment highly inaccurate. As far as magnitudes are concerned, only proportionate accuracy is necessary to sustain Postulate I in Figure 1. Beliefs are proportionately accurate to the extent there is a positive *correlation* between statutory magnitudes and the mean or median perceived statutory maximum or minimum. If the beliefs are totally inaccurate in every sense, then Postulate I in Figure 1 is invalid; and there is no way that statutory penalties alone could deter. Yet Postulate II, Postulate III, and Theorem I could be valid even if Postulate I and Theroem II are invalid.

As to the importance of perceived normative scope, all previous perceptual properties are relevant only if potential offenders know the scope of the punishment in question. Thus, when potential offenders are asked about the certainty, severity, or celerity of a prison sentence for robbery, the assumption is that they believed, before the questions were posed, that a prison sentence for robbery is possible, meaning statutory or prescribed.

Given the proportion of potential offenders in each political unit who ostensibly believe that a particular punishment is prescribed for the type of crime in question, those proportions are possible correlates of the crime rate; and the correlation coefficient would be a test of Theorem I (Figure 1). However, both the sign and the magnitude of the coefficient are contingent on other properties of that punishment.

Actual scope of statutory or prescribed legal punishments. This property pertains to the relative frequency with which the type of punishment in question has actually been applied to instances of the type of crime in question. One formula for expressing actual scope is $AS = (Nx/N)$, where Nx is the total number of times the type of punishment has been applied to instances of the type of crime over some period and N is the total number of actual punishments during the period regardless of the type of punishment or the type of crime.

The property's importance is that actual punishments may largely determine a potential offender's belief as to *possible* legal punishments. Research undertaken to assess that relation would not entail comparisons of crime rates. Suppose that potential offenders have been asked this perceptual question about a particular type of punishment and a particular type of crime: If you were convicted of that crime, could you receive that punishment? Given the proportion of affirmative answers in each political unit, researchers can compute the correlation among those units between the proportions and the actual scope (AS) values. The correlation would bear on Postulate I in Figure 1; and if all such correlations are negligible, it would be difficult to argue that actual punishments even partially determine perceptions of possible punishments for the type of crime in question.

Given an AS value for a particular type of punishment and a particular type of crime in each of several political units, the question would become: What is the correlation between those values and crime rates? Each correlation would bear on Theorem II (Figure 1), but the coefficient's sign and magnitude would be contingent on other properties of that punishment.

Perceived actual scope. Suppose that potential offenders are asked a question something like this about each type of punishment that has been actually applied at least once to an instance of the type of crime under consideration: Of the last 100 cases of this crime, what is your guess as to the number that resulted in this punishment? The average of the responses would represent the perceived *actual* scope of the type of punishment for the type of crime. The perceptual question differs from that pertaining to perceived certainty in that it elicits an implied estimate of *general* risk rather than *personal* risk. Conventional arguments and practices notwithstanding, deterrence theory and research should encompass both conceptions of punishment risk.

Perceived actual scope values should vary directly among political units with actual scope values, and the correlation coefficients would be a test of Postulate I. There would be a series of tests for each type of crime, with a separate test for each type of punishment. Finally, the correlation between perceived actual scope values and crime rates would bear on Theorem I (Figure 1), but the coefficient's sign and magnitude would be contingent on other properties of the type of punishment in question.

Crime Rates in General Deterrence Research

Although a general deterrence theory could be tested by comparing individuals, the crime rate is the dependent variable in Figure 1. The rates in deterrence research are commonly based on police reports, and doubts about their reliability are perennial. However, even if absolutely reliable, official crime rates are ill suited for deterrence research.

THE UNINFORMATIVE NATURE OF OFFICIAL CRIME RATES

Suppose that the 1983 official robbery rate for a city of 25,000 residents is 20 per 100,000 population. Even if absolutely reliable, the rate means nothing more than this: five robberies took place in the city during 1983. As such, the rate would not answer three questions. First, were the perpetrators and victims city residents? Second, of all individuals who committed at least one robbery in the city during 1983, what was the average number of robberies? And, third, how many of the perpetrators had been legally punished before their first 1983 robbery?

Without an answer to the third question there is no basis for conjectures pertaining to the distinction between general deterrence and specific deterrence. So assume that no offender ever had been arrested before a 1983 robbery; and then assume this answer to the second question: The average number was five, meaning that one individual or group committed all five robberies. The answer suggests that with regard to robbery in that city there was more absolute general deterrence than restrictive general deterrence.

SPECIAL CRIME RATES

Ideally, in computing rates for general deterrence research, the first step would be to exclude all offenders who had an arrest history before the offense in question. As such, no rate would reflect specific deterrence. However, an argument could be made for excluding *only* those offenders who have been punished for the type of crime in question. Another argument is that the criterion for exclusion should be some particular type of substantive punishment, such as imprisonment, and not merely an arrest. Since there has been no research on either argument, reference is made henceforth only to "unpunished" individuals.

The categorical impunitive rate (CIR). The formula for this special crime rate is $CIR = Uc/Tu$, where Tu is the estimated average daily number of *unpunished* individuals who were members of some stipulated population over some period (e.g., 1983–1984) and Uc is the number of such individuals who committed the type of crime in question at least once during the period. Unlike a conventional rate, CIR pertains to the relative number of criminals rather than crimes; as such, it is more nearly a measure or prevalance than of incidence.

Regardless of the correlation between punishment properties and the conventional crime rate, no conclusion is warranted about the relative importance of particular types of deterrence. By contrast, the correlation between punishment properties and the categorical impunitive crime rate provides a basis for inferences about absolute general deterrence.

The repetitive impunitive rate (RIR). The formula is $RIR = Nc/Uc$, where Uc is again the estimated average daily number of *unpunished* individuals who were members of some stipulated population over some stipulated period and who committed the type of crime in question at least once during the period and Nc is the total crimes of that type committed by such individuals during the period. Since individuals who did not commit the crime even once are excluded, the rate expresses the average frequency with which perpetrators committed the crime. Hence, RIR is more nearly a measure of incidence than of prevalence.

Just as there is a logical connection between CIR and absolute general deterrence, so is there between RIR and restrictive general deterrence. Specifically, knowledge of the correlation between punishment properties and RIR furthers inferences about restrictive general deterrence.

The data problem. Given the glaring defects of official crime rates, criminologists evidently use them only because they are readily available. In any case, official data cannot be used to compute the special crime rates just described.

Of the major kinds of unofficial data, only self-reported crimes can be used to compute special rates. However, traditional research must be expanded to include reports of being subjected to legal punishments.

Evidential Problems in General Deterrence Research

The great illusion in the debate over deterrence is that arguments about rationality or free will can be substituted for research findings. Those findings are inconclusive not because of insufficient research but because of evidential problems. The two major problems cannot be solved by considering more punishment properties in research or by using special crime rates.

NONDETERRENT PREVENTIVE MECHANISMS

Since legal punishments may prevent crimes several ways other than through deterrence (Gibbs, 1975, p. 57), a negative correlation between a punishment property and crime rates is not evidence of deterrence. Space limitations permit an examination of only one nondeterrent preventative mechanism—incapacitation. Defined explicitly, a punishment incapacitates to the extent that its imposition makes it difficult for the offender to commit another crime. Thus, car thieves cannot readily practice their craft while incarcerated.

Incapacitation poses a glaring evidential problem when we contemplate a substantial negative correlation between the objective certainty or presumptive severity of imprisonment and the crime rate, but to date attempts to estimate the incapacitation effects of imprisonment have not been convincing. The failure is hardly surprising, because the foremost question cannot be answered without conjecture: How many crimes would convicts have committed had they not been incarcerated?

Estimates of the incapacitation effect should be continued if only because of two policy implications. First, incapacitation is a questionable rationale for capital punishment without a defensible estimate of the homicides prevented by executions. Second, because only actual punishments incapacitate and long prison sentences are very costly, general deterrence may cost far less than incapacitation.

EXTRALEGAL CONDITIONS

No deterrence advocate claims that legal punishments alone determine the crime rate, and there is every reason to assume that extralegal conditions play a major role in criminal etiology. That is the case even if it is understood that perceptual properties of legal punishments are not construed as extralegal conditions.

Only possible illustrations of two relevant classes of extralegal conditions can be given. One class can be designated "extralegal generative," and one possible illustration is unemployment. Accordingly, if variation in unemployment is a major cause of variation in the crime rates under consideration, then unemployment rates should be controlled in tests of Theorems I and II in Figure 1.

The other class of conditions is best designated "extralegal inhibitory," and one possible illustration is suggested by Sutherland's notion of definitions unfavorable to crime (Sutherland Cressey, 1974). Sutherland was vague about the notion's meaning and about the sources of such definitions. One plausible argument is that unfavorable definitions prevail where crime is widely and intensely condemned. If that argument is accepted, social condemnation of crime should be controlled in tests of Theorems I and II, and those controls should extend to extralegal punitive reactions to crimes and fear of such reactions (see, e.g., Tittle, 1980).

An extralegal condition should be controlled only if it is assumed that it is a major cause of variation in the crime rate. The best defense of that assumption is a widely accepted etiological theory, but there are no such theories in criminology. Indeed, claims by researchers notwithstanding, the well-known theories, such as Sutherland's, are not subject to *systematic* tests. Hence, without an innovation akin to randomization in experimental methodology, conclusive findings on general deterrence must await testable and defensible etiological theories on crime. Several distinct theories may be needed. Consider incentives (including opportunities) and expected gains from crime, two etiological considerations emphasized by economists and social psychologists (see Carroll, 1978, Cook, 1980). Those considerations may be far less relevant in comparing the crime rates of political units than in comparing types of crimes or individuals.

A Brief Survey of Research on General Deterrence

Extensive research commenced some forty years ago, with the first stage ending in the 1950s. Research was renewed in the late 1960s, and that second stage is "recent" in that it continues today.

EARLY RESEARCH

Most early research pertained to the death penalty. Because the methodology and findings were remarkably uniform, the research can be described briefly.

Comparisons of states. The death penalty was abolished more than a century ago in some of the United States, and in making interstate comparisons early deterrence investigators evidently *assumed* that the legal punishment for murder becomes less severe with abolition. Hence, they argued that the deterrence doctrine implies a higher homicide rate for abolitionist states.

No one is likely to dispute this summary of the early findings: If there was any significant difference in the homicide rates, abolitionist states had lower rates. Note that the summary extends to comparisons extending over several decades up to the 1950s (for references, see Archer, Gartner, & Beittel, 1983; Bedau, 1982).

Longitudinal comparisons. Some American states have never abolished the death penalty, a few have abolished and never reinstated it, others have abolished it only to reinstate it, and still others have abolished it at least twice (Bedau, 1982, p. 23). Early investigators treated these changes as bearing on the deterrence doctrine.

Again, the findings can be summarized briefly and indisputably. There was nothing like a consistent increase in the homicide rate after abolition of the death penalty or a consistent decrease after the penalty's reinstatement. Rather, changes in the homicide rate were negligible and seemingly random.

Major defects. Had it been found that the homicide rate is significantly lower where and when execution is the statutory penalty for murder, the association might reflect incapacitation. The incapacitating effect of execution appears indisputable, but the volume of crimes prevented is unknown. The early death penalty studies indicate that the prevention is negligible, and the findings are consistent with evidence of a very low repetitive homicide rate. Incapacitation has an appreciable effect on the conventional rate for some type of crime only if the ratio of the repetitive rate to the categorical rate is high. However, repetitive rates for murder and not rates for criminal homicide in general are needed to assess the incapacitating effects of executions, and even one recidival murder fuels demands for the death penalty.

Nondeterrent preventive effects pose no problem when tests of a deterrence proposition are negative, but a failure to control relevant extralegal conditions is a problem regardless of test outcomes. Extralegal causes of murder were not controlled satisfactorily in the death penalty studies; perhaps this is an inevitable defeat in the absence of a defensible etiological theory.

The early death penalty studies entailed an unstated assumption—that execution is more severe than life imprisonment. Some recent but very limited research (see Bedau, 1982, p. 110) indicates that people perceive execution as more severe; but the difference is not great, which is all the more important because early investigators ignored the objective and perceived certainty of execution and imprisonment. Although estimates of the certainty of execution for first-degree murder before 1960 are little more than informed guesses, none is greater than 5%. By contrast, the estimated objective certainty of imprisonment for criminal homicide in South Carolina as of 1960 was 22%, and the corresponding figure for Utah was 87% (Gibbs, 1975, p. 243). So before 1960 the objective certainty of imprisonment for murder in abolitionist states could have been between 4 and 18 times that of execution in retentionist states; and that vast difference is one reason some informed advocates of deterrence, including Jeremy Bentham, have opposed capital punishment.

A special defect and a policy consideration. The use of criminal homicide rates in the early death penalty studies was unfortunate but understandable, because it is difficult to compute the "capital" murder rate. The practice is to assume that the two rates are highly correlated, and that practice remains debatable.

Despite their defects, the early death penalty studies are relevant in debating capital punishment. In reinstating the death penalty, legislators have changed nothing more than a statutory penalty. Hence, the early studies are relevant in contemplating this question: What will happen to homicide rates in states where the death penalty has been reinstated? The early studies clearly suggest this answer: Nothing will happen. However, the findings of the early death penalty studies prompted many social and behavioral scientists to reach this conclusion: If executions do not deter, surely lesser penalties cannot. The conclusion is dubious because it equates murder with other crimes and ignores the defects of the early death penalty studies. Although more recent findings (see, e.g., Archer, Gartner, & Beittel, 1983; and references in commentary by Bedau, 1982, p. 97, on Bailey's research) also question the deterrent efficacy of capital punishment, the early studies terminated research prematurely.

RECENT RESEARCH ON GENERAL DETERRENCE

After a hiatus of some fifteen years, deterrence research was revived, with an emphasis on the certainty and severity of *actual* legal punishments, imprisonment in particular. Initially, however, researchers continued to compare the crime rates of political units.

The length of the prison terms. Since 1967 several researchers have reported a negligible correlation among states between crime rates and length of prison sentences served (for references, see Blumstein et al., 1978; Cook, 1980; Gibbs, 1975, p. 147; Tittle, 1980, p. 9). It is not a matter of substantial correlations in some studies but negligible ones in others; rather, the vast majority of correlations are negligible for numerous types of crimes and time points. So at least one version of Theorem II in Figure 1 appears false (see, however, Tittle, 1980, p. 9).

It would be difficult to exaggerate the policy implications. More than 10 years ago the rehabilitation ideal began giving way to long and mandatory prison sentences. Far from justifying that policy change, deterrence research suggests that American legislators suffer from a monumental illusion in their belief that long prison sentences will reduce the crime rate.

The objective certainty of legal punishment. The second major finding is a substantial correlation among states between the objective certainty of imprisonment and the crime rate. That correlation holds for various types of crime over several time points (for surveys, see Blumstein et al., 1978; Cook, 1980; Gibbs, 1975, p. 147; and Tittle, 1980, p. 8). While the finding has sustained deterrence research, there is a thicket of evidential problems. Since the number of crimes is the denominator of the certainty measure but the numerator of the crime rate, the negative correlation between those two ratios is allegedly a statistical artifact (Logan, 1982); but no one has devised a methodology to resolve the debate. Even if the correlations are not artifacts, a great increase of crimes could overload the criminal justice system and decrease the objective certainty of punishment. Hence, so the argument goes, high crime rates tend to produce low objective certainty (e.g., Greenberg & Kessler, 1982).

A solution of the evidential problems will require shifting research from synchronic or cross-sectional comparisons to longitudinal or diachronic comparisons. Advocates of causal modeling or path analysis to the contrary, causal assertions cannot be tested through synchronic comparison; rather, it must be shown that the correlation is much greater when the crime rate is lagged than when objective certainty is lagged. The all-too-few studies along that line do not support the deterrence doctrine (e. g., Greenberg & Kessler, 1982), and the only mitigating qualification has to do with data (but see Gibbs, 1975, p. 172). The reliability of objective certainty measures and crime rates becomes even more of a problem in longitudinal research, because short-run changes are negligible in comparison with synchronic contrasts among political units. Moreover, the most appropriate time lag can be estimated only by crude induction, and official data are not suited for exploratory research along that line.

Perceptual properties of legal punishment. Perceived certainty has received extensive attention, but its relation to crime rates has been examined in only one major line of research (Erickson & Gibbs, 1977). Consistent with Postulate I in Figure 1, the researchers reported a significant positive correlation *among types of crimes* in the same metropolitan area between the *objective* certainty of arrest and the *perceived* certainty of arrest; and, consistent with Theorems I and II, they also reported a significant negative correlation between both certainty variables and the official crime rate. However, contrary to a prediction suggested by Figure 1, the perceived certainty correlation was not greater than the objective certainty correlation. More important, when a measure of the social disapproval of each type of crime was introduced through partial correlation, Postulate I, Theorem I, and Theorem II were not corroborated. The findings indicate that variation in the rate *among types of crimes* is largely a function of variation in social disapproval of crime. Moreover, most people may perceive punishment certainty largely in terms of what they think it should be, meaning greatest for the types of crime they most disapprove; and objective certainty could be correlated with perceived certainty because the police invest more resources to investigate those crimes that the public disapproves of the most. Of course, law-abiding citizens and hard-core offenders probably differ considerably as to perceptual determinants. Yet little is known about the contrast, and a recent report that the perceptions of experienced drug dealers are shaped largely through their interaction with each other (Ekland-Olson, Lieb, Zurcher, 1984) illustrates a truly neglected kind of deterrence research.

Because enormous resources are needed to examine the association between perceptual properties and crime rates, in recent years general deterrence research has shifted from comparisons of political units or types of crimes to comparisons of individuals. Virtually all findings indicate an inverse relation *among individuals* between the perceived certainty of punishment and the frequency of self-reported offenses, whether crimes or delinquencies; but the relation never has been truly substantial despite statistical controls for extralegal conditions (see references in Paternoster, Saltzman, Chiricos, & Waldo, 1982). Indeed, some findings raise doubts about the significance of the relation once extralegal conditions are controlled (e.g., Paternoster, Saltzman, Waldo, & Chiricos, 1983, p. 474; Tittle, 1980). Comparisons of individuals make it more feasible to consider extralegal conditions, such as the frequency of association with offenders and personal disapproval of particular types of offenses. However, only a few conditions have been considered, and in the absence of a defensible etiological theory all are questionable. Moreover, granted that self-reports of offenses are preferable to arrest records, the reliability of self-reports remains debatable; and few self-reports have pertained to felonies. Virtually all of the research has been limited to juveniles or college students, and one of the few studies of adults (Tittle, 1980) is largely an exception to the previous summary of findings.

No study has thrown much light on these questions: How do potential offenders come to perceive properties of legal punishment, and how are those perceptions altered? Indeed, the questions bear on a major defect in the several studies where researchers have reported a relation among individuals between perceptions of punishment and the self-reported frequency of *previous* offenses. There is now evidence (e.g., Paternoster et al., 1983) that the relation is substantially affected by the influence of previous experience on present perceptions; hence, future research must consider the relation between perception of punishment and *subsequent* offenses. Tittle's use (1980) of a measure of "anticipated offenses" is not likely to become an accepted alternative (see Hagan, 1982, pp. 34–35).

Just as deterrence research has shifted from objective certainty to perceived certainty, so it has moved from presumptive severity to perceived severity. There are now a few reports of an inverse relation among individuals between perceived severity and self-reported offenses; but the relation is less substantial and more inconsistent than for perceived certainty, and reports of no significant relation are common when comparisons are not restricted to individuals who perceive a high probability of punishment. Because of inconsistent findings (e.g., Grasmick & Bryjack, 1980; Tittle, 1980), brief summary statements are debatable. The inconsistencies may be due in large part to divergent ways of eliciting perceptions of severity, many of which confound perceived severity and perceived certainty.

Before-and-after research. The most careful before-and-after study was conducted by H. L. Ross (1984) on the British adoption of a device to measure intoxication and other measures to make the legal punishment of drunken driving more certain. Comparisons of various kinds of rates before and after those enforcement changes led Ross to conclude that drunken driving did decline as a consequence.

Like all similar studies, Ross's research would have yielded even more compelling evidence had it encompassed extensive surveys to detect changes in perceived severity and certainty. Nonetheless, Ross deserves praise for dealing with several difficult problems, and his experience equipped him well for a subsequent assessment of recent widespread attempts to reduce drunken driving. Stating his conclusion (1984) briefly: Many attempts have been successful, but only in the short run because of the failure to maintain the initial intensity of enforcement.

One long line of before-and-after research may have come to an end with McFarland's recent study (1983). All research in that line has focused on daily or weekly homicide trends before and after executions, and in citing previous studies McFarland rightly emphasized the inconsistent findings. Whereas some researchers have reported a decrease in homicides (absolute or relative to other periods) just before an execution and an increase after, others have reported the opposite pattern; and still others have reported only a decline in homicides after an execution. Then there have been reports of no significant change before or after executions, with McFarland's report being the most recent. He examined weekly trends in homicides in the United States in connection with four executions, commencing with that of Gary Gilmore in 1977. Only in the case of Gilmore was there a significant dip in the weekly number of homicides, and McFarland deserves great credit for presenting evidence that the dip was due to a blizzard in many eastern states at the time of the execution. So this conclusion appears warranted: If executions have any short-run effect on homicide trends, it is contingent on unidentified conditions.

Experimental research. No research on general deterrence is truly experimental unless some property of punishment is varied *random-*

ly among individuals, populations, or situations. Since such research has been extremely rare, there is scarcely any preponderant
finding (writers such as Moffitt, 1983, often fail to recognize that
most experimental research bears on specific deterrence, not general deterrence). Hence, the present commentary is limited to a few
brief observations on two illustrative experiments.

Although any change in criminal laws or their enforcement can be
thought of as a policy experiment, few such changes have been
guided by even an approximation of a genuine experimental design.
The best known is the Kansas City experiment over 1972–1973 (see
references in Zimring, 1978, pp. 142–144). Briefly, two *experimental
situations* were created: discontinuance of routine patrols in some
police beats, the reactive beats; and as much as a tripling of routine
patrols in some beats, the proactive beats. Those beats identified for
special study but without any change in routine patrols can be
thought of as *control* beats.

During the ensuing year the incidence of either victim-reported or
police-reported crimes did not change significantly more in the two
experimental situations. The research design, the small number of
cases, and the manner of reporting the findings preclude defensible
observations of change in the objective or perceived certainty of legal punishment in the two experimental situations. Although it has
been argued that discontinuation of routine patrols did not prevent
frequent responses of police cars to calls within the reactive beats or
visible patrols in adjacent beats, that argument does not explain the
relatively stable crime rate in the proactive beats (intensified patrols). However, although the findings cannot be dismissed by
appealing to design flaws or the small case numbers, an informative
and incontrovertible interpretation of the Kansas City experiment is
simply not possible, especially in the absence of extensive replica-
tions. The same can be said, unfortunately, of all "policy experiments" on general deterrence over 1970–1975 (see Zimring, 1978).

Schwartz and Orleans (1967) randomly assigned individuals who
had filed 1961 federal income tax returns to one of four groups. An
attempt was made to interview everyone in the "sanction threat"
group so as to communicate the legal penalties for false tax reports.
Interview questions for the "conscience appeal" groups were designed to accentuate moral reasons for compliance with tax laws.
The interview questions for the "placebo group" did not touch on
the threat of sanctions or appeal to conscience, and members of the
untreated control group were not interviewed.

Three dependent variables were considered, each pertaining to

1962 dollars minus 1961 dollars on 1962 tax reports of adjusted gross income, total deductions, or income tax after credits. The average 1961–1962 increase in reported adjusted gross income was much greater for the sanction threat group and the conscience appeal group than for either the placebo or the untreated control group, with the increase far greater for the conscience appeal group. Those differences also held for income tax after credits, but there were no consistent group differences in total deductions.

Despite the randomization, it appears that about 25% of the placebo and experimental subjects were not interviewed. Perhaps more serious, it is not clear exactly what properties of punishment were manipulated, which is a major defect even if the experiment is construed as yielding evidence of deterrence that cannot be attributed to extralegal conditions or nondeterrent mechanisms.

MAJOR DEFECTS IN RECENT GENERAL DETERRENCE RESEARCH

Some 15 years since the revival of deterrence research, no study has considered more than 2 of the 12 possibly relevant punishment properties. Concern in the early death penalty studies with statutory penalties has not been perpetuated; and though the shift to comparisons of individuals rather than political units has facilitated research on perceptual properties, the shift made objective penalties irrelevant. Most serious of all, methodological innovations in deterrence research (see, e.g., Hagan, 1982) have scarcely lessened the evidential problems.

Extralegal variables. Little progress has been made toward identifying and controlling relevant extralegal variables. The problem is illustrated by Ehrlich's widely publicized research on capital punishment and critical reactions (for key references see Forst, 1983). Ehrlich's research improved on the early studies in that it included estimates of the objective certainty of execution as a possible correlate of the annual trend in the criminal homicide rate in the United States from 1933 to 1969. However, his conclusion that on the average each execution prevented some eight homicides was greeted with astonishment in several quarters, and numerous critics promptly offered contrary evidence. The reaction was hardly surprising, if only because plotting annual trends in the estimated certainty of executions and the criminal homicide rate from 1933 to 1969 reveals a clear inverse relation only in the 1960s. However, the critics advanced much more complicated findings to refute Ehrlich. Those findings stemmed from a reanalysis of Ehrlich's data, including diverse control variables (e.g., labor force participation rate, per capita income). There is no defensible etiological theory of homicide that justifies those control variables. However, since critics of Ehrlich considered essentially the same variables and units of comparison, the incompatible conclusions reflect divergent choices in the use of econometric techniques (see commentary by Forst, 1983). Any technique that permits such divergent choices is a dubious contribution to deterrence research, especially when applied to indefensible control variables.

Short of genuine experimental work, before-and-after research offers the greatest prospects for controlling extralegal conditions. Such research offers something better than *statistical* controls of particular variables, which at best are likely to be incomplete. The association between daily or weekly crime incidence and actual punishments is not likely to be influenced appreciably by any well-known possible extralegal determinant of crime, such as unemployment, differential association, or anomie. Those variables apparently change slowly, but McFarland's study (1983) points to the possible relevance of short-run weather changes.

Nondeterrent preventive mechanisms. Of several possible nondeterrent preventive effects of legal punishments, only incapacitation has received extensive attention (see Cohen, 1983). As long as conventional crime rates are used in deterrence research, incapacitation can be directly taken into account only by estimating the offenses that offenders would have committed had they not been punished. The estimates have been riddled with debatable assumptions, which is not surprising because the estimates are really answers to counterfactual questions.

The evidential problem created by incapacitation makes before-and-after research all the more strategic. Not even an execution incapacitates more than one potential offender. Hence, if the daily number of offenses declines markedly at the state or national level after a widely publicized actual punishment, the decline could not readily be attributed to incapacitation.

Reliance on conventional crime rates. The distinction between absolute and restrictive general deterrence will remain theoretical until researchers begin using two special crime rates, the categorical impunitive and the repetitive impunitive. Moreover, impunitive rates are necessary for defensible conclusions about the relative importance of general and specific deterrence, and those rates would make it feasible to ignore incapacitation.

The failure of researchers to use special crime rates is puzzling, especially given the shift to self-reported offenses. Before that shift, the reliance on police reports of crimes precluded special rates. Now, however, special rates can be computed if researchers include in survey schedules or questionnaires questions that elicit self-reports of legal punishment as well as self-reports of offenses.

Toward a Theory of Specific Deterrence

In reporting research on specific deterrence, authors write as though no theory was needed to guide the research. They are typically content to report the recidivism rates of two sets of offenders, one of which has been subjected to a more severe punishment than the other; and they interpret the contrast this way: If those offenders who have been punished the most severely have a significantly lower recidivism rate, the contrast reflects specific deterrence.

Although the interpretation is partially correct, all such research is grossly defective. When two punishments differ qualitatively, judgments of differential severity are questionable. Even ignoring that problem, the research has been limited to the presumptive severity of punishment. Most important, researchers never pose this question: Why would punishing an offender prevent his or her repetition of the offense? The deterrence doctrine must be construed as implying this answer: The punishment increases the offender's *perception* of punishment severity and/or punishment certainty. Even so, the answer is not a theory; and Figure 2 is a step in that direction.

POSTULATES AND THEOREMS PERTAINING TO SEVERITY

Most tests of Theorem 1 in Figure 2 have been questionable if only because of researchers' debatable judgments of the severity of punishments. Moreover, assume a positive test of Theorem 1, meaning an inverse relation among individuals between the presumptive severity of punishment and subsequent recidivism. Now assume that the recidivism data are absolutely reliable. Even so, without evidence corroborating Postulate 1 there is no basis to argue that posi-

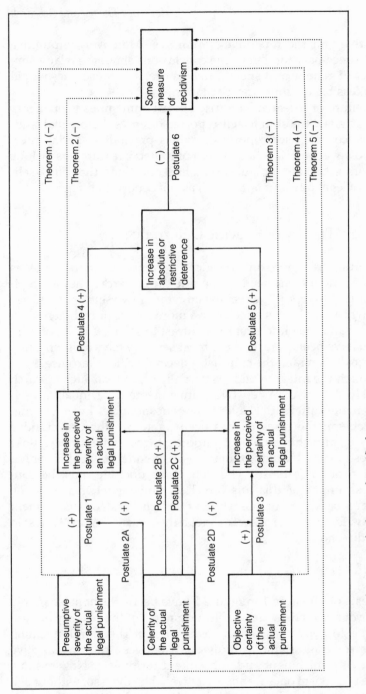

FIGURE 2. Suggested structure of a theory of specific deterrence

Note: See Figure 1 for explication of ⟶, (+), and (−).

tive tests of Theorem 1 reflect an increase in the perceived severity of punishment; but Postulate 1 has never been tested.

Now assume negative tests of Theorem 1 but positive tests of Postulate 1. Theorem 2 should be false, and its test would be evidence for inferences about Postulate 4. That postulate, along with Postulates 5 and 6, cannot be tested directly. However, even though Postulate 1, Theorem 1, and Theorem 2 are directly testable, the tests should entail controls for objective celerity, objective certainty, and increases in perceived certainty.

The requisite research. To repeat, only Theorem 1 in Figure 2 has been tested (see, however, Moffitt, 1983, pp. 139, 147, 148), and gathering data for other tests will require considerable resources. The research could take the form of a panel study of numerous juveniles, in which data are gathered at no less than two time points on self-reported offenses, self-reported legal punishments, and perceptions of the severity of various types of legal punishments. The data on self-reported offenses and self-reported punishments could be used to test Theorem 1, but tests of Postulate 1 would be more strategic. Those tests would require three values for each of several individuals. One value, PS_1, would represent the individual's perception of the severity of a particular type of punishment, one with an objective magnitude, before experiencing it. The second value, M, would represent the presumptive severity (objective magnitude) of some type of punishment, one actually imposed on the individual at some point during the panel study. The third value, PS_2, would be the individual's perception of the punishment's severity *after* having experienced it. The change in perceived severity would be expressed either as the ratio of PS_2 to PS_1 or as PS_2 minus PS_1. In either case, the hypothesis derived from Postulate 1 would be: Among individuals, the greater the value of M, the greater the increase in PS.

The comparison just described would require hundreds of research subjects to assure that several are punished during the panel study and also to assure great variation in presumptive severity. The initial interview would elicit each individual's perceptions of the severity of several types of punishments, so that, regardless of the actual punishment subsequently imposed, the individual's perception of severity *before* the punishment's imposition would be known.

Two tests should be conducted of each theorem in Figure 2. In one test the dependent variable would be the *individual* version of the repetitive recidival rate—the number of self-reported offenses per unit of time after the punishment. In the other test the dependent variable would be binary—whether or not the individual reported committing the offense at least once after punishment, with statistical control of time since punishment. The individual categorical recidival rate would correspond to the notion of absolute specific deterrence, and the individual repetitive recidival rate would correspond to the notion of restrictive specific deterrence. Finally, tests pertaining to Figure 2 may or may not include individuals who report commission of the offense in question but no legal punishment. If they are included, their presumptive severity values, objective celerity values, and objective certainty values would have to be zero.

POSTULATE 2 AND THEOREM 5

Figure 2 is less than a theory, if only because of doubt about the relevance of objective celerity. Some doubts stem from experimental findings in punishment research conducted by psychologists. Those findings indicate that certain behaviors cannot be suppressed unless punished fairly quickly (see van Houten, 1983, p. 22; Moffitt, 1983, p. 140). Since the celerity of legal punishment can be years rather than seconds, celerity may be irrelevant when stating a theory of specific deterrence.

Even if relevant, celerity's role in specific deterrence is debatable. Figure 2 suggests several possibilities, one being that celerity increases perceived severity or perceived certainty but not necessarily both. Similarly, celerity could influence the association between one or both perceptual properties and the corresponding objective properties. So there are 16 possibilities, including no celerity postulate at all. If all versions of Postulate 2 are eliminated, so is Theorem 5.

POSTULATES AND THEOREMS PERTAINING TO CERTAINTY

What has been said of severity also applies to certainty. However, none of the postulates or theorems pertaining to certainty have been tested; and because an individual either has or has not been punished, it may appear that objective certainty cannot be measured. But consider the cluck who is arrested after his or her 1st robbery and someone else arrested only after his or her 20th robbery. The contrast surely suggests that objective certainty was much greater for the cluck.

One formula for measuring individual objective certainty (*IOC*) is $IOC = Np/Nc$, where *NP* is the number of times the punishment in question has been imposed on an offender for the type of crime in question and *Nc* is the number of times the offender has committed the crime. So the objective certainty of arrest was 1 for the cluck but only 0.05 for the offender arrested after his or her 20th robbery.

Requisite data. Data for tests of Postulate 3, Theorem 3, and Theorem 4 could be gathered only in the panel study previously described. Each individual would be asked two questions about each combination of various punishments and various offenses. Both questions would elicit an estimate of the probability of suffering the designated type of punishment should he or she commit the designated type of offense. The two questions would be identical, but one would be asked at the beginning of the panel study and the other at the end.

Whereas severity questions would be asked only about punishments, there would be a *certainty* question for each combination of various offenses and various punishments. Indeed, at the beginning of the panel study the questions should extend to a subject not recognized in Figure 2—potential offenders' beliefs about the scope of statutory penalties, meaning what the legal punishment for an offense *could be*. Deterrence should increase when the offender perceives a type of punishment as very severe but not applicable to the type of offense, then suffers that punishment for the offense. By contrast, deterrence should decrease when an offender perceives a type of punishment as severe and applicable to some offense but does not suffer that punishment for the offense because it is actually not applicable (for observations on relevant research findings see Moffitt, 1983, p. 147). Both possibilities can be described in terms of changes in perceived certainty or perceived severity; but the changes stem from alterations in the beliefs about the scope of penalties, something not suggested by Figure 2.

Principal Findings of Specific Deterrence Research

There are literally thousands of research reports on offenders' responses to legal reactions, and in many instances the researchers compared recidivism rates (see Lipton, Martinson, & Wilks, 1976). So it may appear that there is vast research literature on specific deterrence, but most of those studies were concerned with "treatment procedures" that supposedly rehabilitate and thereby reduce recidivism. Because such research is not concerned with the effect of *punishment* on recidivism, it does not bear on specific deterrence.

OBJECTIONABLE RESEARCH ON SPECIFIC DETERRENCE

The bulk of findings indicate that offenders are not deterred when punished. More precisely, numerous researchers have reported either that recidivism is greater for offenders who have been punished the most severely or that there is no significant relation between punishment severity and recidivism. Note, however, that the findings appear less uniform and more contradictory in the case of juvenile offenders (see partial survey by Moffitt, 1983).

A dramatic illustration of negative evidence. One early study yielded findings that appear exactly opposite what the specific deterrence argument anticipates. Caldwell (1944) reported a 57% official recidival rate for individuals who were imprisoned and whipped at least twice in New Castle County, Delaware, during 1920–1939, but a rate of only 31% for individuals who were placed on probation in 1928. So the findings appear to support the theory of secondary deviance, which is commonly described as being the exact opposite of the specific deterrence argument (see Gibbs, 1975, p. 10). However, most findings on specific deterrence indicate no significant difference in recidivism rates despite contrasts in the severity of punishment.

Caldwell's study is typical in that he gathered no data on the perceived severity, and there are serious doubts about his recidivism data. Yet there is a greater flaw, one that is a major defect of virtually all specific deterrence studies.

The major defect. Numerous findings suggest a fairly substantial positive association among offenders between number of previous arrests or convictions and the severity of the sentence on last conviction. Accordingly, sentencing tends to produce an association that contradicts the specific deterrence argument. With or without punishment, offenders having the longest criminal records are the most likely to repeat an offense, and they are the most likely to be punished severely if convicted.

To understand the problem better, suppose that a judge can impose only one of four sentences for burglary: a suspended sentence without probation, 5 years of probation, 5 years of imprisonment, or 10 years of imprisonment. Now suppose that the judge agrees to impose each of those four sentences randomly on 25% of all convicted burglars. If so, any significant association between sentence severity and previous criminal record would be improbable. However, any such randomization would reek of injustice; and no judge is likely to randomize sentences that differ appreciably in severity, the very thing that is needed in specific deterrence research. Moreover, statistical control of previous criminal record is not a satisfactory substitute for randomization of punishments, because previous criminal record may be only one of several antecedent correlates of recidivism that should be taken into account.

Rare positive findings. Research evidence of specific deterrence is truly rare. One instance is especially noteworthy because it pertains to "chronic" juvenile delinquents. Murray and Cox (1979) report that during the two years after legal intervention the monthly arrest rate declined the most for juveniles who were involuntarily removed from the community and placed in a custodial context for an indefinite duration. Moreover, the decline in the arrest rate was greatest for juveniles who were institutionalized, and the amount of decline appears to have been clearly a direct function of the number of prior arrests.

The findings are puzzling, and all the more so because Murray and Cox considered the possibility of maturation, regression, and selectivity effects. As Murray and Cox argue (1979, p. 177), the findings indicate a dramatic deterrent effect; but in the absence of data on perceived severity and perceived certainty it is difficult to see how or why deterrence flourished.

More nearly defensible research. Because research with randomized punishment is extremely rare, three illustrations will suffice. In the first study (Berecochea, Jaman, & Jones, 1973) two sets of California convicts were selected at random. All 494 convicts in one set were released on parole six months before regularly scheduled, and all 515 in the other set were released on schedule. Because the two sets were selected randomly, those convicts released earlier served shorter sentences on the average than those released on schedule; hence, the two sets differed as to the presumptive severity of actual punishment. However, because the two sets did not differ significantly in "parole success" during the first year after release, the findings contradict Theorem 1 in Figure 2. But in the absence of data on perceived severity and without unofficial measures of recidivism, doubts about the findings are justified.

In the other study (Mecham, 1968) juvenile traffic violators in Salt Lake City were randomly assigned to one of four groups, with the court disposition of a case being a fine, an order not to drive, an order to attend a driving school, or an order to write a paper on traffic safety. The percentage of juveniles with a subsequent record of traffic violation was the lowest for the group who wrote papers. So if it is assumed that the offenders perceived writing a paper as less painful than the other legal reactions, then the findings contradict Theorem 1 in Figure 2. However, the research illustrates the difficulty of judging the severity of qualitatively different legal reactions, and the reliance on official measures of recidivism is another source of doubt.

One of the very few justifications for further research on Theorem 1 in Figure 2 is Sherman and Berk's comparison (1984) of the three groups of domestic assault suspects in Minneapolis. The members of one group were arrested; those of another group were ordered by police officers to leave the residence for eight hours; and members of the third group were given "advice" by the investigating officers, including informal mediation in some cases. Both official and victim-reported recidival data indicate a lower rate of domestic violence for the arrested group during the subsequent six months. Although the groups were created by ostensibly random assignments, the findings are evidence of specific deterrence only if the suspects perceived arrest as more painful than a separation order or advice. The assumption is plausible. Nonetheless, without data on perceived severity in all studies of specific deterrence, there is no basis for assessing this possibility: the types of legal reactions in the Sherman and Berk study differed more as regards perceived severity than did types of legal reactions in other experiments (e.g., Mecham, 1968). Of course, as Lempert (1981–1982) suggests in reporting his study of enforcement of child-support laws, inconsistent findings on specific deterrence may reflect contrasts in the offenses considered, the characteristics of offenders, other extralegal conditions, and differences in legal reactions that cannot be described readily in terms of severity, certainty, or celerity.

UNUSUAL LINES OF RESEARCH

Perhaps because severity is the most dramatic property of punishment, researchers have been preoccupied with Theorem 1 in Figure 2; and methodological innovations have been largely limited to randomization procedures. So some lines of work are not just unusual; they are all too unusual.

Celerity of punishment and specific deterrence. The few findings on the subject are limited to Theorem 5 in Figure 2, and they indicate no relation whatever between punishment celerity and recidivism. For example, Shoham (1974) reports no significant association in Israel between recidivism and the length of the interval from a traffic violation to sentencing.

It is unfortunate that Shoham could not randomize punishments and control other properties of punishment. The suggestion is not that celerity must be relevant after all; rather, more compelling evidence of celerity's irrelevance is needed to justify ignoring it completely in all future deterrence research.

Experimental research on extralegal punishments and specific deterrence. Even if it were possible and ethically defensible to randomize legal punishments, it may well be that the controls needed can be realized only through research on extralegal punishments in fully experimental situations, some of which simulate a criminal justice system more closely than others. Only recently has work in that direction been undertaken (e.g., Gray, Miranne, Ward, & Menke, 1982). The researchers face a hostile audience (see commentary by Moffitt, 1983), some of whom (e.g., Pettigrew, 1983) summarily dismiss the possible relevance of experimental evidence in assessing the deterrence doctrine. The dismissal is little more than a knee-jerk reaction.

For the findings to bear on the specific argument, it is necessary only that the experimental design encompass two or more situations that differ appreciably with regard to the presumptive severity of punishments and two or more situations that differ appreciably with regard to objective celerity. The severity of experimental punishments, no matter how judged, can never remotely equal some legal punishments; but if the experimental relation holds or becomes closer as severity increases, there is a basis for generalizing to legal punishments and recidivism. Of course, such a generalization would be only a hypothesis (not, contrary to Moffitt, 1983, an *ap-*

plication of learning theory in criminal justice); but that is true also when generalizing from any finding in *observational* research. What has been said of severity applies also to celerity, except legal punishments are *less* celerious (just the opposite of severity) than is feasible in the case of experimental extralegal punishments.

Although psychologists have conducted numerous experiments on extralegal punishment, they rarely view that work as bearing on specific deterrence. For instance, the term deterrence is not in the subject index of *The Effect of Punishment on Human Behavior* (Axelrod & Apsche, 1983). Yet summaries of experimental findings are remarkably consistent with the specific deterrence argument. Describing the principal findings in terms familiar to psychologists, response reduction or behavior suppression in experimental situations appears directly related to the intensity (severity), continuity (certainty), and immediacy (celerity) of punishment (van Houten, 1983; Moffitt, 1983). True, the relations are contingent, but many of the contingencies are relevant in speculating about the apparent rarity of specific deterrence in criminal justice. For example, experimental findings indicate that punishment is most effective when introduced at full intensity rather than increased gradually, which is exactly opposite the usual sequence in an offender's career. Of course, the apparent rarity of specific deterrence in criminal justice may stem largely from the fact that legal punishments do not obviate the rewards for crime, nor do they reward subsequent legal conformity (i.e., alternative behavior). Both considerations loom large in experimental research on extralegal punishments (see Moffitt, 1983), and eventually those variables should be manipulated in experimental research on specific deterrence.

Although experimental psychologists are understandably reluctant to generalize from extralegal to legal punishments, it is not imperative that they do more than show that the relation in question holds when punishment celerity decreases and severity increases. Such comparisons have received insufficient attention in the few experiments on extralegal punishments explicitly concerned with specific deterrence. It is not enough to show, as experimenters have done, that the emission rate for a type of behavior varies inversely with the objective certainty and the presumptive severity of punishment. Analysis of those bivariate relations can lead to important discoveries, such as a recent experimental finding of a *direct* relation between punishment celerity and the frequency of the punished behavior (Gray et al., 1982). However, experimental work must go beyond bivariate relations to questions that are not answered by Figure 2: Are the effects of presumptive severity, objective certainty, and objective celerity interactive? And if so, what is the nature of the interaction? The questions are all the more strategic for experimental studies because they appear unanswerable through observational research (see commentary by Gray et al., 1982, p. 207). But only a few experimental studies have addressed the questions; and though some of the findings indicate both additive and interactional effects, there is no consistent and readily comprehensible pattern. The findings will become even more complicated when experimental work is extended to the perceptions of experimental subjects, as it should be. In that connection, the step away from radical behaviorism to cognitive behaviorism (e.g., Meichenbaum, 1977) could lead to kinds of psychological research that are directly relevant in formulating deterrence theories.

A Word to the Extremists

The deterrence doctrine has never lacked fierce foes or dogged defenders, and both camps yearn for a categorical answer to this seemingly simple question: Do legal punishments deter?

OF COURSE LEGAL PUNISHMENTS DETER

That answer is often suggested by economists. Savor Gordon Tullock's arguments (1974, pp. 104–105): "Most economists who give serious thought to the problem of crime immediately come to the conclusion that punishment will indeed deter crime. The reason is perfectly simple: Demand curves slope downward. If you increase the cost of something, less of it will be consumed. Thus, if you increase the cost of committing a crime, there will be fewer crimes."

Now consider a quite different statement: Some individuals are deterred from some crimes some of the time by some threat of some legal punishment. No thoughtful critic will disagree with it, but a less informative statement is difficult to imagine. Moreover, the statement ignores the awful fact that researchers have rarely confronted, let alone answered, three crucial questions about deterrence. First, what types of individuals are the most deterrable? Second, what is the relative deterrent efficacy of the various types of punishment? And third, what types of crimes are the most deterrable?

Dogged defenders of the deterrence doctrine are prone to confuse two questions. First, is it possible for legal punishment to deter effectively? Second, are the legal punishments in particular jurisdictions such that they deter effectively? An affirmative answer to the first question implies no answer to the second, and a negative answer to the second question implies no answer to the first. To illustrate, dogged defenders of the deterrence doctrine respond this way to evidence that criminal homicide rates are much higher in the South, the citadel of the death penalty: The rates would be even higher without the death penalty. The point is that defenders of the doctrine tend to think in terms of hypothetical conditions.

OF COURSE LEGAL PUNISHMENTS DO NOT DETER

At one time it was seemingly an article of faith in criminology that legal punishments never deter, but common experience suggests otherwise. Imagine for example, someone's claiming never to have driven an automobile so as to reduce the risk of a fine.

Should opponents of the deterrence doctrine claim that research supports their argument, they will have overlooked more than findings pertaining to the certainty of punishment. The research most likely to support the doctrine has never been conducted. To date, all research has pertained to *marginal* deterrence, meaning that in all situations compared there was some threat of legal punishment for the type of behavior in question. The comparison has never been such that the behavior is subject to some legal punishment in one situation but none in the other, as when comparing the incidence of public gambling in Salt Lake City and Las Vegas. Should anyone say that incidence is surely greater wherever public gambling is legal, they will have implied a belief in deterrence. Yet research on nonmarginal deterrence would not be free of evidential problems, and its only value might be to sober extreme opponents of the deterrence doctrine. The real challenge would continue to be these questions: What variables determine the amount of deterrence realized through the threat of legal punishments in any given condition? And what formula is needed to relate those variables?

REFERENCES

Archer, D., Gartner, R., & Beittel, M. (1983). Homicide and the death penalty. *Journal of Criminal Law and Criminology, 74,* 991–1013.

Axelrod, S., & Apsche, J. (Eds.). (1983). *The effects of punishment on human behavior.* New York: Academic Press.

Bedau, H. A. (Ed.). (1982). *The death penalty in America.* (3rd ed.) New York: Oxford University Press.

Berecochea, J. E., Jaman, D. R., & Jones, W. A. (1973). *Time served in prison and parole outcome.* Sacramento, CA: Department of Corrections, State of California.

Blumstein, A., Cohen, J., & Nagin, D. (Eds.). (1978). *Deterrence and incapacitation.* Washington, DC: National Academy of Sciences.

Caldwell, R. G. (1944). The deterrent influence of corporal punishment upon prisoners who have been whipped. *American Sociological Review, 9,* 171–177.

Carroll, J. M. (1978). Psychological approach to deterrence. *Journal of Personality and Social Psychology, 36,* 1512–1520.

Cohen, J. (1983). Incapacitation as a strategy for crime control. In M. Tonry & N. Morris (Eds.), *Crime and justice,* Vol. 5 (pp. 1–84). Chicago: University of Chicago Press.

Cook, P. J. (1980). Research in criminal deterrence. In N. Morris & M. Tonry (Eds.), *Crime and justice,* Vol. 2 (pp. 211–268). Chicago: University of Chicago Press.

Ekland-Olson, S., Lieb, J., & Zurcher, L. (1984). The paradoxical impact of criminal sanctions. *Law and Society Review, 18,* 159–178.

Erickson, M. L., & Gibbs, J. P. (1977). Objective and perceptual properties of legal punishment and the deterrence doctrine. *Social Problems, 25,* 253–264.

Forst, B. (1983). Capital punishment and deterrence. *Journal of Criminal Law and Criminology, 74,* 927–942.

Gibbs, J. P. (1975). *Crime, punishment, and deterrence.* New York: Elsevier.

Grasmick, H. G., & Bryjack, G. J. (1980). The deterrent effect of perceived severity of punishment. *Social Forces, 59,* 471–491.

Gray, L. M., Miranne, A. C., Ward, D. A., & Menke, B. (1982). A game theoretic analysis of the components of punishment. *Social Psychology Quarterly, 45,* 206–212.

Greenberg, D. V., & Kessler, R. C. (1982). The effect of arrest on crime. *Social Forces, 60,* 771–790.

Hagan, J. (Ed.). (1982). *Deterrence reconsidered: Methodological innovations.* Beverly Hills, CA: Sage.

Lempert, R. O. (1981–1982). Organizing for deterrence. *Law and Society Review, 16,* 513–568.

Lipton, D., Martinson, R., & Wilks, J. (1976). *The effectiveness of correctional treatment.* New York: Praeger.

Logan, C. H. (1982). Problems in ratio correlation. *Social Forces, 60,* 791–810.

McFarland, S. G. (1983). Is capital punishment a short-term deterrent to homicide? *Journal of Criminal Law and Criminology, 74,* 1014–1032.

Mecham, G. D. (1968). Proceed with caution. *Crime and Delinquency, 14,* 142–150.

Meichenbaum, D. (1977). *Cognitive-behavior modification.* New York: Plenum.

Moffitt, T. E. (1983). The learning theory model of punishment. *Criminal Justice and Behavior, 10,* 131–158.

Murray, C. A., & Cox, L. A. (1979). *Beyond probation.* Beverly Hills, CA: Sage.

Paternoster, R., Saltzman, L. E., Chiricos, T. G., and Waldo, G. P. (1982). Perceived risk and deterrence. *Journal of Criminal Law and Criminology, 73,* 1238–1258.

Paternoster, R., Saltzman, L. E., Waldo, G. P., and Chiricos, T. G. (1983). Perceived risk and social control. *Law and Society Review, 17,* 457–480.

Pettigrew, T. F. (1983). Toward uniting social psychology. *Contemporary Sociology, 12,* 6–8.

Ross, H. L. (1984). *Deterring the drinking driver.* Lexington, MA: Heath.

Schwartz, R. D., & Orleans, S. (1967). On legal sanctions. *University of Chicago Law Review, 34,* 247–300.

Sherman, L. W., & Berk, R. A. (1984). The specific deterrent effect of arrest for domestic assault. *American Sociological Review, 49,* 261–272.

Shoham, S. G. (1974). Punishment and traffic offenses. *Traffic Quarterly, 28,* 61–73.

Sutherland, E. H., & Cressey, D. R. (1974). *Criminology* (9th ed.). Philadelphia: Lippincott.

Tittle, C. R. (1980). *Sanctions and social deviance.* New York: Praeger.

Tullock, G. (1974). Does punishment deter crime? *Public Interest, 36,* 103–111.

Van Houten, R. (1983). Punishment. In S. Axelrod & J. Apsche (Eds.), *The effects of punishment on human behavior* (pp. 13–44). New York: Academic Press.

Zimring, F. E. (1978). Policy experiments in general deterrence: 1970–1975. In A. Blumstein, J. Cohen, & D. Nagin (Eds.), *Deterrence and incapacitation.* Washington, DC: National Academy of Sciences.

The Efficacy of Law as a Paternalistic Instrument

Richard J. Bonnie

University of Virginia

Introduction: The New Paternalism

Major reviews of public health policy issued in the United States and other Western countries in recent years have emphasized that unhealthy and unsafe personal habits play critical predisposing roles in the development of many serious illnesses such as heart disease and cancer and in causing major injuries that consume a large share of health and welfare resources (U.S. Department of Health, Education, and Welfare, 1979; Institute of Medicine, 1982; Lalonde, 1974). Accordingly, these reports emphasize the desirability of changing life-style as a means of reducing the social burden of disease and injury. The usual targets of what I will refer to as the "new paternalism" include alcohol and drug abuse, cigarette smoking, poor eating habits, and unsafe driving.

There is much evidence of public receptivity to the tenets of the new paternalism. The jogging epidemic and the proliferation of health food stores are concrete evidence of a major change in public attitudes toward health. The pervasive impact of these changing attitudes is also evident in the intellectual redefinitions now occurring in the academic community. The public health literature reflects an explosion of interest in "behavioral epidemiology." A new subspecialty in psychology ("health psychology") has emerged to develop the behavioral foundations of life-style modification policies. Three major books on "injury control" have been published by public health specialists in the past year alone (Baker, O'Neill, &

Karpf, 1984; Robertson, 1983; Waller, 1985). Perhaps the most revealing indication of the intellectual trend is the characterization of
automobile safety and interpersonal violence as public *health* problems.

These developments also signify an important ideological shift in
public attitudes toward the relation between the individual and the
state. The liberal belief that each person is—or should be regarded
as—the best judge of his or her own best interests is being eroded
by a general recognition that we all bear the costs of injury and disease. In this sense each person has a financial stake in the well-being
of others. A Blue Cross and Blue Shield advertisement, cited in Bonnie (1978), makes the point:

> If we take better care of ourselves, we're going to need
>   less health care.
> And this will slow down the rise in health care costs. . . .
> We're not asking you to become a Puritan, to stop enjoying
>   life.
> Just to take better care of yourself.
> Please don't overeat, don't oversmoke, don't overwork.
> And, if you're going to drink to someone's health, don't
>   overdo it.

This ideological shift is also evident in legislative activity. The minimum drinking age is being raised. Smoking is being banned in
places of public accommodation. Every state appears to have enacted a law requiring that children be restrained in safety seats in
cars. Warning labels on cigarettes have been strengthened. Political
support for legalizing marijuana and mitigating the severity of the
drug laws has virtually disappeared, and a new "hard line" is evident in the statutory bans on advertising and selling of drug paraphernalia.

In the 1985 session of the Virginia General Assembly, for example, bills were introduced to raise the drinking age, to require drivers and front-seat passengers to wear seat belts, to ban "happy
hour" discounts in bars, and to require hunters to wear orange
vests.

This is not to say that libertarian values have been erased or that
the vested economic interests threatened by the new paternalism
will quickly yield to its initiatives. Indeed, the only one of the paternalist bills to be enacted by the Virginia legislature was the one
raising the minimum drinking age; the "happy hour" ban, the man-

datory seat-belt bill, and the hunter's vest bill were all buried in committee. No doubt the General Assembly was reflecting the sentiments of columnist James J. Kilpatrick (1985), who denounced the mandatory seat-belt law as a violation of the "right to be foolish." Although the tobacco industry does not put the point so bluntly, the R. J. Reynolds Company has launched an advertising counteroffensive in support of the individual's right to make his own choices, however unhealthy they may appear to the nonsmoking majority.

The clash between the new paternalism and ingrained libertarian attitudes and vested economic interests will be played out in the political process in the years ahead. It is not my purpose in this paper to address the issues of political philosophy and legal theory raised by paternalist policies. Instead, I want to survey the state of knowledge about the *utility* of law as an instrument for discouraging unsafe or unhealthy personal choices. I will focus, in other words, on descriptive questions, not prescriptive ones. However, because the leap from data to policy—from *is* to *ought*—is so problematic, and because the philosophical issues are never very far beneath the surface, a brief sketch of my own views about the legitimacy of paternalist interventions will help anchor the subsequent discussion.

I view these issues from the perspective of a liberal paternalist. On the one hand, I reject the libertarian position that decisions to risk one's health or safety are embraced within a sphere of choice over which the individual is entitled to exercise a "sovereign prerogative." Although decisions to smoke, drive unbelted, or eat too much cholesterol do not directly endanger anyone else, the aggregate consequences of these behaviors impose a burden on society's health and welfare resources—and I believe these effects should count in the formulation of public policy. Thus I believe it is legitimate for government to discourage unsafe or unhealthy personal choices. Similarly, I reject the libertarian idea that certain types of interventions are categorically impermissible. Specifically, coercive interventions may be justifiable if the social benefits (measured by reductions in social burden derived from reduction in the unsafe or unhealthy behavior) demonstrably outweigh the costs of the intervention. Based on the data reviewed below, for example, I regard enactment of mandatory motorcycle helmet laws as a legitimate paternalist initiative.

On the other hand, I also reject the "hard" paternalist position that seems to posit health (if not perpetuation of life) as the supreme value. I do not regard a paternalist intervention as justified solely upon a showing that the health and welfare resources conserved as a result of the policy exceed the quantifiable costs of implementing it. Personal autonomy in choosing how to live one's life is a countervailing value; accordingly, the affront to autonomy, and the general erosion of liberty, must be counted among the costs of an intrusive paternalism.

I have said that paternalistic objectives are legitimate and that utilitarian values do not impose categorical limits on the means of intervention, and I have endorsed a cost benefit methodology. Yet I have said that liberty counts. How does it count? The answer lies in the burden of justification: when government restricts individual choice in order to reduce the likelihood of anticipated harm—harm that is realized in the aggregate, but not usually in a given instance —it bears the burden of justification. This is so not only because deliberate action reduces the risk of mistake but also because it reflects our shared taste for liberty.

To say that the government should bear the burden of justifying paternalistic interventions says nothing about the weight of that burden. Rational social action requires some empirical basis for believing that any proposed intervention will make a difference. But government would be disabled from acting at all if uncertainty about the consequences of any proposed action were enough to preclude it. Under what conditions must the government's case be based on convincing empirical proof that the proposed approach will work? Conversely, when is informed speculation enough? Answers to these questions should be contextual. The burden of empirical justification should vary, it seems to me, according to the sweep and intrusiveness of the restriction—that is, according to the affront to libertarian values.

These observations fix the role of empirical investigation in the assessment of paternalist policies. A single-minded libertarian would not regard data on the projected social benefits of paternalist intervention as relevant to the making of public policy; the libertarian mind is not cluttered with empirical questions. However, a single-minded paternalist tends to focus *only* on empirical questions, dismissing libertarian objections as soft-headed impediments to the well-being of the social organism. In my view, data on the efficacy of paternalistic interventions (and on the quantifiable social costs) should play a critical, though not determinative, role in the formulation of public policy. Competing values must be recognized and weighed; they cannot be quantified or hidden in an econometric equation.

Risk-Taking Behavior and the Law

This paper addresses the efficacy of legal interventions as instruments for implementing paternalist public policies—policies aiming to prevent or discourage unsafe or unhealthy personal choices, that is, risk-taking behavior. One should therefore ask at the outset whether any distinctive features of risk-taking behavior bear upon the potential efficacy of paternalistic legal interventions. Further, in order to mark the boundaries of the inquiry, it is necessary to define what one means by legal interventions. These issues are addressed, in turn, below; this discussion will establish the framework for the remainder of the paper.

THE BEHAVIORAL CONTEXT: THE PSYCHOLOGY OF RISK TAKING

The conception of human behavior I find most useful in exploring the behavioral impact of legal regulation is one based on the idea that people make decisions according to the expected utility of alternative behaviors. Whether or not a person's decision-making process is deliberate, the outcome implicitly reflects an assessment of the likely consequences of behavioral alternatives. Such an assessment encompasses the person's *beliefs* about the probable consequences of the behavior (expectancies) and his or her *preferences* concerning those consequences (values).

In the present context, the common dimension of decisions to smoke cigarettes or use marijuana, or to drive without wearing a seat belt or while intoxicated, is that the behavior involves a risk to the person's health or safety—a consequence I will assume to be negatively viewed by almost everyone. Presumably the person's decision will be influenced by his or her beliefs about the probability and magnitude of the adverse consequences associated with the behavior (including the perceived probability of injury or disease), by the value he or she places on avoiding or reducing the risk that such consequences will occur, and by the intensity of his or her preferences for (what are believed to be or have been experienced as) the beneficial consequences of the behavior.[1]

1. In this statement of the expected utility model, I have collapsed the two dimensions of the formula developed by Fishbein and Ajzen (1975)—the personal or attitudinal factor and the social or normative factor. That is, by referring to consequences associated with the behavior, I mean to refer not only to those directly related to the

Risk perception. It follows that the literature on the cognitive psychology of risk appraisal and decision making is relevant to a study of legal regulation of personal health and safety. Several findings from this literature seem especially pertinent.

First, there is evidence that people tend to be insensitive to the risks of low-probability events and that they tend to discount the risk unless it crosses some critical threshold. When probabilities drop to very low values, people tend to become insensitive to losses, even large ones, and their behavior is governed mainly by the unlikelihood of the undesirable outcome (Tversky, 1974; Tversky and Kahneman, 1973). For example, an extensive analysis of decisions regarding the purchase of flood insurance found that most eligible individuals failed to purchase the insurance even though the federal government subsidized 90% of the cost (Kunreuther, 1976).

This tendency illustrates what Tversky and Kahneman (1973) have characterized as the "availability heuristic." Because floods, fatal car crashes, and deaths due to smoking-induced disease are rare and remote events, instances are not readily imaginable. Conversely, use of the availability heuristic can exaggerate the salience of a low-probability occurrence if the individual has actually experienced the relevant event. Researchers have found, for example, that purchase of earthquake and flood insurance increases sharply after such an event occurs and then decreases as memories fade (Kunreuther et al., 1978; Steinbrugge, McClure, & Snow, 1969, appendix A). Kunreuther has described this as a sequential model of choice whereby the potential consequences of a low-probability event are ignored unless and until the event is experienced.[2]

The tendency to discount the risks of low-probability events is exacerbated by an apparent tendency to underestimate the probability that the accident or disease will occur to oneself, or to be overconfident of one's own ability to control the likelihood that it will occur. In effect, people tend to regard themselves as less vulnerable than everyone else and to view themselves as personally immune from hazards (Fischoff, Lichtenstein, Slovic, Derby, & Keeney, 1983, p. 30).

---

performance of the behavior itself, but also to the individual's beliefs about the social response to the behavior and his attitudes toward the anticipated responses of various social referents. Thus, the favorable reaction of peers and the unfavorable reaction of parents may be regarded as desirable consequences of marijuana use while the risk of criminal punishment is viewed as an adverse consequence.

2. Although I have not identified pertinent studies, I suspect that people tend to wear seat belts after they (or someone they know) have experienced an accident.

For example, Robertson (1977) asked a random national sample of new car buyers ($N = 1,017$) whether their risk of being injured or killed in a car crash is greater than, the same as, or less than that of "people like yourself." He found that only 6% of the buyers saw their own chances as greater than those of people like themselves while 36% saw their chances as being less than average. Svenson (1981) reports similar findings in Sweden.

In another study, 1,500 licensed drivers were asked to assess the likelihood (based on five choices ranging from one in five to one in a thousand) that they would be "involved in an automobile accident of any kind in the next year, either one caused by you or someone else." Only 23% of the respondents chose an alternative with odds equal to or less than the societal average (one in ten), while the majority selected odds of one in a hundred or greater (Teknekron, 1979). Moreover, when asked how much control they had over preventing accidents, more than 80% answered "a lot of control" or "almost total control."

These data show the pervasiveness of the belief that automobile crashes "won't happen to me." When combined with a general tendency to misperceive and discount the probability of a crash, these findings demonstrate a significant error in risk perception among the driving population.

The same point can be demonstrated for smoking. The data show that cigarette smoking is strongly addictive and that giving it up is extraordinarily difficult (Pollin, 1984). However, people who begin smoking (especially adolescents) believe that they, at least, will be able to quit whenever they choose. Since smoking is generally perceived to cause disease only after many years of smoking, the belief that one can stop when one chooses (and be only a temporary smoker) reflects a fundamental error in risk perception (Doron, 1979).[3]

Preferences. Risk perception is not the only dimension of psychological theory that is pertinent to an analysis of the efficacy of legal

---

3. Research by Zuckerman (1979) suggests that variations in risk perception may be related to affective factors as well as cognitive ones. Specifically, some individuals (high sensation seekers) tend to perceive less risk, and respond with less anxiety, in situations most people avoid because the risk is perceived to be too high. High sensation seekers may be less amenable than others to efforts to correct cognitive errors in risk perception. Moreover, when people engage, with beneficial consequences, in risky behavior without experiencing harm, the level of anxiety will be reduced in subsequent encounters, reflecting the tendency to discount the risk of harms that are not experienced.

interventions for risk-taking behavior. The impact of the law will also depend on the distribution and intensity of individual preferences for various types of risky behavior. Obviously individuals vary in their preferences and in their attitudes toward risk, and these individual variations are associated with a range of demographic, sociocultural, psychological, and situational variables—variables that differ for various types of risk-taking behavior.[4]

An understanding of the factors accounting for individual or group preferences is indispensable in framing educational and counseling interventions (and in some contexts therapeutic ones) targeted to specific individuals or groups. However, etiological considerations are less likely to be pertinent in framing and assessing preventive interventions addressed to the general population. In this connection it will usually be enough to know the pervasiveness and intensity of the aggregate preference for the behavior.

One dimension of the phenomenology of risk-taking behavior that is especially pertinent to a study of legal intervention is the degree to which the behavior is habitual. A risk-taking behavior is least susceptible to modification if it is longstanding, is frequently displayed, leads to immediate rewards, and is interwoven with other habitual behaviors. On this dimension, driving unbelted and cigarette smoking reflect considerable differences in intensity of preference and are, for this reason, unlikely to be equally susceptible to modification by legal intervention.

The association between risk taking and adolescence should also be noted. Adolescents and young adults are at higher risk than other age groups for injury and death from driving, interpersonal violence, and other causes (Baker, O'Neill, & Karpf, 1984). Moreover, habitual risk-taking behaviors such as cigarette smoking and other forms of substance abuse are typically established during adolescence (Kandel, 1984; Kandel & Faust, 1975; Schuckit & Russell, 1983). It thus appears that the efficacy of legal intervention

4. One psychological factor that appears to have generic significance for all forms of risk-taking behavior is individual propensity to seek adventure, sensory stimulation, and novel experiences and to be aversive to repetitive or routine tasks or experiences. The so-called sensation-seeking trait has been found to be associated with drug, alcohol, and smoking experiences, with risky recreational behavior such as skydiving, and with choice of risky occupations. While high sensation seekers tend to be less aversive to risk than low sensation seekers, sensation seeking is not risk seeking, per se. Instead, the sensation-seeking trait is associated with variations in individual preferences for the perceived benefits (including "psychophysiological state of arousal") of the risky behavior (Zuckerman, 1979).

depends substantially on its impact on adolescent and young adult behavior. Yet the behavior of this population may be especially resistant to intervention—risk perception tends to be least accurate, physical vulnerability tends to be underestimated, the immediate benefits of risky behavior tend to be overvalued in comparison with the risks of low-probability events or remote harms, and risky behaviors often represent assertions of independence from adult norms.

One final point should be kept in mind. Economic analysis suggests that an individual's incentive to reduce risky behavior is generally decreased to the extent that he or she will not bear the full costs of injury or disease. To put it the other way, patterns of risk-taking behavior might differ considerably if the monetary costs (e.g., the costs of hospitalization or a reduced income owing to disability) were not as widely spread as they are today. In economic terminology, the availability of ex post subsidies (in the form of health and disability insurance) may lessen a person's incentive for ex ante risk-reducing behavior.

THE LEGAL CONTEXT: MODES OF LEGAL INTERVENTION

This paper addresses the efficacy of *law* as an instrument for implementing paternalist policies aiming to prevent or discourage risk-taking behavior. To establish the boundaries of the inquiry, it will be useful to identify those government activities that I take to represent uses of the law and to distinguish these from other forms of government action.

Law as constraint by the state. I want to focus on those interventions by the state that constrain individual and corporate conduct. Thus I shall draw three distinctions: first, between intervention by government and similar interventions by other social institutions; second, between government acting as sovereign and government acting as employer, service provider, or insurer; and finally, between those government interventions that constrain conduct and those that aim to influence conduct by persuasion or inducement. These distinctions are schematically depicted in Table 1.

Government versus private regulation. Government is not the only social institution with effective power to impose significant constraints on personal choice. Employers may condition employment on compliance with occupational safety rules or, more relevant

Table 1
Role of Government

Type of Intervention	Sovereign	Service Provider, Employer, Insurer, Etc.

Constraint	General prevention
	    Market regulation
	    Information regulation
	    Direct regulation
	        (deterrence)
	    Individual prevention
		Withholding benefits and privileges (disincentives for unsafe or unhealthy behavior)

Persuasion or inducement	Subsidies Regulatory incentives Government speech	Incentives for safe or healthy behavior

here, with smoking bans. Insurers may condition rates or even coverage on conformity with prescribed risk-reduction requirements. I do not mean to suggest that such private interventions are irrelevant to my topic, but they do not constitute uses of *the law*.[5] Indeed, later on in my presentation I will call your attention to the potential efficacy of private institutional efforts to implement paternalistic social policies.

Government as sovereign. Not all government activity purports to exercise the unique powers of the state. When the government interacts with its own employees, it is functionally indistinguishable from other employers; when government provides health care or transportation, it is offering services that could be furnished by the private sector. The government may use its leverage over its employees, over consumers of its services, and over beneficiaries of its insurance programs to promote safe or healthy behavior, but when it does so it is exercising a prerogative no different in principle from that exercised by private employers, service providers, or insurers. Thus, if one is interested in the efficacy of paternalist interventions by employers, service providers, or insurers, there is no conceptual

5. This is not meant to be a jurisprudential statement. Government does, of course, make legal institutions available to enforce the results of private arrangements. However, for present purposes, I mean to focus attention on the role of government as regulator rather than as enforcer of private regulation.

or empirical reason to distinguish between the public and private sectors.[6] I acknowledge one qualification to this assertion; when government has an effective monopoly over a necessary service or has assumed the responsibility of providing fundamental necessities of life for the poor or disabled, it is functioning in its unique capacity as sovereign.

Constraint versus persuasion or inducement. Government (at all levels) has the authority and resources to try to influence risk-taking behavior by informing or persuading the citizenry and by subsidizing, or offering incentives for, the desired behavior. Expenditure of public funds or use of regulatory incentives should be distinguished from the imposition of legal obligations that constrain people's freedom to act as they please.

The distinction is not without ambiguity. Government speech may be so powerful as to drown out other voices even if those voices are not constrained.[7] Government subsidies for desired behavior may be so substantial as to have a coercive effect on individual choice.[8] Withholding an "essential" government-provided service (such as education, welfare, or a driver's license) from those who behave in an undesired manner may be functionally equivalent to a direct constraint on individual choice. Notwithstanding the ambiguities at the boundaries, however, the conceptual core of the distinction has both legal and empirical significance. *The critical issues relating to the efficacy and legitimacy of law as a paternalist instrument relate to those government interventions that impose constraints on individual or corporate conduct as a means of reducing the occurrence of unhealthy or unsafe behavior.*

6. When the government is functioning in its capacity as employer, insurer, and service provider, its actions are typically subject to *legal* constraints (such as constitutional provisions) that are different from those governing private activities. In some contexts government also has more power than any private employer would have (such as in the military setting). From a behavioral standpoint, however, the relationships between the employer and employee, insurer and insured, and service provider and recipient are the same whether the relationship lies in the public sector or the private sector.

7. Under traditional constitutional analysis, the First Amendment bars government from abridging the freedom of others to speak; it does not constrain the power of government to use its resources to express its own views. However, the distinction has recently become controversial. See, for example, Shiffrin (1980) and Yudof (1983).

8. This was the heart of the constitutional dispute in the abortion funding cases: *Harris v. McRae* (1980); *Maher v. Roe* (1978). In these cases a majority of the Supreme court rejected that argument that by funding childbirth and refusing to fund abortions the government "coerced" poor women to carry their children to term.

Modes of legal intervention. Another preliminary distinction is also necessary. Legal theorists have traditionally distinguished between two general categories of behavioral intervention: *general prevention* and *specific* (or individual) *prevention. When the law is used as an instrument of general prevention, it aims to prevent or reduce the undesired behavior in the aggregate, by the general public as a whole or by a targeted class of individuals.* Thus the general preventive effects of the law are ascertained by determining the *prevalence* of the undesired behavior. In contrast, *when the law is used as an instrument of individual prevention, it aims to modify the behavior of a particular individual to whom the intervention is addressed.* Techniques of individual prevention include intimidation through punishment, incapacitation through confinement, and compulsory education or treatment. The efficacy of individual prevention is ascertained by monitoring the behavior of the specific individual or class of individuals subjected to the particular interventions.[9]

Paternalistic policies are commonly implemented by techniques of individual prevention. Persons apprehended for driving while intoxicated may be required to participate in educational or clinical rehabilitation programs, may be jailed, may be deprived of their driver's licenses—all as a means of reducing the likelihood of their repeating the behavior. Persons who attempt suicide may be committed to a psychiatric facility to prevent the suicidal behavior and to reduce the likelihood of such behavior in the future. Persons apprehended for possessing drugs may be required to participate in drug education or treatment programs to reduce the likelihood of further drug use.

Rather than addressing the efficacy of individual interventions in modifying unsafe or unhealthy behavior, I want to address the uses of the law as an instrument of general prevention. I will organize my presentation acording to four modes of legal intervention designed to reduce the prevalence of undesired risk-taking behavior.

First, *by structuring or regulating the marketplace, government can eliminate or reduce the opportunity for the undesired behavior or increase its price.* The injurious consequences of automobile crashes have been reduced by requiring that cars be equipped with padded dash-

9. Some interventions may be employed to achieve both general and specific preventive effects. For example, the conviction and imprisonment of a violator of a criminal law may be designed to deter others from violating the law (a general preventive effect) and to reduce the likelihood that the convicted and imprisoned defendant will recidivate.

boards. Similarly, the opportunity for children to ingest drugs and household cleaning products containing hazardous chemicals has been substantially reduced by requiring that such products be packaged in child-resistant containers. A related mode of general prevention through market intervention is to depress consumption of a disfavored good by increasing its price. Raising taxes on cigarettes is the prime example.

A second mode of legal regulation is to *regulate the flow of information and messages regarding the target behavior*. The government may initiate its own informational efforts in order to influence attitudes and beliefs. This is "government speech." However, the government may also attempt to influence the content of messages generated by nongovernment institutions by proscribing certain messages or by regulating or restricting the content of private communications. Such restrictions have generally taken two forms— mandatory warnings or proscriptions of certain types of messages.

A third mode of legal control is to *deter risk-taking behavior directly by prescribing and imposing sanctions or punishments for undesired behavior or by withholding benefits or privileges to which the individual would otherwise be entitled.*[10] Thus the law may proscribe certain types of substance use or other risk-taking behavior altogether, or it may prohibit such behavior in certain specified circumstances. Examples of total bans include unauthorized possession and consumption of marijuana and other controlled drugs and consumption of alcohol by persons under the minimum age. Situational prohibitions include laws against consuming alcohol in public, against smoking tobacco in certain public areas, or against motorcycling without a helmet.

Whether or not a legal control has a *direct* impact on the marketplace or the prevalence of the disapproved behavior, it may *symbolize and express the official government view of the behavior and may generate derivative effects on behavioral patterns by influencing attitudes and beliefs.* To the extent that citizens customarily defer to and respect the law or are influenced by messages of official approval or disapproval, a declaration of illegality may serve an "educative" or didactic role. However, under conditions of signifiant normative dissensus, the knowledge of the official preferences may actually encourage the disapproved behavior among disaffected, outsider

10. It bears repetition that the focus here is on the *general* deterrent effects of prescribing these sanctions and of imposing them in individual cases rather than on the behavioral effect of the intervention on the punished offender or group of offenders.

groups; threats to freedom may induce "resistance motivation," generating "reverse" effects. In either case, the task of measuring such "symbolic" effects is notoriously difficult because of the need to isolate these hypothesized effects from other influences on attitudes and beliefs. Nonetheless, the salience of symbolism in debates about the law suggests that the indirect or derivative consequences of legal controls should be of greater interest to empirical investigators. For example, the specification of the minimum drinking age, regulation of the availability of drug paraphernalia, and sanctions for possession of illicit drugs may all generate these symbolic effects even if the measurable direct effects tend to be modest.

In the following sections I will survey what is known about the efficacy of legal interventions designed to acheive paternalist objectives. The data will be organized in terms of the four modes of legal intervention just described: market regulation; information regulation; direct regulation of risk-taking behavior; and declarative effects of legal regulation. By way of comparison, the succeeding section will present the modest information now available on the use of incentives, rather than legal intervention, to reduce risk-taking behavior.

Market Regulation

REDUCING THE OPPORTUNITY FOR RISKY BEHAVIOR

I referred earlier to the regulation of automobiles and household products as successful instances of risk reduction through market regulation. These interventions reduced the risk of injury by making the environment safer rather than by trying to make drivers drive more safely or to make children less curious; the behavioral objective was achieved by effectively eliminating the opportunity for the undesired behavior. Even if some consumers would prefer to pay less for cars without crash protection or for household products without childproof tops, this choice is not available to them: the less safe but less expensive commodities are not legally available, and no illicit supply arose to satisfy the residual demand for them.

Market regulations that do not generate an illicit market or evasive behavior (as did the seat-belt interlock system) represent something of a pure type. Because these interventions effectively eliminate the opportunity for the consumer to make the "unsafe" choice, achievement of the regulatory benefits is not contingent in any way on changing consumer motivation. It should be noted in passing, however, that the overall social utility of these market regulations depends on whether these benefits (in terms of reduced injury and death) exceed the social costs of achieving them. For example, the government and the automobile industry have been debating for a decade the costs and benefits of a proposed regulation that cars be equipped with "passive restraints" (air bags or passive seat belts). The issue remains unresolved.

Robertson (1983) reports an intriguing illustration of how a product regulation can reduce the opportunity for a choice that seems peculiarly unsusceptible to such an effect. Carbon monoxide was removed from coal gas used for household cooking in Birmingham, England. As a result, suicide from coal gas inhalation declined by 86%. But, we may ask, what about the substitution effect? Did suicidal individuals find other instruments for achieving the socially undesired result? Most apparently did not: the overall suicide rate declined by more than 50%. This finding supports the idea that many suicidal acts are impulsive and will not occur if a lethal instrument is not at hand. This has also been an argument for gun control.

It should not be assumed that product regulation is always successful. The efficacy of the intervention depends on whether it has the anticipated behavioral impact. Orr (1982b) provides the following illustration of the behavioral limits of product regulation. In the late 1970s, the Consumer Product Safety Commission proposed standards for strengthening the three-step ladder typically used for changing light bulbs and performing other household tasks. Undoubtedly the regulation would have had demonstrable success in reducing the frequency of injuries attributable to falls from three-step household ladders. However, such an analysis would be misleading if, as the ladder industry had projected, the new ladders (now twice as heavy) had cost 50% more than the old ones. Fewer ladders would have been purchased, more ladders would have been stored in basements or garages, and more people would have had accidents changing light bulbs while standing on chairs.

Reducing health and safety risks through market regulation is more complicated if people will still "demand" the product that has been banned or made less accessible, and if an illicit supply arises to meet this demand. It should be emphasized, however, that the persistence of consumer demand and the evasion of the market restriction do not necessarily demonstrate the failure of the intervention. The regulation is effective to the extent that the undesired behavior (and associated morbidity and mortality) are actually reduced; however, the initiative may nonetheless be socially undesirable if the costs outweigh the public health gains. Alcohol prohibition is just such a case; here the demonstrable reduction in per capita consumption and in alcohol-related morbidity and mortality were far offset by the social costs incurred as a result of the intervention.

Existing laws governing availability of controlled substances and alcohol provide controversial illustrations of the behavioral complexities of market regulation. In the remainder of this section I address what little is known about the effects of the current prohibitory legal regime restricting legitimate availability of controlled substances to medical and scientific uses, and then I turn to alcoholic beverage control.

Effects of drug prohibitions and their enforcement. As I have noted, we should not assume that a prohibitory regime is a failure simply because an illicit market arises. The utility of any prohibitory scheme depends on whether the social costs sustained in the effort to enforce the prohibition, together with the aggregate social costs of illicit use, are less than the social costs that would be incurred in connection with less restrictive policies.

Critics of marijuana prohibition have challenged the basic premises of the paternalist approach to this drug. They argue, for example, that the risk of individual impairment arising from use of the drug is not great enough to justify restrictions on personal choice and that government may not legitimately aim to discourage all use in order to prevent excessive or otherwise unhealthy use. These arguments aside, however, they also argue that prohibition is not an effective way to implement the public health model, contending that the costs of current prohibitory policies exceed the presumed aggregate costs that would be incurred under a regulatory regime, even one that resulted in substantially increased consumption (Bonnie & Whitebread, 1974; Hellman, 1975; Kaplan 1975).

It seems logical to assume that cannabis products, though widely available on the illicit market, are currently less accessible and more costly than they would be under a different legal regime and that the inconvenience, cost, and social risk associated with black-market transactions depress consumption. But how much? Obviously this question cannot be answered with confidence, as the answer would depend on unverifiable assertions about what would happen to consumption patterns under any of several alternative legal arrangements. But the question deserves more systematic attention than it has thus far received.

Similarly, the restriction of access to heroin—especially the lack of more or less controlled availability of the substance to heroin-dependent persons—has been challenged on the ground that the costs of the total prohibition exceed the presumed aggregate costs that would be incurred under a regime that permitted heroin to be available to addicts, even if this resulted in an increase in the number of addicts and an increase in the intensity or duration of their addiction. Again, the consequences of an alternative legal regime cannot be established with confidence; however, many commentators have speculated about the likely effects of alternative schemes under which heroin would be legitimately available to the heroin-dependent population (Blum, 1979; DuPont, 1979; Goldstein, 1979; Kaplan, 1983; Rosenthal, 1979; Trebach, 1982). The key variables in this discussion are the relation between heroin use and criminal behavior and the likely impact of licitly available heroin on the incidence, prevalence, and patterns of heroin use and dependency. This debate is likely to continue, although policy is likely to remain the same.

The promulgation and enforcement of controls against nonmedical availability of controlled substances has the primary effect of shaping the behavior of those who operate on the legitimate market; however, since a black market inevitably will spring up to meet the demand for proscribed uses, the way the law is enforced against the illicit suppliers will affect the price and accessibility of the illegally marketed substances and can presumably affect the patterns and consequences of their illicit use. A focus on enforcement behavior calls attention to the "regulatory" effects (influencing price and other conditions of availability) that can be achieved within the framework of a prohibitory regime.

Although too little is now known about the ways different enforcement strategies and procedures (and different penalty schemes) shape the behavior of dealers and consumers, a significant contribution to our understanding of this subject has been made by Mark Moore (1977). After describing the basic features of the heroin distribution system, with special attention to the market in New York City, Moore analyzes the available enforcement strategies and describes the patterns of police behavior in New York. He then recommends an enforcement strategy for "using domestic law enforcement agencies to enforce the prohibition of heroin." Moore's main contribution lies in his effort to develop the implications of viewing the enforcement system as an instrument for affecting price, accessibility, and consumer behavior.

Some prospect for building on this foundation may lie in continued improvement of our capacity for monitoring trends in availability (price, accessibility) on the illicit market. Moreover, the work of the urban ethnographers promises to enhance our understanding of the interaction between various enforcement strategies and the behavior of persons involved in illegal distribution (Akins & Beschner, 1980). These ethnographers have made an invaluable contribution to the literature on prostitution, and a coordinated research strategy would be of immeasurable value in the drug area.

Effects of the minimum drinking age. The potential impact of alcoholic beverage control laws on patterns of alcohol consumption and on the prevalence of alcohol problems is now receiving substantial attention from investigators and policymakers (Medicine in the Public Interest, 1979; Moore & Gerstein, 1981). For present purposes I will focus on one feature of alcoholic beverage control—the effect of the minimum drinking age. Here a demonstrable social benefit has been achieved despite the unabated demand for the prohibited product in the target population.

Between 1970 and 1976, 29 states reduced the minimum drinking age, usually as part of a more general measure reducing the age of majority to 18 (Wagenaar, 1983). However, proposals to restore a higher minimum age were soon introduced, based largely on claims that alcohol-related crashes had significantly increased among teenagers and young adults. In response, by June 1984, 21 of these states had rolled the minimum age back to some higher age, but usually to 19 or 20 rather than 21 and not covering all alcoholic beverages (Bonnie, 1985). A nationwide return to a minimum age of 21 for all alcoholic beverages is a virtual certainty because the states now stand to lose federal highway funds if they fail to do so.

Impact on consumption. Legal restrictions on availability of alcohol to those under the prescribed age preclude neither access nor consumption. Despite the universal bans against distributing alcohol to persons *under 18,* younger adolescents have been drinking in larger numbers, at earlier ages, and with greater frequency in recent years. About 80% of 12- to 17-year-olds report having had a drink, more than half drink at least once a month, and nearly 3% drink daily. Nearly 80% of male high-school seniors drink at least once a month, and about 8% drink daily (compared with 3% of the females). Since

1966, the number of high-school students who report that they become intoxicated at least once a month has more than doubled from 10% to almost 25%. In a 1982 national survey of high-school seniors, 40% reported that they had taken five or more drinks in a row on at least one occasion during the two weeks before the survey, and 30% reported that most or all of their friends get drunk at least once a week (Bonnie, 1985).

One can safely assume that alcohol consumption is even more prevalent among 18- to 21-year-olds, even in jurisdictions that have set the minimum drinking age at 21. However, most of the research on youthful drinking practices has been based on self-reports by high-school students, usually seniors. Therefore, few data are available concerning drinking practices of 18- to 21-year-olds or on whether their drinking practices vary in states with lower or higher minimum drinking ages. McFadden and Wechsler (1980) surveyed New England college students in 1977 and found that students from states with a low drinking age consumed alcohol more frequently than students from states with a high minimum age. Two studies (Douglass & Freedman, 1977; Wagenaar, 1982) have documented significant increases in on-premises beer consumption after reduction in the minimum age, and most observers have interpreted this finding to reflect increased teenage consumption (Smart, 1980). (Similar effects have not been found in overall alcohol sales, but young drinkers consume such a small proportion of liquor that one would not expect such an effect to be discernible.)

Proponents of a higher than 18 minimum age obviously do not expect to purge drinking from the lives of young adults. These laws do not effectively preclude access to alcohol by the underage population, and the minimum drinking age does not appear to have a substantial effect on the number of abstainers. However, the available data suggest that the law *does* affect the frequency and circumstances of consumption: underage drinkers probably drink less frequently than they would if alcohol were conveniently and readily available to them, and they are probably far less likely to be drinking in on-premises locations, where the age restriction is most easily enforced. Thus, the legal restriction at least pushes aggregate behavior in the desired direction. The question of interest, of course, is the magnitude of this difference and the magnitude of any derivative difference in the prevalence of impaired driving by the underage population.

Effect on alcohol-impaired driving. The first question is whether more 18- to 20-year-olds drive while alcohol-impaired in lower age jurisdictions than in those with a higher minimum age. The best available data on this question are found in the results of a national roadside breath test survey conducted in 1973 by the Highway Safety Research Institute. Wolfe (1974) reported that almost one-fifth of the 18- to 20-year-old drivers had been drinking, and that 11.2% had at least .05% blood-alcohol content (BAC). He found further that these figures were significantly higher in the states with a lower minimum age than in those that had not reduced the minimum drinking age. It is also noteworthy that 8% of the 16- to 17-year-old drivers had a BAC of at least .05%; this figure demonstrates again the prevalence of teenage alcohol consumption and reinforces the conclusion that the minimum drinking age is best understood as a device for containing the level of consumption and shifting its location. A derivative effect is a reduction in the number of underage teenagers who drive while drunk.

Effect on injuries and fatalities. Ultimately the dependent variable of greatest interest in assessing the effect of minimum age laws is the number of alcohol-related crashes involving young drivers. Several studies were done in the early and mid-1970s on the effect of reducing the minimum age, and more recently investigators have been trying to assess the effects of the new wave of laws raising the minimum age. The methodological difficulties encountered in such studies have been summarized by Whitehead (1980), and I will not repeat them here.

In general it appears that lowering the minimum age during the early 1970s resulted in "statistically and socially significant" increases in all types of alcohol-related collisions among the underage population (Douglass, Filkins, & Clark, 1974). Most researchers used nighttime crashes (or single-vehicle nighttime crashes) as surrogates for alcohol-related crashes, and most found that the crash rates increased among the age groups affected by the reduced drinking age (Douglass et al., 1974, 1982; Smart & Goodstadt, 1977; Whitehead & Shattuck, 1976).

Cook and Tauchen (1984) recently attempted to assess the cumulative effect of the minimum age reductions of the early 1970s. They used annual state data on auto fatality rates (not just nighttime/daytime rates) for the relevant age groups for an eight-year period (1970–1977). Their principal finding was that "a reduction in the minimum drinking age from twenty-one to eighteen for all alcoholic beverage types will result in an increase in the auto fatality rate for eighteen-to-twenty-year-olds of about 7 percent and a somewhat smaller increase for sixteen-to-seventeen-year-olds."

Data are now accumulating on the impact of the recent increases in the minimum age. These data must be interpreted cautiously, because the minimum age was often increased only by one or two years, because any short-term effects may erode over a longer term, and because any decrease in crashes may be attributable to factors other than the change in the minimum age. However, the available studies do seem to show a significant and immediate reduction in alcohol-related crashes involving underage drivers.

The most comprehensive study was conducted by Williams, Zador, Harris, and Karpf (1983) for the Insurance Institute for Highway Safety. In this study the investigators paired nine states that had raised the minimum drinking age during the period 1976–1979 with comparison states in which the minimum drinking age remained unchanged. Concentrating on the frequency of nighttime crashes, in which alcohol is particularly likely to be a factor, Williams and his colleagues concluded that in eight of the nine states that had raised the minimum drinking age there were net reductions in nighttime fatal crashes among the age groups to which the drinking age laws applied. Moreover, in the law-affected groups, the ratio between nighttime fatal crash frequency and daytime fatal crash frequency was reduced more in law-change states than in the comparison states. They estimated the magnitude of these reductions to range from 6% to 75%, with the average reduction being 28%.

INCREASING THE PRICE OF RISKY BEHAVIOR

The economic effect of a water fluoridation program is to increase the price of water for those who wish to purchase nonfluoridated water. Similarly, as I have already indicated, the economic effect of a prohibitory scheme that bans legitimate availability of an unsafe commodity is often to increase its price. In each of these situations, however, it is generally assumed that such major market interventions alter consumer preferences and depress consumption of the prohibited or unpreferred commodity to a degree well beyond that attributable to the increase in the price.

It may be unfeasible for the government to restructure the market for some potentially unsafe commodities, either because the commodities have socially desirable uses, because the costs of doing so would be too high, or because vested economic interests make such action politically impossible. Firearms and cigarettes are illustrative—and controversial—cases. However, where the commodities are legitimately available in the marketplace, taxes may be used as a device for raising the price and reducing aggregate consumption of (demand for) the commodities.

Cigarettes. Available data on the relation between price and cigarette consumption suggest that, though price elasticity is relatively low, a large tax increase would nonetheless have a significant effect on consumption, especially among teenagers. As summarized by Lewitt and Coate (1982), estimates of the price elasticity of demand for cigarettes by adults range from -.1 to -1.5 with the best estimate being approximately -.4. This means that a 10% increase in the price of cigarettes will decrease total consumption by 4%. Most of this decrease appears to reflect decisions to stop smoking or not to start rather than decreases in daily consumption by continuing smokers. Based on these figures, Harris (1982) has estimated that the recent doubling of the federal excise tax (from 8¢ to 16¢ per pack) should lead to a 3% decline in the number of adult smokers. Warner (1981a) has estimated that a more substantial tax increase (increasing the tax to 30¢) could decrease adult consumption by 15%.

What may be more important is the finding by Lewitt, Coate, and Grossman (1981) that teenage demand for cigarettes is highly elastic (-1.4)—a 10% price increase would depress consumption by 14%. Accordingly, Harris (1982) has estimated that doubling the federal excise tax will result in a 15% decline in the number of teenage smokers. Warner (1981a) estimated that an increase in the tax to 30¢ would depress teenage consumption by more than 50%.

The responsiveness of teenagers to price regulation is especially pertinent from a public health standpoint. Epidemiologists have consistently found that the persistence of adult smoking behavior is closely related to the age of onset. The likelihood that a person will be a smoker as an adult is radically reduced each year that he or she does not begin smoking after reaching the age of 16, and the chance is near zero if he or she reaches age 25 as a nonsmoker. Moreover, to the extent that the increased price will depress cigarette consumption among preteens and younger teenagers, it may reduce the likelihood of use of other drugs as well.

Alcohol. Most econometric studies indicate that alcoholic beverage consumption is price elastic, although the degree of elasticity appears to vary according to place, time, and type of beverage. In the United States, for example, demand for beer has generally been relatively inelastic and demand for spirits relatively elastic. Taxation has not been used as a regulatory device in this country. In fact, federal taxation levels have been essentially unchanged since 1951; state taxes have risen moderately. The prices of alcoholic beverages have increased much more slowly than the Consumer Price Index and have declined relative to disposable income (Medicine in the Public Interest, 1979).

It has been argued that a significant increase in the price of alcohol through taxation might depress aggregate consumption but would not reduce the level of alcohol problems because high-risk drinking behavior would not be affected. However, there is evidence that the level of alcohol problems varies directly with the aggregate level of consumption. Cook (1981) found a strong relationship between price of alcohol and cirrhosis mortality (a standard indicator of the level of alcoholism) and has estimated that doubling the federal excise tax would result in a 20% decline in cirrhosis mortality.

A recent longitudinal study of drinking patterns in a Scottish sample (Kendell, de Roumanie, & Ritson, 1983) found a significant decline in consumption and in associated adverse effects over a three-year period during which alcohol prices rose more steeply (by 61%) than the general price index. They also reported that the drop in consumption was as large among heavy drinkers as it was among lighter drinkers.

SUMMARY

The existing literature on the behavioral effects of paternalistic market regulation is largely topical. Aside from econometric studies of demand elasticity, little attention has been devoted to a generic analysis of the factors affecting the prevalence of evasive responses to prohibitory interventions and the nature and magnitude of behavioral responses to variations in the price and accessibility of legally available commodities. What is most noteworthy is the absence of any unified behavioral perspective on the effect of legal controls on use of alcohol, tobacco, and controlled substances. Although epidemiological research on substance abuse has eroded the procrustean distinction between legal and illegal drugs, behavioral analysis of legal regulation is still clouded by the widely divergent political contexts of alcohol and tobacco regulation on the one hand and controlled substance prohibition on the other.

Contemporary controlled substance laws are predicated on the assumptions that the prohibitory regime depresses consumption and that its costs are socially tolerable. Unfortunately, in the absence of comparative study of alternative legal regimes, these assumptions defy definitive empirical investigation. However, much can be learned about the influence of variations in enforcement strategy on the accessibility and price of illegal drugs, and ultimately on the prevalence and patterns of consumption. Moreover, because legal regulation of alcohol and tobacco is in transition and often varies across jurisdictions, it is possible to study the effects of various market controls on the accessibility and price of these substances, and ultimately on their consumption. The opportunity for research presented by recent variations in the minimum drinking age has been recognized and exploited. Other dimensions of the regulatory systems—such as taxation and density and location of retail outlets—also merit investigation. Special attention should be paid to the effect of regulatory controls on adolescent behavior.

Information Regulation

Unless market regulation has effectively precluded the opportunity for the undesired behavior, implementation of paternalist policies will depend upon modes of intervention designed to promote individual compliance—to encourage desired behavior, discourage the disfavored behavior, or both. One of the techniques, already discussed, is to increase the price of the disfavored conduct. Another is to regulate the flow of information concerning the target behavior.

Even the most committed libertarian concedes the legitimacy of government efforts to promote informed individual choice. While government may be bound, under libertarian principles, to respect the individual's sovereign prerogative to weigh the risks and benefits of smoking cigarettes or driving without wearing a seat belt according to his own preferences, government is permitted to provide information about the consequences of alternative choices. Similarly, even Chicago-school economists accept the legitimacy of government interventon to correct for the failure of the market to provide adequate or accurate information.

There is an ideological difference between efforts to *inform* and efforts to *dissuade*. The tobacco industry thinks that the distinction is an important one and that the government has crossed the line—as indeed it has. However, beginning with Mill himself, many libertarian philosophers have conceded the legitimacy of efforts to persuade the individual to refrain from harming himself or placing his health or safety in unreasonable jeopardy. Ideology aside, however, the social utility of paternalist policies turns ultimately on changes in behavior, not changes in knowledge. Thus, the efficacy of information regulation should be assessed not only in terms of increased awareness but also in terms of reduced risk-taking behavior (or reduced injury and disease).

As I noted earlier, government may aim to influence individual risk perception and decision making in two ways—by using its own voice ("government speech") or by telling others what they are required or permitted to say. Although my main interest is in the regulation of speech, let me comment briefly on what is known about the utility of "government speech" as an instrument of behavior modification—at least in the context of personal choices about health or safety.

GOVERNMENT SPEECH

In a society in which the state does not control the means of mass communication, govenment's power to inform and persuade by using its own voice is inherently limited by its inability to command the attention of the general population. Further, because access to privately owned media ordinarily costs money, expenditures for paternalistic initiatives will be limited by competing demands for taxpayer dollars. It should come as no surprise, therefore, that mass media campaigns aiming to discourage unhealthy or unsafe behaviors have had little demonstrable effect.

Even in the public school system, where the govenment is better able to command the attention of the target audience, the efficacy of health and safety education programs has been a subject of ongoing dispute. Although it is clear that well-designed programs can improve risk perception, the influence of educational programs on attitudes and behavior is hard to assess because the effects of the exposure are hard to isolate and because it is difficult to know whether any perceived effect will persist.[11]

A comprehensive review of the literature on public information campaigns and educational programs ranges beyond my topic and

11. For recent reviews of the evaluation literature for injury education and substance abuse education, see Robertson (1983, pp. 91–92), Moore & Gerstein (1981, pp. 89–96), and Bukoski (1981).

my expertise. However, a review of recent studies assessing the efficacy of mass media information campaigns promoting seat-belt use and discouraging drunk driving will illustrate the state of the art in the field. Initially, it is important to emphasize that most of these campaigns have not been evaluated or have not included a well-designed evaluation component. A major methodological problem in evaluating media campaigns is the difficulty of identifying the population actually "exposed" to the message. Another typical defect in evaluation design is that outcome variables are often poorly described, especially in relation to the postulated link between changes in beliefs or attitudes and changes in behavioral intention or behavior.

For the most part, the experts appear to agree on one point: in the absence of experimental design it has not been possible to determine whether these campaigns have worked. As to whether media campaigns could be effective, some experts are optimistic about the potential efficacy of such efforts if they are based on sound principles of mass communication theory. Others are more dubious, doubting that such efforts can have much impact on attitudes and motivation even if they improve the level of knowledge. The best of the recent studies are reviewed below.

Seat-belt usage. A field experiment was carried out in three demographically similar California cities to measure the effects of a five-week series of radio and television public service announcements on seat-belt usage (Fleischer, 1971). Two cities were assigned to the campaign condition, and one was assigned to the no-campaign condition. Belt use by drivers was observed before, during, and after the campaign at selected sites in the three communities. The principal conclusion was that the campaign had no effect on either attitudes or seat-belt usage. The authors concluded that broadcast announcements of this type were not likely to reach the intended audience and were therefore unlikely to have any significant effect.

A subsequent study conducted by the Insurance Institute for Highway Safety (IIHS) (Robertson et al., 1974) attempted to increase the likelihood that a pertinent message would reach the intended audience by designing separate messages for three audiences (children, women, and men) and by showing the relevant messages at times when these target groups would predominate in the viewing audience. The messages were also designed to portray the consequences of a serious automobile injury in a manner that would be personally relevant and would make the risk more salient.

A precampaign survey indicated that seat-belt users tended more often than nonusers to have known someone injured in a crash (a reflection of the "availability heuristic"). Thus the messages aimed at adults emphasized the possibility of disfigurement or disability resulting from an accident, portraying surrogates for the injured friend: a woman and teenage girl with facial scars attributed to a crash, and a teenage boy with leg braces on his way to a football game with his father. The children's message attempted to persuade children to remind their parents to exercise responsibility: a child was shown telling the parents to recover a seat belt that had been hidden by the "wicked car witch."

These messages were shown on one cable of a dual cable television system, distributed throughout a community in a checkerboard fashion, which was used to research commercial campaigns. During a nine-month period, the messages were shown 943 times. The campaign had no discernible effect on observed seat-belt use. At no point before, during, or after the campaign was there a statistically significant difference in seat-belt use between drivers from households receiving the experimental and control cables or between these drivers and drivers from households not receiving either cable.

The IIHS study has generally been interpreted to demonstrate the ineffectiveness of public information efforts designed to promote highway safety. This was the best shot, the skeptics say, and it failed. Perhaps this conclusion is premature. Perhaps the message failed to reach a large enough portion of the intended audiences; longer and more intensive exposure might have had a more significant effect. Also, it is possible that the message was ineffective because it aroused negative affect, thereby creating viewer resistance, or because it failed to overcome the general tendency to discount and ignore the risk of a crash.

Slovic, Fischoff, and Lichtenstein (1978) designed an experimental study in which presentation format was varied to overcome the tendency to discount the low probability of an auto crash. One group of subjects was given information concerning the infinitesimal probability of a serious accident on any particular trip—a fatal accident occurs only about once in 3.5 million person-trips and a disabling injury occurs only about once in 100,000 person-trips. The second group of subjects was given lifetime driving data; they were told that over a period of 50 years (about 40,000 trips), the probability of being in a fatal accident is one in a hundred and that the probability of receiving a disabling injury is one in three. The researchers found that 39% of those given lifetime probability data said they expected to increase their use of seat belts, while only 10% of those given single-trip data said this.

The promising results of this test and additional pilot studies (see Schwalm & Slovic, 1982) induced the National Traffic Safety Administration to support further research on the efficacy of televised seat-belt messages designed to improve risk perception including emphasis on lifetime risk. According to Slovic (1985), study participants were repeatedly exposed to the three messages that appeared most promising in pretesting, and their actual seat-belt use was monitored. The three messsages conveyed information concerning lifetime risk; attempted to convey an intuitive appreciation of the substantial physical forces involved even in moderate-speed collisions; and drew an analogy between using seat belts and other repetitive protective actions that most people take. Slovic reports that the messages had no apparent effect on seat-belt use.

Drunk driving. Public information campaigns relating to drunk driving have become increasingly sophisticated during the past decade. Several recent programs have been based on generally accepted theories of mass communications and on behavioral research and have included well-designed evaluation components. In general, experts in the field have repeatedly concluded that though these campaigns have been effective in increasing knowledge about the effects of alcohol on driving skills, there is little evidence that they have changed either attitudes or behavior (Jones & Jocelyn, 1978).

The most promising results were reported by Worden, Waller, and Riley (1975), who conducted a field experiment to assess the effectiveness of a drunk driving campaign in Vermont. As a prelude to the campaign, the researchers had conducted a baseline survey of the target audience (males aged 16–29) to ascertain media habits, knowledge, attitudes, and life-styles. They had also performed a content analysis of other drunk-driving campaign materials to identify the most suitable messages, and they selected their own material after pretesting a series of messages. The messages were placed at the times and places most likely to be exposed to the target audience (radio stations playing soft-rock music, newspaper sports pages, and billboards at auto racetracks).

The media campaign was conducted in two geographically dispersed communities, one of which was also exposed to increased enforcement of the drunk-driving laws. A third community, which was not exposed to the media campaign or to increased enforcement, served as the control for the study. Effect on knowledge (e.g., how many beers would make a person "legally intoxicated") and on attitudes and behavior was assessed by using roadblock surveys before, during, and after the program.

The principal finding was that risk perception had significantly improved in both of the experimental communities compared with the control community. (For example, there was a significant reduction in the proportion of the high-risk target drivers who believed they could drive safely after consuming six beers in one to two hours.) In addition, the proportion of drivers with BACs of .05% or more was reduced in the experimental communities while remaining essentially unchanged in the control community, although the difference was statistically significant in only one of the experimental jurisdictions. There was no effect on crash frequency.

Summary. There is at present little evidence that discrete, time-limited media campaigns are effective in promoting healthy or safe behavior. While such campaigns may reinforce the attitudes and behaviors of persons who are already inclined to behave safely, they appear to have little impact on the "high-risk" populations—in the context of driver safety, teenage and young-adult working-class drivers. Yet some mass communications experts believe that carefully designed campaigns, targeted at the high-risk populations and based on sound communication principles, could have significant effects (Solomon, 1982). The Vermont CRASH project is mildly supportive of this view. Other experts are less sanguine (Lau, Kane, Berry, Ware, & Roy, 1980).

It would be a mistake, however, to conclude that government speech has no effect. As Wallack (1984) has suggested, sustained information campaigns may be an important feature of integrated paternalist strategies. An often-cited example is the Stanford three-community Heart Disease Prevention Program. Two of the three northern California communities were exposed to interventions relating to cigarette smoking, hypercholesterolemia, and hypertension. Both of the experimental communities were exposed to an intensive and extensive media campaign, including advertisements, television and radio commercials, newspaper columns, billboards, and direct mailings. In one of the communities the media campaigns were supplemented with educational intervention for identified high-risk individuals. Calculations of the additive effects of reported changes in food consumption and smoking suggested an overall reduction of 16% in the three risk factors for the media-only community and 20% for the media-plus-educational-counseling community, each as compared with the control community (Macoby, Farquhar, Wood, & Alexander, 1977).

Sustained informational efforts are also an integral component of strategies aiming to promote compliance with direct legal interventions such as smoking bans, seat-belt laws, or changes in drunk-driving laws. As will be discussed below, the attitudinal and educational effects of these laws may be more significant than the deterrent effect per se.

Finally, the effect of the government's antismoking efforts over the past 20 years should not be overlooked. The Surgeon General's Report, issued in 1964, constituted "government speech" in the classic sense. The publicity generated by that report, and the sustained informational initiatives that have followed, are generally credited with having reduced smoking. However, because the government's antismoking effort has not been confined to using its own voice, it will be discussed below.

LEGAL REGULATION OF SPEECH

A government seriously aiming to discourage what it perceives as unhealthy or unsafe behavior is not likely to be satisfied with the influence of its own messages and may seek to regulate communication by others. This can be done in two ways. First, government may require individuals or organizations to use their voices to convey the government's desired message. Second, government may ban communication of messages that it regards as undesirable. In either case, of course, government efforts to regulate or restrict the flow of information raise serious questions under the First Amendment, which bars the government from "abridging the freedom of speech or of the press" and which has been read by the Supreme Court to protect commercial messages.[12]

Mandatory warnings. Mandatory information and warning requirements have become a fairly standard feature of product safety

12. Although courts and commentators had long assumed that commercial messages were outside the sphere of "speech" protected by the First Amendment, the Supreme Court ruled otherwise in *Virginia Board of Pharmacy v. Virginia Citizens' Consumer Council, Inc.* (1976).

regulation and an emerging feature of drug regulation (through patient package inserts). Warning lights and buzzers serve a similar purpose for seat belts. There is a growing literature on the efficacy (and design) of consumer product information and on the regulatory implications of the developing knowledge about risk perception and the psychology of judgment and decision making (Kahneman, Slovic, & Tversky, 1982). In the present context, the most pertinent issues are the efficacy of the government-required warnings about the dangers of cigarette smoking and the potential utility of package warnings for alcoholic beverages.

Cigarette warnings. It is generally agreed that the widespread dissemination of information regarding the health hazards of smoking has accounted for the significant decline in per capita consumption and for the shift in user preference toward low-tar, low-nicotine cigarettes. Moreover, no one doubts that "government speech" has played a central role in these developments. What is harder to determine, however, is whether the government's regulatory actions (e.g., requiring package warnings) have also contributed and whether the stronger warnings now required will reduce consumption even further.

Per capita comsumption rose throughout the 20th century until 1963. In the 20 years since the Surgeon General's Report in 1964, per capita consumption has moved generally downward. The proportion of adult males who smoke has dropped markedly, from 51% in 1965 to 34% in 1982; and the proportion of adult women smokers has dropped slightly, from 33% to 29% over the same period (Remington et al., 1985). Warner (1981b) has estimated that per capita consumption would have been 40% higher than it was in 1978 had it not been for smokers' responses to antismoking information and publicity. However, the *absolute number of smokers* is higher now than it was in 1964, and the proportion of teenagers who smoke remains roughly the same as it was in 1968.

Health warnings on cigarette packages were first required by the Cigarette Labeling and Advertising Act of 1965. In 1969 Congress strengthened the warning and authorized the Federal Trade Commission (FTC) to require health warnings in cigarette advertising. It is difficult to untangle the effects of these warnings from the effects of other sources of information about the health dangers of smoking. However, in the face of industry opposition, Congress in 1984 amended the act and required the manufacturers to display, in rotation, four specific health warnings (relating, respectively, to heart disease, cancer, addiction, and pregnancy). This legislation was explicitly based on a congressional finding that the previously required general warnings had failed to provide sufficient information to consumers on the risks of smoking. This finding, in turn, was based on data presented by the FTC staff in a 1981 report (Myers et al., 1981). Because the FTC analysis identifies continuing errors in risk perception concerning the dangers of smoking, it merits attention here.

Based on an analysis of a dozen national surveys and other studies, the FTC staff concluded that the public underestimates the health hazards of cigarette smoking. For example, 30% of the adult population and 41% of the smokers did not know that "a 30-year-old person reduces his life expectancy if he smokes at least one pack a day." Nor did the public grasp the magnitude of the loss in life expectancy; when asked to estimate the expectancy loss for a 30-year-old who smokes a pack a day, more people, especially more smokers, tended to underestimate the loss (which is about five years) than to overestimate it.

The FTC staff also found that a significant portion of the public is not aware of the major health consequences of smoking. For example, a 1978 Gallup poll indicated that 32% of the population, and 37% of the smokers, did not know that cigarette smoking causes heart disease. In response to an open-ended question in the 1980 survey sponsored by the FTC ("name all the causes of heart attack you can think of"), 67% of the respondents did not mention smoking. Even when given a multiple-choice question, 40% of the public did not know that smoking is the *major* cause of heart disease. Moreover, in the 1980 study, 47% of the women did not know that smoking during pregnancy significantly increases the risk of miscarriage or stillbirth. Finally, even though most people are aware that smoking is associated with bronchopulmonary disease (chronic bronchitis and emphysema) the majority (59%) did not know that smoking causes most cases of emphysema.

The director of the FTC's Bureau of Consumer Protection concluded that consumers are not aware of the "overall risk of smoking" even though nearly everyone knows of the hazards of smoking in general terms (Muris, 1983). In support of the pending legislation, the director stated that the proposed rotational warnings would probably communicate the information more effectively than the existing warnings for three reasons: their novel or unexpected features would compete more successfully for the consumer's attention than the now-stale general warning; they are more specific and concrete and therefore more likely to be converted into mental images; and they are more likely to be viewed as personally relevant.

It remains to be seen whether the new warning requirements alter risk perception and, if so, whether they depress cigarette consumpton. It will be especially interesting to see if the warnings have any impact on the behavior of pregnant women. The FTC Consumer Protection Bureau director argued that the case for this warning was particularly strong because knowledge of the hazard is directly and specifically relevant to a definable target audience to whom the information is important even if they have an accurate understanding of the "overall risk" of smoking.[13]

Alcohol warnings. Similar arguments have been made in support of a package warning for alcoholic beverages, designed to inform consumers of the risk of alcohol use during pregnancy. Indeed, a report issued by the secretaries of Health and Human Services and Treasury in 1980 concluded that such a warning label would "fit some of the conditions under which such labels tend to be effective—the threat to health is unequivocal, will be manifested relatively quickly, and requires only a short term behavior change" (U.S. Department of the Treasury and U.S. Department of Health and Human Services, 1980). Notwithstanding the predicted utility of the warning, the secretarial report did not endorse pending legislation to require one, in part because the multiple hazards of pregnancy would be "more successfully conveyed through a public information campaign covering all significant risks to pregnancy rather than through a labeling effort directed toward the single risk of alcohol consumption, with corollary efforts singling out smoking and caffeine." Another problem identified in the report was the difficulty of framing a concise but accurate statement of the nature of the risk in relation to the amount of alcohol consumed.

There is much evidence of imperfect understanding of the risks of drinking alcohol during pregnancy among women of childbearing age as well as among the general public. Although people appear to be generally aware that excessive drinking can be harmful, they do

13. The effects of maternal smoking on fetal development are reviewed in a recent Surgeon General's Report (U.S. Department of Health and Human Services, 1983). It has been suggested that these effects merit a descriptive diagnostic term, "fetal tobacco syndrome" (Nieburg, Marks, McLaren, & Remington, 1985). A recent study has indicated that reduced fertility is also a reproductive hazard of cigarette smoking (Baird & Wilcox, 1985).

not appear to know that even one or two drinks a day significantly increases the risk of spontaneous abortion and of fetal abnormalities (Little, Grathwohl, Streissguth, & McIntyre, 1981). Perhaps there is reason to doubt that container warnings would be an effective mechanism for communicating the necessary information. However, I am inclined to think that a warning in print advertising would be effective in improving risk perception.

I should emphasize, parenthetically, that product regulation is not the only legal mechanism at government's disposal for using other people's voices to get its message across. It is also possible to employ the threat of tort liability as a means of imposing an obligation to warn on persons in a reasonable position to do so. The best example is the threat of malpractice liability for obstetricians who fail to warn pregnant women of the risk of fetal alcohol syndrome. This example is compelling because the risk is a significant one that women underestimate, and because the legal obligation does not seem to impose an unfair burden on the physician.

There is some evidence that warnings by physicians and other authority figures may have a greater influence on patient behavior than warnings by others. Reisinger et al. (1981) compared the behavior of an experimental group of mothers who received physician counseling on the use of infant car restraints with the behavior of a control group of mothers who did not receive such counseling. They found that use of restraints in the experimental group was higher by 23% in one month and 72% in two months, though it declined to 9% and 12% in four and 15 months respectively.

Whether or not legal obligations are imposed, the effect of direct involvement by physicians and other health care professionals should be further explored.

Proscribing undesirable messages. Requiring product manufacturers to include information on or with their products is a well-accepted means of government regulation of the marketplace. So too is regulating advertising to prevent false or misleading claims. However, a paternalist program might also be carried a step further: government may seek to *suppress* a message because it is thought to encourage disapproved behavior.

A recurrent assertion in the paternalist literature is that the continued high prevalence of smoking is at least partly attributable to the influence of cigarette advertising. It is argued that the pervasive prosmoking messages generated by the industry's advertising reinforce attitudes favorable to smoking, especially among teenagers and young adults, and that these messages drown out the occasional antismoking message. The answer, it is said, is to ban cigarette advertising. The industry responds that advertising affects what people smoke, not whether they smoke or how much. A ban would not decrease consumption, they argue, and would reduce the consumer's access to important information regarding tar and nicotine content.

A parallel dispute has arisen in connection with controversial proposals to ban alcohol advertising. Those who advocate a public health approach toward alcohol control claim that alcohol advertising tends to increase consumption, while the industry claims that advertising affects market shares, not aggregate consumption.

What is known about the impact of cigarette and alcohol advertising? Did bans on television advertising of cigarettes reduce consumption? Would bans on print advertising reduce it further? Does alcohol advertising promote consumption? Because the literature on alcohol advertising is easier to summarize, I will present it first.

Alcohol advertising. Findings from econometric studies have been equivocal, partly because of the difficulty of unraveling the variables that influence consumption patterns and of drawing causal inferences from correlational data. An econometric analysis of alcohol consumption in the United Kingdom from 1956 to 1975 conducted by McGuiness (1979) found that alcohol advertising modestly increased total consumption, but other econometric studies have found no such relationship (e.g., Ogborne & Smart, 1980). Two quasi-experimental studies reported time-series comparisons between a Canadian province that had banned alcohol advertising and a demographically similar province that had not (Ogborne & Smart, 1980; Smart & Cutler, 1976). Although neither study found that banning advertising reduced consumption, the effectiveness of the bans was compromised by continued exposure to advertisements originating outside the province. A major study was recently conducted by Atkin and Block (1981) for several federal agencies. They reported positive correlations between alcohol-advertising exposure and alcohol consumption among adolescents and adults, but the methodology has recently been criticized by Strickland (1984).

Finally, Kohn and Smart (1984) conducted a field experiment on the effect of televised beer commercials on immediate consumption. They concluded that limited exposure to the commercials briefly stimulated consumption, but that additional exposure did not contribute to further consumption and that, over the course of the experiment as a whole, amount of advertising had no significant effect on consumption.

At present there appears to be no convincing empirical support for the idea that alcohol advertising increases consumption or, conversely, for the claim that a ban would reduce it.

Cigarette advertising. Several economists have attempted to ascertain the impact of the congressional ban on broadcast advertising of cigarettes that took effect in 1971. The analysis is complicated by the fact that from 1967 to 1970, a Federal Communications Commission (FCC) ruling required broadcasters who carried cigarette advertising to provide free air time for messages on the health hazards of smoking. This ruling was an application of the FCC's "Fairness Doctrine." Estimates of the value of this "free" air time have ranged from $40 to $75 million per year. When the industry's advertising disappeared in 1971, so too did most of the antismoking ads; it has been estimated that total expenditures, both public and private, for antismoking ads now amount to about $5 million per year.

A number of investigators have conducted econometric studies, using data on per capita cigarette consumption in the context of time-series demand functions, in order to ascertain the effects of the advertising ban and the Fairness Doctrine. There are two views. One view is that while advertising may have a modest tendency to increase consumption, the antismoking messages required under the Fairness Doctrine depressed consumption more than the pro-cigarette advertising stimulated it (Doron, 1979; Hamilton, 1972; Warner, 1977). Under this view, the broadcast advertising ban may have backfired, because the antismoking messages fell dramatically after 1970. This view is supported by the fact that cigarette consumption declined each year from 1967 to 1970 but began to rise again in 1971, turning downward again in 1973. The opposing view is that advertising significantly stimulates consumption and that the ban on advertising made an important contribution to the continuing decline in smoking (Ippolito, Murphy, & Sant, 1979). According to this view, the decline in consumption supposedly attributable to the Fairness Doctrine probably reflected a lagged behavioral response to the issuance of the Surgeon General's Report in 1964.

Another feature of the debate relates to the impact of the Fairness Doctrine and the advertising ban on teenage consumption. It can be argued that even if advertising does not affect overall consumption (and even if a ban would not suppress overall consumption), it may have an effect on teenage consumption (the decision to initiate smoking, in essence, rather than the decision to terminate or cut down). Teenage smoking rates apparently increased between 1968 and 1970.[14] Supporters of the advertising ban argue that the Fairness Doctrine was not effective in the case of teenagers, whatever effect it had on aggregate cigarette consumption (Evans, 1976; Gritz, 1977). However, Lewitt et al. (1981) have presented data showing that during the period of the Fairness Doctrine, the teenage smoking rate was 3% lower than in the previous 16-month period; specifically, the smoking rate fell 5.2% during the first year but rebounded thereafter. They interpreted these data to mean that the introduction of the Fairness Doctrine "represented a 'shock' to the underlying upward trend in teenage smoking in the mid 1960's and early 1970's" and that the effects of the antismoking ads thereafter were dominated by the underlying trend. They concluded that "the mechanism at work was the responsiveness of teenagers to antismoking messages that stress the health hazards posed by smoking."

At present, attention has been focused on advertising in the *print* media. Cigarettes are the most widely advertised consumer product in America; $1.5 billion was spent to promote them in 1983 (Warner, 1985). It is not possible to demonstrate whether print advertising stimulates consumption. However, as with broadcast advertising and the Fairness Doctrine, another dimension of the debate is the relation between advertising and antismoking messages. It has been argued that the print media's dependence on cigarette advertising revenue has led to pervasive self-censorship: these media, it is said, tend to suppress any discussion of the relation between smoking and health and are unwilling to carry antismoking advertising. With the experience under the Fairness Doctrine in mind, and mindful of possible constitutional objections to a print advertising ban, proponents of paternalist initiatives have argued that those media accepting tobacco advertising should make compensatory space available, at no cost, for antismoking messages (Warner, 1985; Myers et al., 1981).

I am inclined to believe that advertising does not stimulate demand for commodities such as alcohol or cigarettes. Other psychological and social influences are much more potent in determining whether people will drink or smoke and in shaping their patterns of

14. The rate of smoking among high-school seniors peaked in the mid-1970s and decreased thereafter; but it leveled off between 1980 and 1983 (Johnston, O'Malley, & Bachman, 1984).

consumption. If one's family and peers disapprove of smoking, for example, it seems unlikely that advertising that makes it seem attractive will play a predominant behavior-shaping role.

The dispute about the effects of advertising is now being carried on in the courts in those states that have banned various forms of alcohol advertising.[15] Most courts have deferred to legislative judgments that advertising does tend to increase consumption and have upheld the bans as justified infringements of the companies' rights. However, it seems clear that the courts would scrutinize the data more closely if the prohibited messages were political or artistic rather than commercial. Indeed, the courts have deferred to the legislative judgment precisely because commercial advertising has little, if any, First Amendment value (Jackson & Jeffries, 1979).

The fact remains, nonetheless, that the legislative judgment rests on a weak empirical foundation. If alcohol advertising is banned, the justification lies, in my view, in the symbolic effect of the ban, not in its direct effect on consumption. In the context of commercial advertising, where First Amendment values are not strongly implicated, I regard symbolism as a sufficient justification for suppression.

Entertainment programming. It is useful to pose the question about the efficacy of message suppression in a context where the First Amendment *does* matter—regulation of the entertainment media. The paternalists have not overlooked the fact that movies and television programming may also influence behavior by portraying smoking and drinking in an attractive way. For example, a recent National Institute of Mental Health (NIMH) Report on Television and Behavior (1982) stated that "incidental learning from behavioral stories and portrayals may be contributing to lifestyles and habits that are not conducive to good health." Specifically, it was pointed out that: "Alcohol consumption is common [on television]; it is condoned and is presented as part of the social milieu. When people drive cars, which occurs often on television, they almost never wear seat belts."

The authors of the NIMH Report were not inviting legal regulation of media programming, the constitutionality of which is surely doubtful. They were merely inviting television producers to join the government's health promotion campaign. But I tend to think their

15. For recent cases challenging the constitutionality of state bans on alcohol advertising, see *Dunagin v. Oxford* (1983) and *Oklahoma Telecasters' Association v. Crisp*, (1983).

premise was erroneous. I think it unlikely that the media are shaping unhealthy life-styles. Although the issue is controversial, I believe that media portrayals *reflect* the culture more than they shape it. The quotation from *Television and Behavior* makes the point; it describes normative behavior in American society, on television as well as by real people in their daily lives. It is noteworthy that smoking is *not* mentioned. In fact, television portrayals of smoking have declined substantially, as the report itself noted; the frequency of cigarette smoking on television has dropped tenfold over three decades (Breed & DeFoe, 1984). This pattern undoubtedly reflects emerging public attitudes toward smoking.

Use of illegal drugs is not mentioned in the NIMH Report. In this context, however, the government has occasionally tried (or thought about trying) to purge the environment of messages that are thought to encourage illicit drug use (Bonnie, 1981). One provision of the Model Drug Paraphernalia Act drafted by the Drug Enforcement Administration (reprinted in Corwin, 1981) specifically bans paraphernalia advertising: "It is unlawful for any person to place in any newspaper, magazine, handbill or other publication any advertisement, knowing, or under circumstances where one reasonably should know, that the purpose of the advertisement, in whole or in part, is to promote the sale of objects designed or intended for use as drug paraphernalia."

In 1973 the FCC threatened to revoke the licenses of radio stations whose lyrics were thought to encourage illicit drug use. In 1980 the National Advisory Council on Drug Abuse wrote to the Squibb Corporation to protest its marketing and advertising of a perfume called Opium on the ground that "the marketing campaign . . . tends to romanticize, glamorize, and encourage the use of illicit drugs."

It is probably impossible to establish empirically the attitudinal and behavioral effects of messages thought to portray drug use, cigarette smoking, and other disapproved behavior in a favorable light. By the same token, the efficacy of government efforts to eradicate or restrict the influence of these messages defies meaningful evaluation. That aside, it seems apparent that the impact of the marketing of "Opium" perfume and of the paraphernalia trade pales in comparison with that of the news and entertainment media, which portray and reflect the salience of drug use in Western culture. In short, a government intent on suppressing messages that encourage disapproved (even illicit) behavior has an impossible task in a society that values freedom of expression.

Direct Regulation of Risk-Taking Behavior

Attention has thus far been given to government efforts to reduce unsafe or unhealthy behavior by regulating the marketplace in order to reduce the opportunity for, or increase the price of, the undesired personal choices; and by regulating the flow of information in order to influence beliefs and attitudes about the behavior and thereby to encourage desired choices and discourage undesired ones. Obviously, the government can attempt to affect individual choice more directly by proscribing and punishing the undesired behavior or by withholding benefits or privileges to which the person would otherwise be entitled.

From a purely economic view of human motivation, the distinction between direct prohibition of the disapproved behavior and a market regulation that increases its price may seem artificial. By introducing the risk that a sanction may be imposed, a prohibition may be said to decrease the "expected value" to the individual of engaging in the disapproved behavior. Similarly, the social utility of the intervention rests, in both cases, on the assumption that the increase in its "cost" will reduce the "demand" for the behavior.

Although this analysis may have some explanatory power, I am inclined to think the psychology of deterrence is not so easily converted into an economic demand function. Moreover, when viewed from the perspective of Anglo-American legal theory, the two modes of intervention are fundamentally different. The distinction is that between coercion and inducement. While the individual is always "free" to make a legally prohibited choice if he is willing to pay the price, he is not "free" to do so in a normative sense.

As I mentioned at the outset, the distinction between coercion and inducement may be regarded as dispositive from a libertarian standpoint; a coercive intervention may be categorically objectionable regardless of the nature and severity of the pains inflicted on a person for making the prohibited choice. Although I do not regard the use of coercive intervention as categorically objectionable, I do believe the government bears a heavier burden of justifying such interventions than it does for other interventions. I also regard the nature and severity of the sanction as relevant in determining the weight of this burden. In the present context, for example, the distinction between criminal sanctions and "civil" sanctions is a critical one.

I have said that the distinction between coercion and inducement is fundamental. However, as I mentioned earlier, the distinction is not identical to the difference between regulatory and prohibitory devices. For example, a tax on "excess body weight" (a regulatory intervention that leaves the person legally "free" to act either way) would be more coercive (i.e., a more substantial affront to liberty) than a $50 fine for driving in excess of a posted speed limit (a prohibitory intervention that does *not* leave the person legally free to exceed the speed limit). Thus, what is significant about the category of interventions considered below is that the *mechanism* being employed is a coercive one. Whether this turns out to be objectionable will turn on an assessment of the benefits and costs, as weighted by libertarian values, and on whether utilitarian gains are trumped by superseding principles (such as the principle that the severity of the punishment should not be disproportionate to the seriousness of the offense).

For present purposes, I want to focus on the benefits that have been, or might be, achieved by proscribing risk-taking behavior. Obviously the costs of such interventions will vary according to the nature and severity of the sanctions threatened (and actually imposed) and according to the intensity of the enforcement effort, but I do not intend to focus here on the costs of the interventions. Instead, I will focus on what is known about the benefits—the deterrent effect—of these proscriptions.

Deterrent effects of legal prohibitions are most amenable to empirical investigation if the law is in transition. Natural experiments are possible if the legislature proscribes a previously lawful behavior (or *significantly* increases the severity of threatened sanctions) or, alternatively, if the legislature repeals (or *significantly* reduces) sanctions against previously proscribed behavior. Recent legislative activity in the areas of substance abuse and driver safety has provided a series of natural experiments that should be studied and incorporated into the general literature on deterrence.

I will review the available evidence on the effects of prohibitions in three behavioral contexts: (1) bans against possessing or using illicit drugs, against use of alcohol by persons who are underage, and against smoking cigarettes in prohibited locations; (2) requirements that motorcyclists wear helmets and that drivers wear seat belts; and (3) variations in penalties for driving while intoxicated.

POSSESSION OF ILLICIT DRUGS

What incremental contribution do sanctions for possession of illicit drugs and other consumption-related behavior, and their enforcement, make to the preventive effect already achieved by the proscriptions on nonmedical availability? What is known about the "deterrent" effect of possession laws?

The first thing to be said is "not much." Because possession of all controlled substances other than marijuana is a crime in every jurisdiction, there is no way of knowing whether use patterns would be significantly different if consumption-related behavior were not punishable as a crime. Variations clearly do exist among jurisdictions in the severity of the penalty threatened, the severity of the penalties actually imposed, and the likelihood that a detected offense will be prosecuted. Patterns of police behavior—and therefore the likelihood that offenses will be detected at all—undoubtedly differ from jurisdiction to jurisdiction. However, the degree to which these differences are perceived by the "at risk" population and therefore the degree to which they influence decisions to initiate or continue use of particular illicit drugs are virtual mysteries. There is considerable speculation about these matters (National Commission on Marihuana and Drug Abuse, 1973; Rosenthal, 1979), but very few investigators (Erickson, 1976; Johnson, Petersen, & Wells, 1977; Meier & Johnson, 1977) have attempted to tackle what is obviously a very complicated empirical question (Zimring & Hawkins, 1973).

The repeal of "criminal" sanctions for marijuana possession in eleven states between 1973 and 1978 provided an opportunity to investigate the deterrent effects of criminal sanctions for possession of this drug. Before 1965 all marijuana offenses, including "simple possession," were felonies under federal law and in most states. However, between 1965 and 1972 the entrenched opposition to marijuana use was exposed to public debate for the first time in its 50-year history (Bonnie & Whitebread, 1974). In response to the extraordinary explosion in marijuana consumption and the penetration of its use into the middle class, every state amended its penalties in some fashion between 1969 and 1972, the overall result being a massive downward shift in penalties for consumption-related offenses. Simple possession of less than one ounce was classified as a misdemeanor in all but eight states by the end of 1972 (Bonnie, 1980; Bonnie & Whitebread, 1974). In March of that year the publication of the report of the National Commission on Marihuana and

Drug Abuse, recommending decriminalization of consumption-related offenses (National Commission on Marijuana and Drug Abuse, 1972) marked the beginning of the "decriminalization" movement. During this period the states began to explore noncriminal approaches toward discouraging marijuana use.

In 1973 the National Conference of Commissioners on Uniform State Laws promulgated amendments to the Uniform Controlled Substances Act codifying the recommendations of the National Commission. Some form of decriminalization was endorsed during the same year by a variety of national organizations, including the American Bar Association and numerous state and local bar associations, the National Education Association, the Consumers Union, the National Council of Churches, the American Public Health Association, and the Governing Board of the American Medical Association. In 1973 Oregon became the first state to decriminalize possession of small amounts of marijuana. Over the next four years, ten additional states eliminated incarceration as a penalty for simple possession, usually substituting a $100 fine. Five of these states made possession a "civil" offense; in others it remains a criminal offense, but the law usually contains a provision for expunging criminal records after a specified period. In Alaska, because of a supreme court ruling in that state, possession by adults in the home for personal use is not an offense at all (Bonnie, 1977, 1980).

Although these eleven state laws share the common feature of having eliminated incarceration as a penalty for some consumption-related behavior, at least for first offenders, the reform statutes vary in significant respects. The conduct that has been "decriminalized" is not uniformly defined, and the reform jurisdictions also differ in their prescriptions of the residual sanctions that can still be imposed on persons who are apprehended for, and convicted of, "decriminalized" offenses (Bonnie, 1977, 1980). For present purposes, however, I will asume that the elimination of incarceration, and of the usual record consequences of a criminal conviction, is perceived as a significant reduction in the penalty—and therefore in the "cost" of being apprehended and "convicted" for the unlawful activity.

The question, of course, is whether, as a result of this change, fewer persons are "deterred" from initiating or continuing marijuana use or whether users use the drug more frequently than they would have under the previous legal regime. Or to put it another way, what is the marginal effect on aggregate consumption patterns of "criminal" penalties aginst consumption-related behavior as compared with noncriminal ones or no sanctions at all?

174

Several studies have compared the prevalence and patterns of consumption before and after decriminalization in decriminalized jurisdictions and in jurisdictions where the law has remained unchanged. Although the methodologies of these studies vary in strength (Cuskey, 1981), these data consistently show that there was no significant immediate change in consumption patterns after decriminalization and that consumption trends are essentially the same in decriminalized and nondecriminalized jurisdictions (Bonnie, 1981; Maloff, 1982; National Governor's Conference, 1977). Of course, the issue merits more systematic research; but from the standpoint of the "deterrent" process, the available data strongly suggest that little incremental preventive effect is attributable to the extant "criminal" misdemeanor sanctions, which are so sporadically applied, when compared with "civil" penalties. On the other hand, it is possible that changes in the law do influence attitudes and beliefs about the behavior and that these "symbolic" effects can be assessed only over a longer period. This issue will be addressed below.

DRINKING BY PERSONS WHO ARE UNDERAGE

The issues raised by penalties for underage consumers of alcohol (or tobacco or other substances not legitimately available to them) are substantially the same as those presented by bans against personal possession of marijuana. The only difference is that the ban on marijuana distribution aims to restrict access for everyone, not only those below the minimum age; however, since the prevalence of marijuana use is especially high among adolescents and young adults, the analysis would be the same.

State laws now vary on whether bans on distribution to underage consumers are supplemented by a proscription that penalizes the consumer for purchase, possession, or use (Mosher, 1977), and there are no studies on the preventive effect of such proscriptions. I suspect, however, that there is hardly any marginal effect introduced by the user penalty, beyond what is attributable to the access ban itself. Such an effect seems especially unlikely if, as appears to be the case, the underage user is hardly ever prosecuted.

I recommend that researchers who investigate the impact of changes in marijuana penalties focus particularly on adolescents' knowledge of the law and their perceptions about its enforcement; in so doing they should also assess, for comparative purposes, consumption of alcohol and tobacco, together with perceptions about the law and its enforcement on these subjects as well.

PUBLIC SMOKING

I suspect that the main behavioral effect of bans on possession and use of illicit drugs, and on underage consumption of alcohol is to affect the conditions of use—to drive the behavior into private locations. Of course some proscriptions concerning legitimately available substances apply only in public—for example, drinking alcohol in public or smoking in designated places of public accommodation.

These offenses are visible and readily detected. So long as the legal norm is widely supported, the threat of reproach, and possibly of legal enforcement, is likely to have a discernible effect on behavior. Thus, assuming that smokers comply, in the aggregate, with public smoking bans, we might say the law is an effective mode of behavioral regulation. But we might also ask the next question: Aside from reducing the discomfort of nonsmokers, what contribution do these bans make to the public health? Do smokers smoke less because they are not permitted to smoke everywhere? Do nonsmokers suffer less small-airways dysfunction than they would in the absence of such bans (Lenfant & Lin, 1980; White & Froeb, 1980)? To these questions, of course, we do not yet have answers. But the first, at least, should be susceptible to investigation.

MOTORCYCLE HELMET LAWS

Laws requiring motorcyclists to wear helmets represent a clear case of effective deterrence. In 1966 only three states had such laws. In 1967, following passage of the Highway Safety Act of 1966, the Department of Transportation required states to enact them in order to qualify for federal funding for highway safety programs and highway construction. By 1975 all but three states had done so. Although the legislatures typically prescribed relatively light fines, the probability that the fine would be imposed for a violation was unusually high. Even though helmet use may be characterized as an "expressive" behavior (and therefore may be less susceptible to deterrence than "instrumental" behavior), it is a *public* behavior, and therefore violation of the law is easily detected. Moreover, there is no reason to suspect that police would be unwilling to enforce the law. Not surprisingly, in states with laws applicable to all motorcyclists, usage rates were over 95% (Watson, Zador, & Wilks, 1980). As a result, motorcyclist fatalities declined an average of 30% in states with mandatory helmet laws as compared with unchanged fatality rates in states without the laws (Robertson, 1977).

After Congress repealed the federal funding penalty in 1975, 28 states repealed or weakened their mandatory helmet laws within the next four years. Studies conducted on the effect of the repeal showed that helmet use declined, on the average, to about 50% (Watson et al., 1980).[16] Moreover, the usage rate among motorcyclists involved in accidents is even lower than in the motorcyclist population as a whole, suggesting that the highest-risk cyclists are the least likely to wear helmets voluntarily. In Indiana, for example, the overall usage rate was 95% before repeal; however, the usage rate among accident-involved cyclists, which was 76% before repeal, dropped to 37% immediately afterward (Scholten & Glover, 1984).

Watson, Zador, and Wilks (1980, 1981) assessed the effect on motorcyclist fatalities of 26 instances of complete repeal of or weakening of helmet use laws. They concluded that the change in the laws coincided with an increase of 38% in fatality rates. Similarly, a study of national fatality data conducted by the National Highway Traffic and Safety Administration (1980) showed that the rate of motorcyclist fatalities per 10,000 motorcycles dropped from 12.7 to 8.1 (a 36% drop) during 1966–1969 (when 40 states adopted helmet laws) and increased from 6.7 to 9.7 (a 31% increase) between 1976 and 1979 when 27 states repealed or weakened the laws. Hartunian, Smart, Willemain, and Zador (1983) calculated that about 24% of the motorcyclist deaths occurring in 1980 in the 28 states with repealed or weakened laws would not have occurred had the laws remained unchanged.

Similar findings emerge in studies of serious head injuries. In Iowa, for example, the incidence of head injuries attributed to motorcycle or moped accidents, which was 39% before the mandatory use law, fell to 23.5% while the law was in effect. After repeal it returned to 40% (Scholten & Glover, 1984).

As I noted earlier, helmet use appears to be lowest among the highest-risk group of motorcyclists, especially among the young.

16. Muller (1980) estimated that aggregate helmet use among motorcyclists declined about 51% following repeal.

Indeed, even though many of the current laws continue to require persons under 18 to wear helmets, only half of young cyclists do so (Williams, Ginsburg, & Burchman, 1977). There is an important lesson to legislators about deterrence here. By making the helmet law applicable *only* to the most vulnerable population, legislators actually *reduced* its deterrent effect. This is probably because the partial coverage of the law reduces the likelihood that the police will stop a helmetless driver and therefore reduces the likelihood of detection. Perceiving this, the young cyclists reduce their level of compliance.[17]

SEAT-BELT LAWS

Seat belts, when worn, reduce the likelihood of occupant death in a crash by about 50%. However, roadside observational surveys in the United States indicate that at any given time 90% of passenger car occupants travel unbelted (Opinion Research Corporation, 1980). In fact, manual belt usage rates have actually declined from 20% in the early 1970s to about 10% in 1980. Moreover, usage rates are even lower in the highest-risk groups—teenagers and people under the influence of alcohol (Williams et al., 1983).

The data presented earlier concerning the impact of media campaigns suggest that informational efforts are not likely to increase seat-belt use. The question now on the public agenda is whether a law requiring occupants to belt up will make any difference. We will soon have a chance to find out. Five states (New York, New Jersey, Illinois, Michigan, and Missouri) already have enacted such laws, and other states can be expected to follow suit. (They will be under pressure to do so by the automobile industry which will be required by a United States Department of Transportation ruling [1984] to equip all new cars with airbags or automatic seat belts unless states containing two-thirds of the population have accepted mandatory seat-belt laws by 1989.)

Published studies have not yet appeared on compliance rates in the states that have adopted mandatory seat-belt laws.[18] However,

17. It is also possible that the likelihood of reactance, through protest behavior, is increased by the *selective* imposition of the ban on the liberty of adolescents.

18. Preliminary survey data in four areas of metropolitan New York indicate that between 63% and 76% of the drivers were belted during the first month after the law became effective (Pressley, 1985).

data are available on the impact of mandatory seat-belt laws in 30 countries that have adopted them within the past decade (Graham & Henrion, 1984). Most of them have succeeded in raising usage to at least 50%. Usage in Great Britain apparently exceeds 90%, and Australia has sustained usage in the 70% to 80% range. It should be noted, however, that usage in some countries, such as Japan, is only slightly higher than it was before the laws.

The Canadian experience is perhaps most pertinent to the United States. Four provinces (Ontario, Quebec, British Columbia, and Saskatchewan) adopted mandatory seat-belt laws in 1976 and 1977. Summarizing the available reports in these four provinces, Jonah and Lawson (1984) indicate that belt use increased from about 20% to about 70% immediately after passage of the laws and eventually dropped to about 50% over the next several years. In 1982 New-foundland became the fifth Canadian province to adopt a seat-belt law. Before-and-after observations indicated that belt usage in New-foundland increased from 16% to 77%. Usage in a "control" jurisdiction (Nova Scotia) changed only slightly, from 16% to 19% (Lund & Zador, 1984).

In sum, the international experience suggests that mandatory seat-belt laws are likely to increase usage in this country to at least 50% (Graham & Henrion, 1984). Assuming that this turns out to be an accurate prediction, what would we learn about deterrence? What is the principal finding? Is it the increase in seat-belt use (which, after all, would be five times higher than the current level), or is it the incomplete compliance (one out of two drivers will still fail to wear a belt)?

What we learn is that passage of mandatory seat-belt laws has a significant behavioral impact, but available data do not tell us why. In the absence of studies comparing compliance under different conditions of enforcement, I would speculate that the immediate increase in belt usage is primarily attributable to the declarative or educative effects of the prohibition, to be discussed in the next section, rather than to its deterrent effects (i.e., the threat of punishment).[19] The remaining half of the driver population—that part that does not respond to the declarative effects of the law—represents the population for whom *deterrence*, per se, is relevant. The question is whether, and how much, the level of compliance in *this* group can

19. Hakkert, Zaidel, and Sarelle (1981) offered a similar interpretation of their finding that belt use in Israel increased from 6% to 70% following passage of a seat-belt law.

be affected by variations in the nature of the penalty or the level of enforcement.

I suspect that the level of compliance can be increased by a vigorous enforcement effort but that it will hit a ceiling and that the noncompliant group will include the high-risk drivers. As was the case with motorcyclists, belt-use rates among crash-involved drivers in other countries are substantially lower than usage rates observed in the general driver population. Moreover, research in Canada, Denmark, and West Germany shows that the highest-risk groups (e.g., teenagers and drinkers) are more likely to be unbelted in crashes than typical motorists. It also appears that belt-use rates are lower at night, when detection is less likely and when most crashes occur (Williams & O'Neill, 1979).

DRIVING WHILE INTOXICATED

Aside from the impact of capital punishment on homicide, the topic most often studied in deterrence is the efficacy of various legal measures in reducing drunk driving. The already voluminous literature will be expanding in the next few years as evaluations are reported on the current generation of "get tough" measures. A comprehensive review of the current state of knowledge appears in Ross (1982, 1984). For present purposes, I want only to summarize a few basic points and call attention to one recent development that merits further investigation.

Severity of punishment. First, interventions designed to increase the severity of punishment, without a major effort to increase the (perceived) likelihood of its being applied, have not had a demonstrable influence on the prevalence of drunk driving or, deriv-atively, on alcohol-related crashes and fatalities (Ross, 1984). For example, a comparison of fatality rates, over time, in Chicago and Milwaukee indicated that no significant behavioral change occurred as a result of a "crackdown" on drunk drivers in Chicago in 1971, when highly publicized seven-day jail sentences were imposed (Robertson, Rich, & Ross, 1973).

Andenaes has consistently argued that mandatory imprisonment for driving while intoxicated (DWI) in Norway and Sweden has a preventive effect on driving behavior in Norway not apparent in other countries with less severe penalties (Andenaes 1975). However, Ross has analyzed available data over the period before and after the harsher laws were introduced and has concluded that "the claim that the Norwegian and Swedish laws deter drinking and driving rest at this time upon inadequate and scientifically unacceptable evidence" (Ross, 1975). The debate has been carried on in a recent volume of the Scandinavian Studies in Criminology (Hauge, 1978).[20]

It seems likely that evaluations of the impact of the current generation of mandatory jail terms will produce similar findings (Ross, 1985).

The generally accepted interpretation of these findings is that the population of drinking drivers is probably relatively insensitive to changes in the severity of a punishment that is perceived as highly unlikely to be imposed in the first place. Jones and Jocelyn (1978) have estimated the risk of arrest for DWI to be one in two thousand. It may be that drinking drivers accurately regard the risk of detection as low and therefore tend to discount it anyway, a tendency not affected at all by the magnitude of the punishment. Further, it appears that a substantial portion of drinking drivers (and certainly the *most* impaired) are people who are least likely to be influenced by the deterrent threat (e.g., young drivers and people who have been arrested before).

Probability of punishment. What, then, of the possibility that the deterrent efficacy of the drunk driving laws can be enhanced by increasing the perceived probability of enforcement—at least to the point where it crosses the threshold of negligibility? Existing research does not furnish any examples of programs that have effected a long-lasting increase in the perceived probability of punishment for drunk driving. Instead, studies of enforcement crackdowns have repeatedly shown that a highly publicized enforcement effort that increases the perceived probability of detection—whether or not it is combined with an increase in the severity of the punishment (e.g., mandatory jail sentences)—can lead to a significant *immediate* impact on driving behavior, but that these

20. If drinking and driving occurs less frequently in the Scandinavian countries than in others, which remains unproved, it is entirely possible that the harsher penalties are an effect, rather than a cause, of the public's attitudes; in this sense obedience to the DWI laws may reflect the same comparatively disapproving attitudes toward the behavior that led the legislature to adopt the more stringent laws. The deterrent explanation seems an unlikely one in the absense of evidence that either the perceived or the objective risk of apprehension is high.

effects tend to disappear with the passage of time (Jones & Jocelyn, 1978; Robertson, 1977; Ross, 1973, 1984).

A recent report (Voas & Hause, 1984) of an enforcement crackdown in Stockton, California, between January 1976 and June 1979 is illustrative. With support from federal Alcohol Safety Action Project (ASAP) funding, the Stockton police substantially increased drunk driving patrol on weekend nights. As a result, the risk of apprehension was raised to an estimated likelihood of one in three hundred. According to Ross (1985), the intensity of the Stockton patrol was among the greatest ever experienced in the world, and the duration of the crackdown was the longest ever reported in the literature. Roadside surveys indicated that the proportion of alcohol-impaired drivers declined from 8.8% during the baseline period to 5% after two years of the crackdown. In addition, weekend nighttime crashes (which are a good index of alcohol-impaired driving) were reduced by an average of 15% during the project period. However, according to Ross (1985), the immediate behavioral impact does not appear to have survived the termination of the project.

Administrative license suspension. The recent search for drunk-driving countermeasures has produced one interesting development—administrative license suspension—that merits continuing investigation. License suspension has traditionally been a potential consequence of a drunk-driving conviction, although in the United States this sanction could be regarded as a remote possibility. Under the administrative suspension procedure, police are empowered to revoke the license on the spot if the driver has an "illegal" BAC or refuses to take the test. Although the driver is given a temporary license pending a hearing, the license is not likely to be returned. The procedure was first introduced in Minnesota in 1976 and had been adopted in 17 other states by 1983.

Although the administrative license suspension does not affect the probability of detection, the punishment itself is imposed more certainly and more swiftly. In addition, drivers may regard the punishment as more severe than a fine or even a few days in jail. Although no definitive investigation has yet been reported, some preliminary signs suggest that the policy may have had some effect on some drivers (Ross, 1985).

SUMMARY

One of the characteristic features of most of the risky behaviors targeted by paternalist legal interventions is that they are not exposed to public view. The risk of detection for legally prohibited behavior—driving while intoxicated, possessing or using marijuana (or alcohol by underage consumers), and driving without wearing seat belts—is slight, so slight that it is likely to be discounted by most of the target population, especially those most inclined to engage in the risky behavior. In this context the deterrent efficacy of legal prohibitions seems to depend on whether the perceived risk of detection reaches a psychologically critical threshold level, regardless of the severity of the threatened sanction.

This view of deterrence theory is strongly confirmed by the available data on the effect of drunk driving prohibitions, which suggest that the overall level of compliance with the legally prescribed norm is achieved largely by nonlegal factors rather than the threat of legal punishment. Similarly, the data on marijuana consumption in decriminalized jurisdictions and on underage alcohol use suggest that the threat of sanctions against the consumer generates little preventive effect beyond that achieved by the prohibition against legal access. Finally, although the rate of seat-belt use rises significantly in response to the imposition of a legal requirement, I am inclined to attribute this response to the educative and symbolic effects of the law rather than its deterrent effects.

Some paternalistic legal interventions prohibit conduct that is exposed to public view. Motorcycle helmet laws represent the prototypical case. Nearly universal compliance with these laws is clearly attributable to the deterrent threat, and public smoking bans are presumably equally efficacious. An important lesson can be learned from the experience with incomplete age-linked helmet laws; because the enforcement costs are increased (the police must determine age of the helmetless motorcyclist), the risk of detection is accordingly reduced.

One final point should be noted. Violations of helmet laws and public smoking bans are typically punishable as minor noncriminal infractions. These penalties are not regarded as excessive either by the general public or by the police. Experience wth criminal penalties for marijuana users and with mandatory jail terms for drunk driving suggests that any effort to increase the deterrent effect by raising the severity of the penalty is likely to fail—and generate greater costs—if the penalty is regarded as unduly harsh by those who must enforce it.

Declarative Aspects of Legal Regulation

Government sends messages by its actions as well as its words. By declaring conduct illegal or by using any of the other instruments of legal intervention described earlier in this paper, the government expresses and formalizes social norms. Viewed from this perspective, the law is perhaps the most potent form of "government speech."

To the extent that citizens customarily defer to and respect the law, awareness of these formal expressions of illegality can serve an "educative" or didactic role. Where the law imposes a *criminal* sanction, prohibition also radiates a "moralizing" effect associated with the social meaning of this potent legal sanction (Andenaes, 1974; Zimring & Hawkins, 1973). Where the prohibited behavior is widely disapproved, the law serves mainly to reinforce and perpetuate this attitude. However, the respect or deference the law attracts also makes it possible for a legal intervention to affect public attitudes that are not already deeply rooted or are in transition. This emphasizes the law's affirmative role as an integrated strand of the socialization process rather than something apart from and superimposed on it. It also suggests that the expressions of the law, over time, may affect attitudes about right or wrong and about desirable and undesirable conduct and ultimately—in this indirect way—may influence behavior.

Arguments drawing on the declarative effects of legal regulation are rather routinely employed by proponents of restrictive controls over availability and consumption of alcohol, tobacco, and other drugs. Criminal sanctions against "simple possession" of controlled substances are frequently regarded as indispensable symbols of social disapproval (National Commission on Marihuana and Drug Abuse, 1973). Moreover, graded or stratified penalty schemes, which punish possession of "more harmful" drugs more severely than possession of "less harmful" drugs, are generally regarded as necessary devices for expressing and communicating the relative seriousness of these transgressions even though there may be no reason to believe that the threat of more severe sanctions exerts a significantly greater deterrent effect than the lesser penalties would.

Declarative uses of criminal sanctions have been addressed in some depth in the legal literature (Andenaes, 1974; Zimring & Hawkins, 1973). A critical issue is whether criminal prosecution and punishment of violators of the prohibition can be justified by purely declarative objectives; moreover, enforcement generates costs that may exceed the symbolic benefits achieved by reinforcing the declaration of disapproval. These concerns about legitimacy and cost are mitigated, though not erased, by "civil" or noncriminal penalties of the type usually used in connection with public smoking bans or possession of marijuana in "decriminalized" jurisdictions.

Proponents of such civil penalties ordinarily assume that society must make the conduct "illegal" in order to convey the desired message, whether or not there is any evidence of significant "direct" instrumental effects in suppressing the target behavior. This has been especially apparent in the debate about marijuana decriminalization (Bonnie, 1977, 1980). Similarly, public smoking bans may reduce *public* smoking and thereby protect nonsmokers from the odor and possible ill effect of tobacco smoke (Lenfant & Lin, 1980; White & Froeb, 1980), but many of the proponents assert that one of their goals is also to indicate "that society does not condone smoking as an acceptable social habit" (Christoffel & Stein, 1979). Presumably they hope that unfavorable attitudes will lead, over time, to reduced tobacco consumption. Similarly, I am convinced that the only conceivable instrumental effect of antiparaphernalia laws is to reinforce attitudes unfavorable to recreational drug use and that their proponents would seek such bans even if it were proved that the sale or promotion of paraphernalia would not actually be curtailed.

Statements of legal rules can serve an educative role even if they do not penalize the undesired behavior. Minimum drinking-age laws (which prohibit distribution to persons who are underage) provide a good example, because they denote the norm even if they do not penalize the youthful drinker. Similarly, bans on alcohol or tobacco advertising might be enacted to erase a possible symbol of social approval even though the proponents do not believe that these bans will reduce consumption in any direct way.

Despite the frequent reliance on symbolism in the formulation of legal controls over alcohol, tobacco, and other drugs, virtually nothing is actually known about the validity of the underlying hypothesis. Do legal declarations of disapproval have any independent effect on the development of attitudes and beliefs about the use of these substances? As I mentioned earlier, the task of determining whether these declarative effects actually occur is notoriously difficult because of the need to isolate them from other influences on attitudes and, ultimately, on behavior. It is nonetheless surprising how little research has been conducted in the area. Professors Melton and Saks address the declarative effects of legal regulation in some depth elsewhere in this volume, so I will not dwell on them here. Let me simply call your attention to two contexts in which I think the declarative effects of a legal regulation *can* be empirically demonstrated.

SEAT-BELT LAWS

As I suggested earlier, mandatory seat-belt laws represent a convincing illustration of the declarative effect of a legal prohibition. Based on the Canadian experience, which I expect to be replicated in this country, the mere declaration of illegality significantly increases seat-belt use practically overnight. We *know* that 40% of the driving population who did not wear seat belts before the law was passed, and were not persuaded by educational efforts, began to do so in immediate response to the law. Although it is conceivable that this behavioral response was due to a fear of punishment and will erode over time, I do not find this a plausible explanation. Instead, the law sent a formal message that "failing to wear a seat belt is unreasonably risky, and you should get in the habit of wearing one." When the law was used as the medium of communication, half of the population listened.[21]

CHILD RESTRAINTS

Every state now appears to require drivers transporting children under a designated age (usually 4) to restrain them in a child safety device. Although data have been reported on the effect of laws in Rhode Island (Williams & Wells, 1981b) and California (Guerin & Mackinnon, 1985), the most extensive research has been conducted in Tennessee, which enacted the first such legislation in 1978. Observational studies have indicated that the proportion of children wearing child restraints has gradually increased since the Tennes-

---

21. Hakkert, Zaidel, and Sarelle (1981) suggest that the level of compliance is attributable to a cluster of declarative effects, including enhanced appreciation of the risk and respect for law.

see law was passed, but that compliance is still relatively low: usage has risen from 9% before the law to 16% after the first year and to 29% in the third year. If the parent was driving (as was the case 79% of the time), 34% of the children were restrained, compared with 11% of those being transported by persons other than parents, to whom the law does not apply (Williams, 1979; Williams & Wells, 1981a).

It appears likely that usage is somewhat higher in high-speed interurban traffic than in the slow-moving local traffic where these observational studies have been conducted. A study of state police accident reports in Tennessee indicated that 48% of the children being transported in accident-involved vehicles in 1983 were restrained (Decker, Dewey, Hutcheson, & Scheffner, 1984). Presumably this is a conservative estimate of usage in high-speed traffic, since accident-involved vehicles are likely to involve a disproportionate number of the least risk-conscious drivers.

Violation of a child-restraint law is likely to be somewhat more easily detected than violation of a seat-belt law; however, the probability of detection still appears to be low. Moreover, the prescribed fines are slight (ranging from $2 to $10 in Tennessee, for example). In these circumstances, the increase in usage does not seem attributable to the deterrent effect of the law. As with seat-belt laws, I am inclined to attribute the behavioral change to the declarative and educative effects of the legal change: The law sent the message that having a child unrestrained is both hazardous and a breach of parental duty. I would expect a continuing gradual increase in child restraint use over a period of years.[22]

SUMMARY

Although legal theorists (for example, Andenaes, 1974) have long emphasized the importance of what I have referred to as the declara-

22. We should not overlook the opportunity for *individual* prevention presented by child-restraint laws. As is so often the case with paternalist interventions, the state's ultimate behavioral aim in this context is not clouded by punitive or retributive goals; the only goal is to get parents to protect their children. In these circumstances, the most sensible thing to do after detection of a violation would be to use the threatened sanction as leverage to induce the person to purchase or install the safety device. According to Decker et al. (1984), this is precisely what has been done in Tennessee: Persons cited for violations are offered the loan of a car seat. This seat is reclaimed at the scheduled hearing if the defendant offers proof that he or she has purchased one.

tive effects of legal regulation, there has been little empirical investigation of those effects, especially when compared with the literature on deterrence. One of the methodological difficulties in exploring this issue is ascertaining whether any observed behavioral change is attributable to deterrent or declarative effects. However, this problem can be overcome, it seems to me, in two contexts: where the legal intervention imposes no direct constraint on the behavior that the law seeks to minimize (as is the case, for example, with bans on distribution, but not possession, of pornographic material); and where the prohibited behavior is not exposed to public view and is therefore not susceptible to a significant deterrent threat. Seat-belt and child-restraint laws satisfy this second condition, and I think declarative effects can be demonstrated in both cases.

It should also be noted that the declarative effects of legal rules can be brought within the framework of behaviorist theory, at least up to a point. According to Skinner (1969), rules tend to bring remote consequences into play for behavior that does not have immediate aversive consequences:

> Consequences which have a negligible effect in shaping behavior may yield important actuarial rules. Few people drive a car at a moderate speed and keep their seat belts fastened because they have actually avoided or escaped from serious accidents by doing so. Rules derived from contingencies affecting large numbers of people bring these consequences to bear upon the individual. Ethical and legal consequences work synergistically with the natural consequences which by themselves are ineffective. (p. 168)

In terms of the decision-making model used in this paper, I think the aversive consequences associated with violation of the rule (which are also fairly remote) are less important than its educative effect in bringing the remote consequences of the risky behavior into play.

Incentives for Reducing Risk

In keeping with the theme of this symposium, my emphasis has been on the efficacy of law as a behavioral instrument. For this purpose, I have focused on the idea of law as *constraint*. However, to ensure that my earlier observations are kept in proper perspective, I want to call your attention to what is known about the utility of *incentives* to encourage healthy or safe behavior. Although the scientific literature is limited, some reports suggest that incentive schemes may be comparatively more efficacious than the legal interventions thus far reviewed as devices for achieving paternalist policies.

There are three contexts in which paternalist policies might be implemented through incentive schemes. First, in its role as sovereign, the government may use established regulatory mechanisms, such as licensing, to generate incentives for risk-reducing behavior for the licensed population. Second, employers (whether private or public) can use incentive systems to encourage safe or healthy behavior among employees. Finally, insurers (whether public or private) can use the pricing or coverage of its policies to generate incentives for risk-reducing conduct among the insured population.

LICENSING

Government's licensing authority provides one context in which the state, acting as sovereign, is in a position to manipulate incentives and disincentives. Although the threat of license revocation has often been employed as an instrument of general deterrence,[23] licensing systems have not often been used to generate incentives for safe driving. The one reported exception is an experiment conducted by the California Division of Highways in the early 1970s. According to Wilde (1982, 1985), the Division of Highways mailed letters to 9,971 drivers who had had collisions or violations in the previous year informing them that they would receive a free 12-month extension of their driver's licenses if they had a clear record during the forthcoming year. In addition to the financial incentive (which amounted only to a few dollars), the extension also deferred the obligation to retake the written part of the licensing examination. To evaluate the impact of the program, the Highways Division obtained data on accident involvement not only for the experimental group but also for a control group of 9,976 drivers who had not been offered the incentive.

The program had promising results. In the first follow-up year,

23. The revocation of the license also serves as an instrument of individual prevention, either as incapacitation or intimidation.

drivers in the experimental group had significantly fewer accidents than the control group. The difference was especially significant in the subgroup whose licenses were scheduled to expire within the year following the receipt of the letter; in this group the accident rate was 22% lower than in the appropriate control group. Moreover, the drivers who actually earned the bonus after one year had 33% fewer accidents in the second year than did the controls, suggesting that the beneficial effect on driver behavior may have persisted beyond the period during which it was directly influenced by the incentive program.

EMPLOYMENT

Rewards and punishment are more susceptible to manipulation in the employment setting than among the public at large. By distributing bonuses, promotions, special privileges, and vacations, employers are in a position to implement incentive systems to encourage health-promoting or risk-reducing employee behavior.

Although employers often use incentive systems to promote occupational safety by their employees, there is little experimental evidence regarding their efficacy (Robertson, 1983, p. 107). In one of the few reported studies, Wilde (1985) has described a successful driver safety incentive program operated for 25 years by the German branch of Kraft Foods. The company's fleet of truck and van drivers were told in 1957 that they would receive a bonus of $150 for every half-year of driving without "culpable accidents" (i.e., accidents in which they were judged to be at fault). In 1981 the rate of culpable accidents per 100,000 km was only 14% of the 1956 rate. In addition, the frequency of all accidents (i.e., whether culpable or not) was reduced to 25% of the 1956 rate. Finally, accident costs dropped even more steeply than accident frequency, tending to suggest that the program was particularly successful in reducing the occurrence of more serious accidents.

Employer-sponsored health promotion programs have mushroomed in recent years (Warner & Murt, 1984), but only a small number of them have utilized incentives to encourage healthy behavior. I will mention two. Employees of the Speedcall Corporation receive a bonus of $7 per week if they do not smoke on the job. Within one month of the initiation of the program, the percentage of employees smoking on the job dropped from 67% to 43%. During a four-year follow-up, the percentage fell as low as 13%, and at the most recent reported assessment it stood at 20%.[24]

The efficacy of combining incentives and peer pressure is illustrated by a seat-belt program developed by the General Motors Technical Laboratories. Under this program, employees are encouraged to sign pledge cards promising to use seat belts; actual usage rates are monitored at the entrance to the plant. If the *group* of employees exceeds the specified usage goal, sweepstakes prizes (money and paid vacations) are awarded to winners drawn from among the pledge-card signers. When the program was initiated in the fall of 1982, belt usage increased from 45% to 70% within six weeks, exceeding the group goal of 60%. When a second sweepstakes program was initiated, a goal of 75% was announced, with a 10-day vacation in Hawaii as the major prize. The proportion of employees signing pledge cards increased to 85%, and within 12 weeks 82% of the signers were using their seat belts.

INSURANCE

Insurance, by definition, spreads risk. As a result, many insurance schemes tend to reduce the incentive for risk-reducing conduct that the insured would have if he had to bear the full loss of an injury or disease related to his own conduct. In the insurance literature, this incentive-reducing effect is called "moral hazard." In order to retain economic incentives for healthy or safe conduct, insurers sometimes use variations in *pricing* or *coverage*.

Pricing. Experience rating is widely used in pricing automobile insurance, but there is no evidence that the availability of reduced premiums has inspired safer driving and reduced accident rates. In fact, insurers appear to use experience rating primarily as a marketing strategy, appealing to the consumers' sense of fair payment, rather than as a device to encourage safe driving. The factors typically taken into account in automobile risk rating (e.g., age, sex, area of residence) represent broad categories of risk experience rather than any particular driver's own behavior; as a result, they do

---

24. The success of the Speedcall program may reflect the utility of repeated reinforcement through ongoing periodic cash bonuses as opposed to one-time reinforcement through a single lump sum. It is also likely that the incentive program galvanized peer pressure to help modify attitudes toward smoking behavior.

not generate incentives for safe driving. Although most auto insurers impose a surcharge on drivers who have been involved in an accident within the previous three years, there is no evidence that awareness of the "cost" of having an accident (in terms of increased premiums) actually motivates people to drive more safely. (What it may do is affect accident reporting.)

Premiums for automobile insurance also could be varied to take into account the reduced risk of death and serious injury associated with use of protective devices. Arnould and Grabowski (1981) report that several insurers now offer discounts of up to 30% on premiums for medical or personal injury protection for people who own cars equipped with passive restraints. It is conceivable that similar discounts could be offered to those who promise to use manual seat belts, but the difficulty of monitoring to ensure compliance with such a promise is obvious.

Even if such premium discounts were widely available, it is not clear that they would have a significant influence on driver behavior. Cars equipped with passive seat belts or air bags would cost an extra $100 and $600 respectively. If the annual insurance premium were reduced by $20, it is difficult to know whether car buyers who would not otherwise purchase cars equipped with passive restraints would do so (Arnould & Grabowski, 1981; Kunreuther, 1984). To the extent that car purchasers have a choice, the cumulative reduction of premiums over the life of the car may not offset the out-of-pocket cost of the higher price, especially if consumers organize their mental accounts according to short-term balance sheets (Kahneman & Tversky, 1984).

Proponents of paternalist initiatives have frequently proposed reduced premiums for life and health insurance as a mechanism for encouraging people to stop smoking, lose weight, reduce cholesterol intake, or exercise (Brasley, 1980; Fielding, 1977; Greenwald, 1981; Haggerty, 1977; Stokes, 1983). Although nonsmoker discounts are relatively commonplace in individual life insurance policies, there is no evidence that such premium differentials have induced smokers to quit. In fact, it is doubtful that premium reductions will have much incentive effect unless they are substantial.

Even if premium risk rating would not have a significant impact on the incentive structure for risk reduction, the promise of *refunds for healthy or safe results* may be more effective. An innovative incentive program for driver safety being considered by the Canadian province of Saskatchewan has been described by Wilde (1985). Under the program, not yet implemented, all licensed drivers in specified age groups (especially teenagers) residing in selected communities will be informed that the Saskatchewan government's insurance underwriter expects to pay out, for example, three million dollars during the coming year in claims arising from accidents involving drivers within the particular age group and that any reduction in that amount will be divided among those who have no accidents. As in the General Motors seat-belt program, the amount of the reward would depend not only upon the individual's performance but also upon the performance of the person's peer group. This program therefore aims to generate peer pressure as well as individual motivation for safe driving. Also, it should be noted that the payoff is made each year, in accordance with the idea that incentives are most effective if the reward is relatively immediate rather than remote in time.

If this program is implemented, it merits careful study. From the standpoint of behavioral change, two points should be emphasized. First, it aims to remedy one of the possible causes of "market failure" in the context of individual health and safety—the distortions in the market incentives for safety protection arising from widespread public and private insurance coverage for medical costs of injury and disease. To the extent that individuals do not have to bear the full costs of the consequences of unhealthy or unsafe behavior, their incentive for risk reduction may be lessened. The Saskatchewan program aims to utilize the insurance system itself to provide an incentive for risk reduction. Second, as Wilde has pointed out, the program offers incentives for *results*, thereby aiming to generate a desire to be safe. It reflects Wilde's own view that "lasting accident reductions cannot be achieved by merely confronting road users with more opportunities to be safe, but that safety can be more permanently enhanced by measures that increase people's desire to have no accident" (Wilde, 1982, 1985).[25]

A similar plan could be implemented by private automobile insurers or other accident insurers. Conceptually, the notion of using premium refunds as an incentive can be extended to health insurance. In fact, Kunreuther (1984) reports that the Mendocino County (California) Office of Education has used this approach. Each em-

25. The outcome measure would be distorted to the extent that drivers participating in the program refrain from reporting accidents. However, this would not be likely in the case of any serious accident, and even for minor repairs the reporting disincentive is probably no greater under the proposed program than under an insurance policy that includes a deductible or is experience rated.

ployee was covered by a health insurance policy with a relatively large deductible amount of $500. However, the county set aside $500 to cover the deductible for each employee, and employees were permitted to keep whatever was left over at the end of the year. Kunreuther reports that expenditures on medical care were substantially reduced during the first four years of the program. The problem, of course, is knowing whether the reduced expenditures reflect changes in health and safety behavior or merely changes in utilization of health services or changes in claim-filing behavior.

Coverage. Proposals have also been made to reduce or deny insurance *coverage* to persons whose failure to reduce risk caused the injury or disease for which they seek reimbursement. Fielding (1977) has suggested that a driver with an elevated blood-alcohol level at the time of an accident should recover only a part of his losses. Kunreuther (1984) reports that under Austrian law, hospital payments for treatment of injuries suffered in an auto accident are conditioned on the victim's having worn a seat belt. Warner (1983, p. 52) alludes favorably to this idea. One can imagine extending the argument to the reduction of payments for medical expenses or disability benefits for heart disease or cancer attributable to smoking; but I doubt that even the most ardent proponent of life-style modification paternalism would insist that the smoker bear the full cost of his foolishness.

Incentives and Disincentives

It can be seen that the search for incentives for risk reduction can easily shade into the use of disincentives; and a threatened "disincentive" may be functionally indistinguishable from a threatened "punishment." There is a fundamental difference between an employer policy of offering bonuses or vacations (to those who wear seat belts or refrain from smoking) and a policy of withholding salary or benefits to which the employee would otherwise be entitled (from those who smoke or drive unbelted). This is not to say that disincentives (or punishments) should never be used, but only that they implicate countervailing values and can be more coercive than the direct state-imposed prohibitions (on driving without seat belts or smoking in public places) that have received so much attention.

Moreover, there is another important difference between systems of incentives and of disincentives. One can be relatively confident that employers will not adopt or retain incentive systems unless they are proved cost effective—that is, unless the cost of injuries avoided exceeds the cost of the incentive. In contrast, when the employer uses disincentives, one has less confidence that the employer's balance sheet will reflect the costs of the program (i.e., that they will be "internalized" in an economic sense), because the loss falls initially on those individual employees who fail to respond to the threat. Although the perception that fellow employees have been unfairly treated may impair worker morale and make it harder for employers to hire and retain the most qualified employees, these effects are diffuse and hard to measure. In light of the relatively greater economic power held by many employers, there is reason to be skeptical of the degree to which employers would internalize the full costs of disincentive schemes.

Manipulation of insurance coverage[26] raises a similar difficulty. State Farm has chosen to double the amount payable for certain injuries or death for victims of accidents who were wearing seat belts at the time of the accident. Obviously, the company anticipates that the increased rate of seat-belt use will reduce its payouts more than doubling the benefit payment will increase them. However, if coverage were denied or reduced for persons who failed to wear seat belts, the insureds would absorb the loss. Notwithstanding the social desirability of increasing seat-belt usage, such a drastic consequence is likely to be regarded as unfair.[27]

This discussion has focused on the ways employment relationships and insurance schemes can be structured to influence individual risk-taking behavior. Although the state may also serve as employer or insurer, it is not acting as "sovereign" when it does so, and it is not using "the law" as a behavioral instrument. Thus the entire discussion may appear tangential and perhaps altogether off the point.

I think the discussion is germane for two related reasons. First, from a libertarian standpoint, unduly "coercive" use of any institutional power to affect personal choice implicates the individual's de-

26. As already noted, I do not expect differential premiums to have significant behavioral effects in the context of individual health and safety. However, so long as risk-rated premium sanctions reflect actuarial experience, there is some objectifiable way to ensure that the difference is fairly related to the risk.

27. It could be argued that a driver who does not intend to wear seat belts should have the opportunity to shop for an insurer willing to charge a lower premium for reduced coverage. The likelihood of cognitive errors is so great that this "market solution" should not be permitted.

cision-making autonomy; in this context, an emphasis on coercion by the state can obscure objectionable uses of "private" power. It follows also that unduly coercive uses of economic power by employers and insurers should be regulated by the state. Second, attention to the possible utility of incentive systems as behavioral instruments by employers and insurers places disputes about the uses of legal constraints in a larger context and corrects for the tendency to think of law as the only significant institutional force.

Risk Homeostasis: Another View of the Psychology of Risk-Taking

I have described a range of situations in which some portion of the population appears to behave more healthily or more safely in response to various forms of legal intervention. By regulating the marketplace or individual behavior, the state can affect the prevalence of risky behavior—more people wear seat belts or helmets, fewer people smoke at all or do so in public locations, and, perhaps, people modify the frequency or circumstances of their smoking, drinking, or drug use. Ultimately, however, the crucial variable is whether the change in the prevalence of the target behaviors actually reduces the rates of disease, injury, and fatality. For the paternalistic policymaker, reduction in the risky behavior is expected to save lives and reduce morbidity.

There is some evidence that this does not always happen. For example, although mandatory seat-belt laws have increased belt usage by significant amounts—at least 50% in most countries—it seems clear that the rate (per driver) of serious injuries or fatalities has *not* been reduced by the anticipated amount, and in some countries it has not been reduced at all (Jonah & Lawson, 1984).

This finding—which has been a relatively consistent one—might be explained in two ways. One explanation is that the most careful drivers are the ones who tend to buckle up in compliance with the legal directive; accordingly, to the extent that belt usage remains low among the least careful drivers—say among young males and those who drive while drunk—then the overall injury and fatality rates will not be strongly influenced by the aggregate increase in seat-belt usage. This explanation argues strongly for a technological solution—mandatory passive restraints—rather than one that aims to modify individual behavior.

However, an alternative explanation has been offered: when people are forced to receive more protection than they would choose voluntarily, they respond with riskier driving that more or less offsets the increase in protection attributable to the intervention. Wilde (1982) has characterized the theory as one of risk homeostasis—that is, individuals have a "target level of risk" for various activities and will adjust their behavior to achieve or maintain that level of risk:

> [W]hile driving a vehicle, while involved in an industrial task or recreational sport, or while making decisions in any other behavior domain that may [involve risks to] health or safety, [an individual] is acting in a way that may be understood as a homeostatically controlled self-regulation process. At any moment of time, the instantaneously experienced level of risk is compared with the level of risk the individual wishes to take and decisions to alter ongoing behavior will be made whenever the two levels are discrepant.

The theory of risk homeostasis, as proposed by Wilde, seeks to explain and predict the dynamics of human conduct in the face of risk. The theory implies that interventions that do not change the person's target level of risk (such as mandatory crash protection) will not be utilized to reduce accident loss; instead, people will "consume" the safety gain by driving faster, by following other cars more closely, and in general by increasing "driving intensity." Or as another proponent of this theory has put it, "protecting car occupants from the consequences of bad driving encourages bad driving" (Adams, 1982).

The risk homeostasis (or risk compensation) hypothesis has triggered a vociferous debate in the risk analysis field. It can easily be seen that if this theory is true it calls into question the efficacy of any automobile safety regulation that perceptibly reduces the risks associated with driving without changing the aggregate desire for safety. Indeed, an economist (Peltzman, 1975) reported that the United States occupant-protection regulations of the late 1960s resulted in *increased* numbers of crashes and pedestrian fatalities because of increased driving intensity.

Although the dispute has centered on automobile safety, the theory calls into question all forms of paternalist regulation. Wilde has suggested that the theory is generally applicable to all human behavior "in the face of risk or damage, morbidity and mortality." As he puts it, "when people are made to take less risk in one way, they will take more in another." Thus, he suggests:

The per capita frequency of occupational injuries and fatal accidents will go down to the extent that working hours are reduced, [but] non-occupational accidents will increase commensurately. . . . If larger segments of the population involved themselves in fitness exercises and dieting, the frequency of certain types of morbidity may change, but aggregate morbidity and mortality rates will not be similarly affected. . . .

. . . A strict application of the proposed theory would hold that improvements in lifestyle-dependent health and [in] lifespan can be achieved only to the extent that measures are introduced that are effective in motivating people to live healthier and longer.

If the risk homeostasis theory is true, most of the modes of legal intervention reviewed in this paper are not likely to be effective, over the long term, in reducing death and injury due to risk-taking behavior. Although information regulation may be effective in improving risk perception, regulations of the market or of individual behavior are unlikely to succeed in modifying outcomes; so long as people perceive a reduction in risk, they will adjust their behavior to maintain the "target level of risk." This supposition leads Wilde to emphasize the advantage of systems of incentives, which motivate people to behave more safely or healthily and thereby reduce the target level of risk, as compared with systems of constraints that modify options without modifying risk perceptions or preferences.

How does the psychological model of risk homeostasis differ from the model of risk benefit decision-making described earlier in this paper, and what are its implications for use of the law as a behavioral instrument? It appears that the theories are congruent up to a point. As Wilde has made clear in response to critical comment, risk homeostasis theory does not postulate that people take risks for the sake of taking risks; instead, what he calls the "target level of risk" is a function of the perceived benefits of the behavior. Thus the target level of risk varies for each individual and for each risky activity. When individual target levels of risk for a given activity (driving, smoking, or eating foods high in cholesterol) are aggregated, the resulting risk/benefit preference represents the target level of risk of the population as a whole for that behavior.

Risk homeostasis theory is thus compatible with standard "expected utility" theory. According to expected utility theory, each individual will adjust his conduct to achieve an optimum risk/benefit relationship, and these aggregated preferences reflect the collective optimum level of risk. Thus, if mobility and time are valued, people will "consume" improvements in safety (such as studded tires) to go faster per unit of time exposure. Similarly, reducing the tar and nicotine content of cigarettes has probably not reduced the level of morbidity and mortality associated with smoking because smokers apparently have increased consumption to maintain the same nicotine intake. In this context the increased cigarette consumption achieves a pharmacologic "benefit," equivalent to the increased mobility permitted by studded tires, at a constant (perhaps "optimal") level of risk. In both of these contexts there is no need to postulate a "homeostatic" process; it is sufficient to assume that people are willing to tolerate greater levels of risk in order to achieve greater benefits associated with a particular behavior.

Risk homeostasis theory goes a step further than standard "expected utility" analysis by including nonrational motivational factors. In fact, Wilde explicitly links the theory to the hypothesis that people seek an optimal level of psychophysiological arousal. That is, they drive faster (and offset the reduced risk achieved by studded tires or seat belts) not simply to save time but also to experience an optimal level of arousal:

> The sources of utility are not limited to those appearing "rational" to *homo oeconomicus*, but include the satisfaction of other desires. Salient among these is the need to maintain an optimal psychophysiological arousal level (or levels). People may engage in travel for this purpose and thus satisfy their need for variety, a change of pace, stimulation or relaxation, adventure and curiosity. . . . [Risk homeostasis theory] hypothesizes that the occurrence of road accidents is an accepted consequence if behavior, for the sake of reaching or maintaining an optimal arousal level, takes some form of surface travel. This may seem irrational if one adheres to strict economic views, but it is perfectly plausible from a psychobiological perspective: maintaining optimal levels of arousal (like body temperature and blood pressure) has clear evolutionary and survival value.

This dimension of the theory, which has important implications for achievement of paternalist policy goals, opens a window on controversial issues in basic psychological theory. For example, Zuckerman (1979) has proposed a model of sensation seeking, linked to biological factors, hypothesizing that people seek a level of stimulation or positive arousal that is optimal in relation to the appraised risk and in relation to the level of anxiety (fear or negative arousal) associated with the appraised risk.

As I noted earlier, the risk homeostasis hypothesis has provoked a major controversy in the field of automobile safety regulation. Its proponents contend that the safety benefits of mandatory interventions (by market regulation or by direct regulation of driver behavior) are partially or wholly offset by changes in the behavior of drivers, who take greater risks, thus maintaining the same level of overall risk as before the intervention. Unfortunately, despite all the fuss, there is not much convincing empirical evidence for or against the hypothesis. The need for further research is emphasized by proponents of the theory as well as by its critics.

Most of the available evidence is drawn from studies of changes in the aggregate level of fatalities and injuries before and after changes in safety regulation. When the data are interpreted to show shortfalls in expected reductions in deaths or injuries, changes in driver behavior are posited to explain the shortfall. Few studies have tested the hypothesis directly by observations of driver behavior. However, the most pertinent studies, which have all focused on the effect of seat-belt laws, have all failed to support the risk homeostasis theory. Evans, Wasielewski, and von Buseck (1982) compared "following headways" in freeway driving by seat-belt users and nonusers in Ontario, which had adopted a mandatory seat-belt law, with comparable data previously reported for drivers in Michigan, which had no seat-belt law. They found "no evidence for any difference in driving behavior associated with compulsory seat belt use as compared to voluntary use." This study is limited, of course, because the following headways in Ontario before the law were not known.

Lund and Zador (1984) and O'Neill, Lund, Zador, and Ashton (1984) conducted before-and-after studies of driver behavior in Newfoundland, Canada, and Birmingham, England. The Newfoundland data were also compared with similar data from Nova Scotia, where seat-belt use was not required by law. The measures of driver behavior in the Canadian study included average speed, driving through intersections after lights changed to amber, turning headway at T-intersections, and following headway. The English study measured speed and following headway on four-lane and two-lane roads. In general, the studies found relatively little change in driver behavior.

Do these studies refute the risk homeostasis theory? Perhaps not. Wearing a seat belt does not reduce the risk of an accident; it merely reduces the likelihood of death or serious injury if an accident occurs. Thus the link between the safety regulation and the perceived risk may be too attenuated to expect any offsetting effect on driver behavior. As O'Neill et al. (1984) point out: "It is intuitively difficult to accept that drivers are prepared to be more frequently involved in crashes, with all of their unpleasant and expensive consequences, simply because they perceive that they would be less likely to be injured or to be less seriously injured." However, some proponents of the theory have relied on precisely the opposite intuition in explaining why increases in occupant protection (including padded dashboards as well as seat belts) have not achieved the projected reductions in death or injury (Orr, 1982a, 1982b; Peltzman, 1975). Their suspicion is that people "feel" safer and therefore adjust their behavior to maintain the constant level of perceived risk.[28]

Further experience with mandatory seat-belt laws will produce more definitive data on whether the increase in belt use is associated with a corresponding decrease in fatalities and serious injuries. If not, risk homeostasis will be offered as one of the competing explanations. But this is not the only context in which the hypothesis can be tested. Studies of motorcycle helmet laws and the minimum drinking age, reviewed earlier in this paper, appear to indicate that these interventions have reduced fatalities and serious injuries. This suggests that motorcyclists are not driving more riskily while helmeted than they otherwise would and that teenagers are not driving more riskily while sober in order to achieve the same level of risk achieved while intoxicated.

It could be argued, in response, that motorcyclists and automobile drivers who are forced to be safer on the roads than they would choose to be will compensate in some other unmeasured way. Perhaps motorcyclists and teenage drivers will behave more riskily in recreational activity to offset the reduced stimulation available to them while driving motorcycles or cars (or while drinking alcohol). However, if the truth of the risk homeostasis hypothesis turns ultimately on the existence of such an elastic "substitution effect," the theory is empirically unfalsifiable and therefore of little

28. Wasielewski and Evans (1985) recently collected and reanalyzed previously reported data on the relation between risky driving and size of the car being driven. They concluded that drivers of smaller cars tend to take fewer risks in everyday driving (as measured by following headways, speed, and seat-belt usage) than drivers of larger cars, and that the data are consistent with the conclusion that more cautious driving in smaller cars is substantially reducing the occupant fatality rates that might otherwise be associated with smaller cars. Although Wasielewski and Evans did not link their findings to the risk homeostasis theory, it might also be inferred that drivers of larger cars "feel" safer and are willing to drive less safely to reach their target levels of risk.

interest to behavioral scientists and of virtually no value to policy-makers.

It would be premature, I think, to conclude that the risk homeo-stasis theory is false. It merits further development and empirical investigation. Although I doubt that the theory explains the full range of risk-taking behavior, it does identify a feature of the psychology of risk taking that is probably pertinent in some con-texts.

Moreover, even if the theory is not true, or at least not as robust as its proponents claim, it does call attention to the significance of in-centives in the implementation of paternalist policies. Although I have argued that the use of legal constraints to implement paternal-ist initiatives can be effective, I have also tried to emphasize both the limits of law and the *costs* of legal interventions. Attention to the de-velopment of incentives for safety and health should be one of the critical priorities for the new paternalism.

REFERENCES

Adams, J. (1982). *The efficacy of seat belt legislation: A comparative study of road accident fatality statistics from 18 countries* (SAE Report No. 820819). War-rendale, PA: Society of Automotive Engineers.

Akins, C., & Beschner, G. (Eds.). (1980). *Ethnography: A research tool for policymakers in the drug and alcohol fields.* Rockville, MD: National Institute on Drug Abuse.

Andenaes, J. (1974). *Punishment and deterrence.* Ann Arbor, MI: University of Michigan Press.

Andenaes, J. (1975). General prevention revisited: Research and policy im-plications. *Journal of Criminal Law and Criminology, 66,* 338–365.

Arnould, R. J., & Grabowski, H. (1981). Auto safety regulation: An analysis of market failure. *Bell Journal of Economics, 12,* 27–48.

Atkin, C., & Block, M. (1981). *Content and effects of alcohol advertising* (NTIS No. PB82-123142). Washington, D.C.: Bureau of Alcohol, Tobacco, and Firearms.

Baird, D. D., & Wilcox, A. J. (1985). Cigarette smoking associated with de-layed conception. *Journal of the American Medical Association, 253,* 2979–2983.

Baker, S. P., O'Neill, B., & Karpf, R. S. (1984). *The injury fact book.* Lexington, MA: D. C. Heath.

Blum, R. (1979). Controlling heroin addict crime. *Journal of Drug Issues, 9,* 311–316.

Bonnie, R. J. (1977). Decriminalizing the marijuana user: A drafter's guide. *Michigan Journal of Law Reform, 11*, 3–50.

Bonnie, R. J. (1978). Discouraging unhealthy personal choices: Reflections on new directions in substance abuse policies. *Journal of Drug Issues, 8*, 199–219.

Bonnie, R. J. (1980). *Marijuana use and criminal sanctions: Essays in the theory and practice of decriminalization.* Charlottesville, VA: Michie/Bobbs-Merrill.

Bonnie, R. J. (1981). Discouraging the use of alcohol, tobacco, and other drugs: The effects of legal controls and restrictions. *Advances in Substance Abuse, 2*, 145–184.

Bonnie, R. J. (1985). Regulating conditions of alcohol availability: Possible effects on highway safety. *Journal of Studies on Alcohol*, Suppl. 10, 129–143.

Bonnie, R. J., & Whitebread, C. (1974). *The marijuana conviction: The history of marijuana prohibition in the United States.* Charlottesville, VA: University Press of Virginia.

Brasley, A. (1980). The promotion of health through health insurance. *New England Journal of Medicine, 302*, 51–52.

Breed, W., & Defoe, J. R. (1984). Cigarette smoking on television, 1950–1982. *New England Journal of Medicine, 309*, 617.

Bukoski, W. J. (Ed.). (1981). *A review of prevention theory, program concepts and evaluation results.* Unpublished manuscript, National Institute on Drug Abuse, Prevention Branch, Rockville, MD.

Christoffel, T., & Stein, S. (1979, Winter). Using the law to protect health: The frustrating case of smoking. *Medicolegal News*, pp. 5–9, 20, 28.

Cigarette Labeling and Advertising Act of 1965, 15 U.S.C.A. §1333(a) (1984).

Cook, P. J. (1981). The effect of liquor taxes on drinking, cirrhosis and auto accidents. In M. H. Moore & D. R. Gerstein (Eds.), *Alcohol and public policy: Beyond the shadow of prohibition* (pp. 255–285). Washington, D.C.: National Academy Press.

Cook, P. J., & Tauchen, G. (1984). The effect of minimum drinking age legislation on youthful auto fatalities, 1971–1977. *Journal of Legal Studies, 13*, 169–190.

Corwin, L. B. (1981). Antidrug paraphernalia laws: Void for vagueness. *Boston University Law Review, 61*, 453–476.

Cuskey, W. R. (1981). Critique of marijuana decriminalization research. *Contemporary Drug Problems, 10*, 323–324.

Decker, M. D., Dewey, M. J., Hutcheson, R. H., & Schaffner, W. (1984). The use and efficacy of child restraint devices: The Tennessee experience, 1982 and 1983. *Journal of the American Medical Association, 252*, 2571–2575.

Doron, G. (1979). *The smoking paradox.* Cambridge, MA: Abt.

Douglass, R. L., Filkins, L. D., & Clark, F. A. (1974). *The effect of lower legal drinking age on youth crash involvement* (Report No. UM-HSRI-74-1-2). Ann Arbor, MI: University of Michigan Highway Safety Research Institute.

Douglass, R. L., Filkins, L. D., & Clark, F. A. (1982). *The effect of lower legal drinking age on youth crash involvement.* Ann Arbor, MI: University of Michigan Highway Safety Research Institute.

Douglass, R. L., & Freedman, J. A. (1977). *Alcohol-related casualties and alcohol beverage market response to alcohol beverage availability policies in Michigan* (Vol. 1). Ann Arbor, MI: University of Michigan Highway Safety Research Institute.

Dunagin v. Oxford, 718 F.2d 738 (1983).

DuPont, R. (1979), Controlling heroin addict crime. *Journal of Drug Issues, 9,* 319–320.

Erickson, P. (1976). Deterrence and deviance: The example of cannabis production. *Journal of Criminal Law and Criminology, 67,* 222–232.

Evans, L., Wasielewski, P., & Buseck, C. R. von. (1982). Compulsory seat belt usage and driver risk-taking behavior. *Human Factors, 24,* 41–48.

Evans, R. I. (1976). Smoking in children: Developing a social psychological strategy of deterrence. *Preventive Medicine, 5,* 122–127.

Fielding, J. E. (1977). Health promotions: Some notions in search of a constituency. *American Journal of Public Health, 67,* 1082–1086.

Fischoff, B., Lichtenstein, S., Slovic, P., Derby, S. L., & Keeney, R. L. (1983). *Acceptable risk.* New York: Cambridge University Press.

Fishbein, M., & Ajzen, I. (1975). *Belief, attitude, intention and behavior: An introduction to theory and research.* Reading, MA: Addison-Wesley.

Fleischer, G. A. (1971). *An experiment in the use of broadcast media in highway safety.* Los Angeles: University of California Department of Industrial and Systems Engineering.

Goldstein, A. (1979). Heroin maintenance: A medical view. *Journal of Drug Issues, 9,* 341–347.

Graham, J. D., & Henrion, M. (1984). A probabilistic analysis of the passive-restraint question. *Risk Analysis, 4,* 25–39.

Greenwald, M.(1981). Health promotion and health insurance. *Strategies in Public Health, 16,* 259–266.

Gritz, E. R. (1977). Smoking: The prevention of onset. In M. E. Jarvik, J. W. Cullen, E. R. Gritz, T. M. Vogt, & L. J. West (Eds.), *Research on smoking behavior* (pp. 290–307). Rockville, MD: National Institute on Drug Abuse. Monograph 17.

Guerin, D., & Mackinnon, D. P. (1985). An assessment of the California child passenger restraint requirement. *American Journal of Public Health, 75,* 142–144.

Haggerty, R. J. (1977). Changing life styles to improve health. *Preventive Medicine, 6*, 275–288.

Hakkert, A. S., Zaidel, D. M., & Sarelle, E. (1981). Patterns of safety belt usage following introduction of a safety belt wearing law. *Accident Analysis and Prevention, 13*, 65–82.

Hamilton, J. L. (1972). The demand for cigarettes: Advertising, the health scare, and the cigarette advertising ban. *Review of Economics and Statistics, 54*, 401–411.

Harris v. McRae, 448 U.S. 297 (1980).

Harris, J. E. (1982). Increasing the federal excise tax on cigarettes. *Journal of Health Economics, 1*, 117–120.

Hartunian, N. S., Smart, C. N., Willemain, T. R., & Zador, P. L. (1983). The economics of deregulation: Lives and dollars lost due to repeal of motorcycle helmet laws. *Journal of Health Politics, Policy and Law, 8*, 76–98.

Hauge, R. (Ed.). (1978). *Drinking and driving in Scandinavian studies in criminology.* Oslo: Universitetforlage.

Hellman, A. (1975). *The laws against marijuana: The price we pay.* Urbana: University of Illinois Press.

Institute of Medicine. (1982). *Health and behavior: Frontiers of research on the biobehavioral sciences.* Washington, D.C.: National Academy Press.

Ippolito, R. A., Murphy, R. D., & Sant, D. (1979). *Consumer response to cigarette health information.* Washington, D.C.: U.S. Federal Trade Commission, Bureau of Economics.

Jackson, T., & Jeffries, J. (1979). Commercial speech: Economic due process and the First Amendment. *Virginia Law Review, 65*, 1–41.

Johnson, W., Petersen, R. E., & Wells, L. E. (1977). Arrest probabilities for marijuana users as indicators of selective law enforcement. *American Journal of Sociology, 83*, 681–699.

Johnston, L. D., O'Malley, P. M., & Bachman, J. G. (1984). *Drugs and American high school students, 1975–1983.* Rockville, MD: National Institute on Drug Abuse.

Jonah, B. A., & Lawson, J. J. (1984). The effectiveness of the Canadian mandatory seat belt use laws. *Accident Analysis and Prevention, 16*, 433–450.

Jones, R. K., & Jocelyn, K. B. (1978). *Alcohol and highway safety, 1978: A review of the state of knowledge* (NHTSA Contract No. DOT-HS-5-01217). Washington, D.C.: U.S. Department of Transportation.

Kahneman, D., Slovic, P., & Tversky, A. (Eds.). (1982). *Judgement under uncertainty: Heuristics and biases.* Cambridge: Cambridge University Press.

Kahneman, D., & Tversky, A. (1984). Choices, values and frames. *American Psychology, 4*, 341–350.

Kandel, D. (1984). Marijuana users in young adulthood. *Archives of General Psychiatry, 41*, 200–209.

Kandel, D., & Faust, R. (1975). Sequences and stages in patterns of adolescent drug use. *Archives of General Psychiatry, 32*, 923–932.

Kaplan, J. (1970). *Marijuana: The new prohibition.* New York: World.

Kaplan, J. (1975). Primer on heroin. *Stanford Law Review, 27*, 801–826.

Kaplan, J. (1983). *The hardest drug: Heroin and public policy.* Chicago: University of Chicago Press.

Kendell, R. E., de Roumanie, M., & Ritson, E. B. (1983). Influence of an increase in excise duty on alcohol consumption and its adverse effects. *British Medical Journal, 287*, 809–811.

Kilpatrick, J. J. (1985, February 12). Preserving the freedom to be foolish. *Charlottesville Daily Progress,* p. A4.

Kohn, P. M., & Smart, R. G. (1984). The impact of television advertising on alcohol consumption: An experiment. *Journal of Studies on Alcohol, 45*, 295–301.

Kunreuther, H. (1976). Limited knowledge and insurance protection. *Public Policy, 24*, 229–261.

Kunreuther, H. (1984, September). *Incentives for improving driving behavior: Ex ante/ex post considerations.* Paper presented at the General Motors International Symposium on Human Behavior and Traffic Safety, Warren, MI.

Kunreuther, H., Ginsberg, R., Miller, L., Sagi, P., Borkan, B., & Katz, N. (1978). *Disaster insurance protection: Public policy lessons.* New York: Wiley.

Lalonde, M. (1974). *A new perspective on the health of Canadians: A working document.* Ottawa: Information Canada.

Lau, R., Kane, R., Berry, S., Ware, J., & Roy, D. (1980). Channeling health: A review of televised health campaigns. *Health Education Quarterly, 7*, 56–89.

Lenfant, C., & Lin, B. M. (1980). (Passive) smokers versus (voluntary) smokers. *New England Journal of Medicine, 302*, 742–743.

Lewitt, E. M., & Coate, D. (1982). The potential for using excise taxes to reduce smoking. *Journal of Health Economics, 1*, 121–145.

Lewitt, E. M., Coate, D., & Grossman, M. (1981). The effects of government regulation on teenage smoking. *Journal of Law and Economics, 24*, 545–569.

Little, R. E., Grathwohl, H. L., Streissguth, A. P., & McIntyre, C. (1981). Public awareness and knowledge about the risks of drinking during pregnancy in Multnomah County, Oregon. *American Journal of Public Health, 71*, 312–314.

Lund, A., & Zador, P. (1984). Mandatory belt use and driver risk-taking. *Risk Analysis, 4*, 41–54.

Macoby, N., Farquhar, J. W., Wood, P. D., & Alexander, J. (1977). Reducing the risk of cardiovascular disease: Effects of a community-based campaign on knowledge and behavior. *Journal of Community Health, 3*, 100–114.

Maher v. Roe, 432 U.S. 464 (1978).

Maloff, D. (1982). A review of the decriminalization of marijuana. *Contemporary Drug Problems, 10,* 307–322.

McFadden, M., & Wechsler, H. (1980). Minimum drinking age laws and teenage drinking. *Psychiatric Opinion, 16,* 22–28.

McGuiness, T. (1979). *An econometric analysis of total demand for alcoholic beverages in the U.K., 1956–1975.* Edinburgh: Scottish Health Education Unit.

Medicine in the Public Interest, Inc. (1979). *The effects of alcoholic-beverage-control-laws.* Washington, D.C.: Author.

Meier, R., & Johnson, W. (1977). Deterrence as social control: The legal and extralegal production of conformity. *American Sociological Review, 42,* 292–304.

Moore, M. H. (1977). *Buy and bust: The effective regulation of an illicit market in heroin.* Lexington, MA: D. C. Heath.

Moore, M. H., & Gerstein, D. R. (1981). *Alcohol and public policy: Beyond the shadow of prohibition.* Washington, D.C.: National Academy Press.

Mosher, J. (1977). The prohibition of youthful drinking: A need for reform. *Contemporary Drug Problems, 6,* 397–423.

Muller, A. (1980). Evaluation of the costs and benefits of motorcycle helmet laws. *American Journal of Public Health, 70,* 586–592.

Muris, T. J. (1983). Comments on proposals to amend Public Health Service Act and Federal Cigarette Labeling and Advertising Act [letter to the chairman]. In *Smoking Prevention Education Act: Hearings before the Subcommittee on Health and Environment of the Committee on Energy and Commerce of the House of Representatives* (pp. 208–230). Washington, D.C.: Government Printing Office.

Myers, M. L., Iscoe, C., Jennings, C., Lenox, W., Minsky, E., & Sacks, A. (1981). *Staff report on the cigarette smoking advertising investigation.* Washington, D.C.: U.S. Federal Trade Commission.

National Commission on Marihuana and Drug Abuse. (1972). *Marihuana: A signal of misunderstanding.* Washington, D.C.: Author.

National Commission on Marihuana and Drug Abuse. (1973). *Drug use in America: Problem in perspective.* Washington, D.C.: Author.

National Governor's Conference. (1977). *Marijuana: A study of state policies and penalties.* Washington, D.C.: U.S. Government Printing Office.

National Highway Traffic and Safety Administration. (1980). *A report to Congress on the effect of motorcycle helmet use law repeal: A case for helmet use* (NHTSA Report No. DOT-HS-805-312). Washington, D.C.: Author.

National Institute of Mental Health. (1982). *Television and behavior: Ten years of scientific progress and implications for the eighties* (DHHS Publication No. ADM 82-1195). Washington, D.C.: U.S. Government Printing Office.

Nieburg, P., Marks, J. S., McLaren, N. M., & Remington, P. L. (1985). The fetal tobacco syndrome. *Journal of the American Medical Association, 253,* 2998–2999.

Ogborne, A. C., & Smart, R. G. (1980). Will restrictions on alcohol advertising reduce alcohol consumption? *British Journal of Addictions, 75,* 293–296.

Oklahoma Telecasters' Association v. Crisp, 699 F.2d 490 (1983), *reversed on other grounds sub nom* Capital Cities Cable, Inc., v. Crisp, 104 S.C. 2694 (1984).

O'Neill, B., Lund, A. K., Zador, P., & Ashton, S. (1984, September). Mandatory belt use and driver risk taking: An empirical evaluation of the risk-compensation hypothesis. Presented at the International Symposium on Human Behavior and Traffic Safety Sponsored by General Motors Research Laboratories, Warren, MI.

Opinion Research Corporation. (1980). *Safety belt usage among drivers* (NHTSA Report No. DOT-HS-805-398). Washington, D.C.: NHTSA.

Orr, L. D. (1982a). Incentives and efficiency in automobile regulation. *Quarterly Review of Economics and Business, 22*(3), 43–65.

Orr, L. D. (1982b). Goals, risks and choices. *Risk Analysis, 2,* 239–242.

Peltzman, S. (1975). The effects of automobile regulation. *Journal of Political Economy, 83,* 677–725.

Pollin, W. (1984). The role of the addictive process as a key step in causation of all tobacco-related diseases. *Journal of the American Medical Association, 253,* 2874–2877.

Pressley, S. A. (1985, March 11). Public in middle of U.S. seat belt debate. *Washington Post,* pp. A1, A10.

Reisinger, K., Williams, A., Wells, J., John, C., Roberts, T., & Pod Gainy, H. (1981). The effect of pediatrician's counseling on infant restraint use. *Pediatrics, 67,* 201–206.

Remington, P. L., Forman, M. R., Genry, E. M., Marks, J. S., Hogelin, G. C., & Trowbridge, F. L. (1985). Current smoking trends in the United States. *Journal of the American Medical Association, 253,* 2874–2877.

Robertson, L. S. (1977). Car crashes: Perceived vulnerability and willingness to pay for crash protection. *Journal of Community Health, 3,* 136–141.

Robertson, L. S. (1983). *Injuries: Causes, control strategies and public policy.* Lexington, MA: D. C. Heath.

Robertson, L. S., Kelley, A., O'Neill, B., Wixon, B., Eiswirth, R., & Haddon, W., Jr. (1974). A controlled study of the effect of television messages on seat belt use. *American Journal of Public Health, 64,* 1071–1080.

Robertson, L. S., Rich, R. F., & Ross, H. L. (1973). Jail sentences for driving while intoxicated in Chicago: A judicial policy that failed. *Law and Society Review, 8,* 55–68.

Rosenthal, M. (1979). Partial prohibition of nonmedical use of mind altering drugs: Proposals for change. *Houston Law Review, 16*, 603–665.

Ross, H. L. (1973). Law, science and accidents: The British Road Safety Act of 1967. *Journal of Legal Studies, 2*, 1–78.

Ross, H. L. (1975). The Scandinavian myth: The effectiveness of drinking and driving legislation in Sweden and Norway. *Journal of Legal Studies, 4*, 285–310.

Ross, H. L. (1982). *Deterring the drinking driver: Legal policy and social control.* Lexington, MA: D. C. Heath.

Ross, H. L. (1984). Social control through deterrence: Drinking-and-driving laws. *Annual Review of Sociology, 10*, 21–35.

Ross, H. L. (1985). Deterring drunk driving: An analysis of current efforts. *Journal of Alcohol Studies*, Suppl. 10, 122–128.

Scholten, D. J., & Glover, J. L. (1984). Increased mortality following repeal of mandatory motorcycle helmet law. *Indiana Medicine, 77*, 252–255.

Schuckit, M., & Russell, J. (1983). Clinicial importance of age at first drink in a group of young men. *American Journal of Psychiatry, 140*, 1221–1223.

Schwalm, N. D., & Slovic, P. (1982). *Development and test of a motivational approach and materials for increasing use of motor-vehicle occupant restraints* (Final Technical Report No. PFTR-1100-82-1). Woodland Hill, CA: Perceptronics.

Shiffrin, S. (1980). Government speech. *UCLA Law Review, 27*, 565–655.

Skinner, B. F. (1969). *Contingencies of reinforcement: A theoretical analysis.* New York: Appleton-Century-Crofts.

Slovic, P. (1985, January 30). Only new laws will spur seat-belt use. *Wall Street Journal*, p. 26.

Slovic, P., Fischoff, B., & Lichtenstein, S. (1978). Accident probabilities and seat belt usage: A psychological perspective. *Accident Analysis and Prevention, 10*, 281–285.

Smart, R. G. (1980). The impact of changes in legal purchase or drinking age on drinking and admissions to treatment. In H. Wechsler (Ed.), *Minimum-drinking-age laws* (pp. 133–154). Lexington, MA: D. C. Heath.

Smart, R. G., & Cutler, R. E. (1976). The alcohol advertising ban in British Columbia: Problems and effects on beverage consumption. *British Journal of Addictions, 71*, 13–21.

Smart, R. G., & Goodstadt, M. S. (1977). Effects of reducing the legal alcohol purchasing age on drinking and drinking problems: A review of empirical studies. *Journal of the Study of Alcohol, 38*, 1313–1323.

Solomon, D. (1982). Health campaigns on television. In D. Pearl, L. Beuthelit, & J. Lazar (Eds.), *Television and behavior: Ten years of scientific progress and implications for the eighties (Vol. 2) (DHHS Publication No. ADM 82-1196). Washington, D.C.: Department of Health and Human Services.*

Steinbrugge, K. V., McClure, F. E., & Snow, A. J. (1969). *Studies in seismicity and earthquake damage statistics* (Report No. COM-71-00053). Washington, D.C.: Department of Commerce.

Stokes, J. (1983). Why not rate health and life insurance premiums by risk? *New England Journal of Medicine, 308,* 393–395.

Strickland, D. E. (1984). Content and effects of alcohol advertising: Comment on NTIS pub. no. PB82-123142. *Journal of Studies on Alcohol, 45,* 87–100.

Svenson, O. (1981). Are we all less risky and more skillful than our fellow drivers? *Acta Psychologica, 47,* 143–148.

Teknekron Research, Inc. (1979). *1979 survey of public perceptions on highway safety.* Washington, D.C.: U.S. Department of Transportation.

Trebach, A. S. (1981). *The heroin solution.* New Haven: Yale University Press.

Tversky, A. (1974). Judgement under uncertainty: Heuristics and biases. *Science, 185,* 1124–1131.

Tversky, A., & Kahneman, D. (1973). Availability: A heuristic for judging frequency and probability. *Cognitive Psychology, 5,* 207–232.

U.S. Department of Health and Human Services. (1983). *The health consequences of smoking for women: A report of the surgeon general* (Publication No. 410-889/1284). Washington, D.C.: Author.

U.S. Department of Health, Education, and Welfare. (1979). *Healthy people: The surgeon general's report on health promotion and disease prevention* (PHS Publication No. 79-55071). Washington, D.C.: U.S. Government Printing Office.

U.S. Department of the Treasury & U.S. Department of Health and Human Services. (1980). *Report to the president and Congress on health hazards associated with alcohol and methods to inform the general public of the hazards.* Washington, D.C.: Author.

U.S. Department of Transportation Ruling. (1984, July 11). *Congressional Quarterly Almanac, 40,* 295–296.

Virginia Board of Pharmacy v. Virginia Citizens' Consumer Council, Inc., 425 U.S. 748 (1976).

Voas, R. B., & Hause, J. M. (1984). Deterring the drinking driver: The Stockton experience. Report prepared by the National Public Service Research Institute for National Highway Traffic Safety Administration. Washington, D.C.

Wagenaar, A. C. (1982). Preventing highway crashes by raising the legal minimum age for drinking: An empirical confirmation. *Journal of Safety Research, 13*(2), 57–71.

Wagenaar, A. C. (1983). *Alcohol, young drivers and traffic accidents: Effects of minimum age laws.* Lexington, MA: D. C. Heath.

Wallack, L. (1984). Drinking and driving: Toward a broader understanding of the role of the mass media. *Journal of Public Health Policy, 5,* 471–496.

Waller, J. A. (1985). *Injury control: A guide to the causes and prevention of trauma.* Lexington, MA: Lexington Books.

Warner, K. E. (1977). The effects of the anti-smoking campaign on cigarette consumption. *American Journal of Public Health, 67,* 645–650.

Warner, K. E. (1981a). The federal cigarette excise tax. In *National Conference on Smoking and Health.* New York: American Cancer Society.

Warner, K. E. (1981b). Cigarette smoking in the 1970's: The impact of the antismoking campaign on consumption. *Science, 211,* 729–731.

Warner, K. E. (1983). Bags, buckles, and belts: The debate over mandatory passive restraints in automobiles. *Journal of Health Politics, Policy and Law, 8,* 44–75.

Warner, K. E. (1985). Cigarette advertising and media coverage of smoking and health. *New England Journal of Medicine, 312,* 384–388.

Warner, K. E., & Murt, H. A. (1984). Economic incentives for health. *Annual Review of Public Health, 5,* 107–133.

Wasielewski, P., & Evans, L. (1985). Do drivers of small cars take less risk in everyday driving? *Risk Analysis, 5,* 25–32.

Watson, G. S., Zador, P. L., & Wilks, A. (1980). The repeal of helmet use laws and increased motorcyclist mortality in the United States, 1975–1978. *American Journal of Public Health, 70,* 579–585.

Watson, G. S., Zador, P. L., & Wilks, A. (1981). Helmet use, helmet use laws, and motorcyclist fatalities. *American Journal of Public Health, 71,* 297–300.

White, J., & Froeb, H. (1980). Small-airways dysfunction in non-smokers chronically exposed to tobacco smoke. *New England Journal of Medicine, 302,* 720–723.

Whitehead, P. C. (1980). Research strategies to evaluate the impact of changes in the legal drinking age. In H. Wechsler (Ed.), *Minimum-drinking-age laws* (pp. 73–92). Lexington, MA: D. C. Heath.

Whitehead, P. C., & Shattuck, D. (1976). *Lowering the drinking age in Saskatchewan: The effect on collisions among young drivers.* Regina: Department of Health, Aware Program.

Wilde, G. J. S. (1982). The theory of risk homeostasis: Implications for safety and health. *Risk Analysis, 2,* 209–225.

Wilde, G. J. S. (1985). The use of incentives for the promotion of accident free driving. *Journal of Studies on Alcohol,* Suppl. 10, 161–167.

Williams, A. F. (1979). Evaluation of the Tennessee child restraint law. *American Journal of Public Health, 69,* 455–458.

Williams, A. F., Ginsburg, M. J., & Burchman, P. F. (1977). Motorcycle helmet use in relation to legal requirements. *Accident Analysis and Prevention*, *9*, 69.

Williams, A. F., & O'Neill, B. (1979). *Seat belt laws: Implications for occupant protection* (SAE Paper No. 790683). Warrendale, PA: Society of Automotive Engineers.

Williams, A. F., & Wells, J. (1981a). The Tennessee child restraint law in its third year. *American Journal of Public Health, 71*, 163–165.

Williams, A. F., & Wells, J. (1981b). Evaluation of the Rhode Island child restraint law. *American Journal of Public Health, 71*, 742–743.

Williams, A. F., Zador, P. L., Harris, S. S., & Karpf, R. S. (1983). The effect of raising the legal minimum drinking age on involvement in fatal crashes. *Journal of Legal Studies, 12*, 169–179.

Wolfe, A. (1974). Characteristics of late-night, weekend drivers: Results of the U.S. National Roadside Breath-Testing Survey and several local surveys. In S. Israelstam & S. Lambert, *Proceedings of the Sixth International Conference on Alcohol, Drugs and Traffic Safety* (pp. 41–49). Toronto: Addiction Research Foundation of Ontario.

Worden, J. K., Waller, J. A., & Riley, T. J. (1975). *The Vermont public education campaign in alcohol and highway safety: A final review and evaluation* (CRASH Report No. I–5). Waterbury, VT: Vermont Department of Mental Health, Project CRASH.

Yudof, M. (1983). When government speaks: Politics, law and government expression in America. Reviewed in F. Schauer, Is government speech a problem? *Stanford Law Review, 35*, 373–386.

Zimring, F., & Hawkins, G. (1973). *Deterrence: The legal threat in crime control.* Chicago: University of Chicago Press.

Zuckerman, M. (1979). Sensation seeking and risk taking. In C. E. Izard (Ed.), *Emotions in personality and psychopathology* (pp. 163–197). New York: Plenum.

Empirical Assessment and Civil Actions[1]

Stanley L. Brodsky

University of Alabama

*I*nstitutional class action suits are legal acts filed on behalf of a group or class of residents of a prison or hospital or other institution. Institutional class actions are filed in federal court, and over the past two decades they have been pursued in large numbers. Such suits seem to be exceptions to Galanter's (1983) carefully developed argument that our society is not increasingly contentious and litigious. Galanter writes that "Lack of scholarly development, the pattern of repetition and cross-citation, reappearance of the same atrocity stories, all suggest that the 'litigation explosion' might be thought of as an item of elite folklore, resembling 'urban legends'" (p. 64). The class actions diverge from this perspective because the courts had not previously accepted institutional regulation as fit business for judicial intervention. Prisons, schools for delinquent youth, and hospitals for the mentally disturbed and retarded have been primary targets of such suits. The rulings of many courts have been sweeping and ambitious, and in at least some cases the consequences have been dramatic.

In an earlier review (Brodsky & Miller, 1981), I observed that such suits have documented the effects of living in total institutions, that the court rulings have prescribed minimal standards of institutional life, and that the state has been directed to offer therapeutic services to citizens under its care. These consequences can also be seen as promoting primary prevention of psychopathology by minimizing coercion, stress, and dependency and by maximizing clients' roles

1. I appreciate the help of John Bonazzi in the preparation of this paper.

in decision making as part of a sense of community. Such class action suits can thus be a vital, extraordinarily valuable vehicle for good in our society. The class action suit clearly stands as a commitment to improving the lot and insuring the rights of the poor, the underserved, and the helpless in our care. This view is hardly idiosyncratic to me. A typical assessment is that of Deborah Rhode (1982), who asserted: "On the whole, institutional reform class actions have made and continue to make an enormous contribution to the realization of fundamental constitutional values—a contribution that no other government construct has been able to duplicate" (p. 1184). Yet it is not so simple. Reform outcomes are not the rule and in some suits are no more than the stuff dreams are made on. Even when courts have ruled for the plaintiffs and even when specific remedies are ordered, meaningful changes may be castles in the air. My reading of the nature of these orders and the extent of institutional compliance (Brodsky, 1982) is that myriad paths may be chosen to avoid full compliance. The problem may be redefined, and changes may be illusory. Take the actual case of a large state psychiatric hospital ordered to provide therapeutic programs for all residents able to benefit from them. Within a year the 150 patients who had been assigned to clearing the grounds of litter and mowing the lawn were designated as receiving "landscape therapy."

This form of social slippage between court intent and institutional change is a problem. However, before court orders or consent decrees are issued, we need a prior foundation of empirical knowledge about the harmful effects to be remedied. The bulk of this paper will address the nature of the knowledge base on which such suits are tried and orders issued.

I shall approach the empirical knowledge base by first addressing broad concerns in the attorney/expert interactions that are part of class actions. In almost all class actions experts are brought in to evaluate the institution, testify about some scientific finding related to the issues at hand, or both. Because much attention is directed toward psychological consequences of institutionalization, psychologists and psychiatrists are among the experts most frequently called on. After the issues of subjectivity and nonobvious persuasion have been developed, I will deal with specific prison evaluations, looking at preliminary data gathering and data gathering proper and finally at data interpretation muddles. With that plan outlined, we can move to the beginning point: the literature on inquiry structure and eyewitness accuracy.

Loftus's (1979) research indicates that the nature of the inquiry process influences recall by eyewitnesses. When queries about filmed automobile accidents were phrased as "smashed" versus "contacted," the eyewitnesses recalled higher speeds. There was a decided shaping of recall based on how the questioner phrased the question. During this process, the subjects were never aware of how malleable their memories were.

Inquiry Structure and Other Participants in Legal Events

There is no reason to assume this phenomenon is limited to eyewitnesses. Any information recall and presentation may be shaped by the nature of the inquiry. Consider questions asked during the voir dire examination of potential witnesses in court. In many jurisdictions, and especially those using group voir dire routinely, the questions the attorneys ask (or write for the judge to ask) are required to have a yes/no format. Considerable social science literature points to major limitations on such closed-ended questions (see, for example, Suggs & Sales, 1981). If information other than highly factual data is sought, then closed-ended questions may reflect the views of the questioner as much as those of the respondent. Both personality assessment and survey research accept as a given the restrictive and persuasive elements in such yes/no questions.

A demonstration based on this principle is sometimes used in lecturing to police about their style of questioning. After a volunteer has left the room, the officers are told to answer all the questions the volunteer asks with "yes" if the last word in the sentence ends in a consonant, "no" if the last word ends in a vowel, and "maybe" if the last word ends in y. The volunteer returns and is told he is to determine what principle everyone has agreed on. He may ask anybody, but only yes, no, or maybe answers will be given. A wild variety of hypotheses can emerge.

Mandated closed-ended questions in jury selection have similar limitations. The difficulty is that the panel's preexisting biases are rarely found. In such a format, social-conformity effects wash away the modest amounts of valid bias reporting.

If this applies to veniremen, it may well apply to other participants as well. It appears that no examinations have been made of the inquiry structures applied to expert witnesses. This concern is probably most pressing in the early stages of soliciting information from the expert and querying his or her results and opinions.

The source and form of an inquiry may have substantial and lasting effects on the responses. Few courtroom studies are available in this area, but studies within social psychology have demonstrated consistent effects concerning the nature of the persuader's or communicator's influence on perception and recall. This has been called confirmatory bias. According to Snyder and Swann (1978), people not only remember evidence that confirms present schemata (or beliefs), they also seek out confirming evidence. These researchers looked at what happened when people were told they were going to meet and interview either introverts or extroverts. Not only did the questions the subjects asked confirm this expectation of introversion or extroversion, they also brought out tendencies to be introverted or extroverted in the individuals interviewed.

Parallels to this effect may be observed in the courtroom. Jones (1985) investigated the differential effect of voir dire questioning by judges and attorneys. Items from an Attitudes toward Law and Justice scale were provided before the jury panels were assembled and then asked orally in the course of the voir dire. Subjects gave significantly different answers depending on whether the questions were asked by judges or by attorneys. The veniremen gave more "proper" law and justice attitude answers to the judges.

Whereas this phenomenon is visible to the attentive observer in the courtroom, many such interactions are private and invisible. Such an invisible process occurs in the discussions between attorneys and expert witnesses. Let us consider the roles and behaviors of attorneys and potential experts to illustrate this process and to move toward making the invisible more accessible.

The motivations of attorneys in class action suits may be complex. Even representing a large class of confined, unhappy people can be difficult; it can lead to what might be called a "Moses complex"—let my people go—or to the dispirited malaise of a Willie Loman.

Money may be a motive too. Attorneys in prolonged institutional class actions have earned sums well into six figures. As one Cook County judge (Holzer, 1981) has written: "The practical, legal, and tactical decisions that arise are often sophisticated and subtle. The rewards are often great for the successful litigant. Class action work is not for the faint-of-heart or the conservative Joe or Jane. The odds are high, but the fees are often high as well, a well-deserved reward" (p. 182).

The ideology of class action attorneys may affect how they represent their clients. This topic is rarely explored between class action clients and attorneys. Indeed, no American Bar Association ethical opinions or disciplinary sanctions have ever been imposed because ideological interests were not disclosed (Rhode, 1982). What is likely to happen in attorney/expert interactions if the attorney is a mildly motivated, court-appointed Willie Loman? A lukewarm advocacy is likely to manifest itself in tone of voice, volume, and other means of influence. After all, about 92% of all emotion is communicated through nonverbal modes (Mehrabian, 1981). Even in the more usual case of a firm, energetic commitment and enthusiastic advocacy, the attorney's attitude may influence the expert in a variety of ways.

The initial contact between attorney and potential expert typically is by telephone. The attorney engages in three discrete tasks: first, describing the "facts" of the case; second, ascertaining the expertise of the expert. These appear to be relatively straightforward tasks, and descriptions can be found in a number of guides to legal practice.

The third task is the object of our present concern. The attorney begins trying to influence the expert by posing questions and seeing how the expert responds. Like the eyewitness research outcomes, language choice and outcome may well be related. Indeed, Edward Sapir, Alfred Korzybski, and Paul Watzlawick have all made compelling cases that language use and our interpretation of events are intimately linked.

Before I describe language use itself, let me note that an outright propagandizing effort is often present. The attorney mobilizes the persuasive skills of the profession and seeks to convince the expert. Take, for example, a case in which a woman was raped at knifepoint, while her husband watched, by a patient accidentally given grounds privileges at a nearby psychiatric hospital. The attorney presented me an extensive verbal picture of a woman severely traumatized, unable to resume her normal marital, occupational, and social roles—then he asked me to evaluate her to find out how the assault had affected her.

The second and more subtle aspect of the persuasive attempt occurs in language use. Just as the skilled interrogator can elicit selective eyewitness recall, it is possible for a skilled attorney to introduce proactive perceptions.

Note that the expert is neither passive nor naive in these events. The obviousness of the direct propagandizing makes it possible that little impact will result. Psychological reactance theory, for example, holds that if someone tries to limit our freedom to act or to feel or think something, we tend to respond in the opposite direction. That is why, according to Jack and Sharon Brehm (Brehm & Brehm, 1981), President Johnson retained all of President Kennedy's appointees when the press had predicted he would not. It is the same reason children refuse to eat spinach when they are told they must: to preserve their freedom to act. So it is with experts who are told what they will find. They may bend over backward to be objective.

However, nonobvious language use is a story that awaits telling. It may best be told by experimental study, and I am now conducting such research in which experienced clinicians read standardized case reports. Then, in a procedure similar to that of Loftus (1979), the clinicians are questioned using words designed either to attend to dramatic aspects of a report or to minimize its impact. This will be tried both with a civil case—a personal injury suit—and with a plea of not guilty by reason of insanity. I anticipate that the intensity of the clinicians' reports, as reflected in ratings by judges and other clinicians, will be substantially influenced.

One additional opportunity for influence occurs during the pretrial discovery process. Rules of procedure typically permit opposing attorneys access to opposing counsels' evidence, including what experts will conclude. Thus the attorney frequently meets with the expert in such discovery before submitting the anticipated evidence to the opposing counsel. While this is often routine, the process offers an interesting and essentially unexplored area of influence on the expert. A typical scenario works this way.

The attorney calls the expert and apologetically explains that the other side has asked exactly what the expert will say. In several telephone conversations, the attorney reads the expert drafts of what he understands the expert plans to say. The expert corrects him and describes what he actually means to say during the deposition. In a nonobvious way, this is a period of negotiation. The attorney tests how far the expert will go in anticipated support of the case he is mobilizing. The expert works to draw a clear boundary about the extent of his conclusions and scope of his findings. Social scientists have not examined this bargaining, nor have legal sources dealt with this phase beyond describing the technical and procedural issues involved.

However, this is a critical and fascinating stage. Most civil actions are settled before trial, or at least before the jury or bench verdict. The foundation of such settlements is the perceived relative strength of each side. Although this assessment of relative strength is determined by many sources of information, including depositions, this pretrial preparation of anticipated testimony is a formal, explicit contribution to "sizing up" each other's cases.

Institutional Assessment

SELECTION AND BIAS IN SOURCES OF DATA

Up to this point I have been examining elements of persuasion and subjectivity in expert/lawyer interactions. Potential subjectivity is hardly limited to how the expert reacts to the attorney. A case can be made that there are just as many sources of subjectivity and error in the data phases of the expert's tasks. Thus for the moment I will set aside discussions of the attorney and move to the institutions proper, asking about the ways of assessing total institutions, especially prisons, and the implications for understanding these institutions.

Three dominant issues exist in assessment of prison and mental hospital environments: how the data are gathered, the nature of the data, and how the data are interpreted. I shall consider each of these in turn.

GATHERING THE DATA

No single, standardized procedure is used for gathering institutional effects data. After all, compared with the perhaps 2 million individual evaluations done each year (counting intellectual and achievement evaluations), institutional assessments by psychologists are rare. Between 100 and 1,000 are probably conducted yearly, and the best estimate is closer to the lower number. Few psychologists do any at all, and those who do, perform fewer than half a dozen evaluations—one or two a year would be modal. Thus almost every assessor may be applying some existing methods while at the same time clearing a new path.

Given this caveat, let us look at methods of data gathering. These practices are among the most common means of evaluating institutions.

Visual inspection of the physical plant

Review of incident reports and mental health reports, and medical records

Interviews with on-site administrators and professionals

Discussions with inmates who seek out the evaluators

Discussions with inmates who are visible and readily accessible

Passive observation of specific housing or activity units

Review of secondary documents, such as reports of other evaluators and depositions

Systematic or random inmate interviews

Formal research approaches

There are more possibilities. However, no one of these approaches can be counted on to appear in an assessor's procedure. Part of the diversity of approaches arises because the assessments are global. The task is not to evaluate the quality of mental health services or the impact of living in disciplinary segregation units, tasks that have the potential for being well defined. Instead these assessments are concerned with the effects that an entire institutional milieu has on the residents. I will describe a set of procedures I have developed for such global assessments of prisons.

My procedural checklist begins with structured interviews or tests with systematically or randomly chosen inmates. The interviews can be individual, which is preferred, or with a very small group. They should last at least ten minutes per inmate and attend to specific predetermined items, with queries about the extent of existing problems.

The sampling calls for about 40 to 50 inmates per institution, chosen from an alphabetical roster of prisoners. If the count is 1,000 men, every 20th name is chosen. The procedure thus assumes that no selection bias would be present and that alphabetical units of 20 would reasonably sample inmates throughout living and work units.

Are 40 or 50 men enough to sample a prison? Probably, for a point of diminishing returns affects sample size. After a certain number of subjects, additional interviews do not contribute substantially to the decision-making process. Note that it is *decision making* about which I am talking. No objective external referent exists for validity. The principle is that the absolute size of the sample is much more important than what proportion of the population the sample represents. This is why we accept Gallup polls of 1,200 people to survey population attitudes for the entire United States. However, unnatural statistical operations are sometimes performed just because these are evaluations in class action suits. Two experienced assessors urge that "it pays to invest in far larger samples than one really needs. Experience suggest that a 25% sample seems reasonable in advocacy proceedings, while a 10% sample is often too small. The fact that such figures are typically irrelevant to the real power of one's statistical inferences is beside the point" (Berk & Oppenheim, 1979, p. 135).

The invisible subjects. An interesting subgroup of men appears when prisoners are sampled randomly. This subgroup is composed of individuals who have slipped through the institutional routine without being noticed by anyone and who are puzzled and occasionally distressed that they are to be interviewed. Twenty years ago when I was a psychologist at the United States Disciplinary Barracks in Fort Leavenworth, Kansas, Anthony Perino and I conducted a study of men like this (Brodsky & Perino, 1967). We started with a full prisoner roster. Then we crossed out the names of all men who had disciplinary reports. Subsequently we eliminated the names of men who had applied for job changes, had used the infirmary, had received mental health or counseling services, had been promoted to better cellblocks or dormitories, or were known by name to any of the officers who worked in living units. About 7% of the men remained on the list.

We then interviewed these men and another group selected at random. The study group was extremely difficult to interview. They spoke minimally and were suspicious, so that our time with them passed with agonizing slowness. The control group was interested and lively. We named the study group "uninvolved prisoners," men who were hidden from observation and who had developed efficient mechanisms for remaining unseen. The term uninvolved seemed more prudent than words like schizoid, though such speculative labeling was sometimes generated with sufficient intensity to make a Szaszian rage with linguistic indignation.

Men like these uninvolved prisoners inevitably show up in random procedures. They are detached by choice or by dynamics. To say they are difficult to interview understates the problem. They wish to say little. Most important, these are men who are never seen in other than random or systematic interviews and whose interpersonal style makes it hard to know what effects institutional living has on them.

The unavailable subjects. Attempting to interview from a count within an alphabetical roster clarifies how many men are unavailable for interviewing. If a roster of 50 is generated, 10 or 15 men will not show up as scheduled or will show up three hours late. In prisons with farming operations, men may be miles away driving a tractor or planting soybeans. When they eventually do appear, it generally is just when the allocated interviewing hours are over. They may be sweaty, caked with dust and mud, and quizzical, especially when their interviewer disappears as they come in the door.

Other unavailable men are those in the prison hospital, on death row, in disciplinary segregation, or in protective custody. Interviewing without such organized sampling never permits awareness of those one does not see. The result yields what Zimring and Hawkins (1973) have called the "warden's fallacy," in which the prison warden draws his conclusions about all murderers from observing the men on death row. As difficult as it is to assess the effects of a whole prison, it is far more difficult when we inadvertantly exclude up to half the inmates.

THE NATURE OF THE DATA

The room set aside for interviewing the inmates was a converted laundry storage room with no windows or soft surfaces. The walls, floor, and ceiling were rough concrete, all a dirty gray, and the only furniture was 13 straight-backed wooden chairs, one in front facing three rows of four chairs.

The men filed in quietly and showed mild interest when I asked them to help rearrange the chairs in a circle. The attorney who had brought me there sat outside the circle in the corner. She was not inconspicuous.

I introduced myself as a psychologist brought in to find out what it was like to live in this prison and in this cellbock. Cries of indignation and "tish" (Eric Berne has suggested transposing consonants in unacceptable words) burst out against their treatment within the institution. The tone was familiar: hurt, anger, petulance, and emotional release in the telling. The content was familiar too. "This place treats me like a boy, not like a man. I am a man and I want to be treated like a man, not a boy. You hear?"

The men criticized the officers and complained about lack of access to services. The problems of disturbed inmates were impossible. Too little space. Too much noise. Dirt. Insects. Heat. Cold. Bad food. Hypocrisy.

These assertions are both to be believed and not to be believed. They are to be believed because they are deeply felt reports of the experience of imprisonment—the complaints arise directly from the men's daily living. What they feel is what they say. They do feel infantilized. They are closely confined, often in crowded, dirty, and noisy living conditions.

But these complaints are also not to be believed (or at least not to be overweighted in the assessment process), because they are so much a part of being imprisoned. Men are deprived of freedom and choice and space. Such deprivations exist in all prisons. Furthermore, almost all prisoners fuss angrily about their living conditions. Only naive or inexperienced evaluators make judgments from prisoner complaints alone. Lack of freedom and all it entails is such a profound and fundamental loss that the imprisonment experience evokes these reactions in all but a handful of institutions.

How should these complaints be taken? If the prisoners' reports are not accepted, then what is the basis for judging prison impact? Several answers emerge.

1. Comparative judgments. The severity of the inmates' complaints must be compared with routine inmate complaints in garden-variety institutions. In other words, the signal-to-noise ratio should be ascertained. Standards of reference are still central, but a sense of perspective to level out our personal judgments is important as well. After all, when Maslow identified self-actualization as the epitome of human adjustment, he based it on his ideas of ideal adjustment—Beethoven, Eleanor Roosevelt, and so on—hardly on objective personal values.

2. Pathological signs. If inmates are suffering adverse psychological consequences, most men will show the harm in disturbances of affect, in quality of thinking, in discontinuities of behavior and cognition, and in other manifestations. It is not the words that are of primary importance, but the behaviors.

3. Complaints as hypotheses. Rather than assuming that prisoner complaints are answers, assume they are hypotheses. The assessor's task is to look for multiple sources of information to test these hypotheses. Much like Aaron Beck's concept of "collaborative empiricism" in his model of cognitive therapy (1976), complaints are starting points or potential sources of either support or disconfirmation of existing concerns.

4. Group process. When an inmate bitterly complains, he will sometimes trigger a dramatic chorus of agreement that is a product of group support. This is to be taken less seriously than independent assertions, unless clear and compelling individual examples support it. A social conformity and embarrassment effect limits honest participation by the weak, the shy, and the victimized. Prison

Darwinism leads the powerless to defer to the concerns of the powerful. Assessors also recognize power and often attribute excess weight to the opinions of aggressive and outspoken participants.

Now that I have aired these concerns about perspective in the assessment process, we can return to my earlier comment about material to be believed and not believed. Such a comment is not courtroom appropriate. Rather, it fits into the category of observations that have the potential for wreaking havoc in the course of courtroom testimony.

Norman Poythress (1982) in an open letter to Judge David Bazelon and Stephen Morse, among others, in *Law and Human Behavior*, told what happened when he talked in court about what it meant for psychologists to offer their best professional opinions. As you may know, a long finger has emerged in the literature pointing angrily at those who give or are cajoled into giving professional judgments on ultimate legal opinions on responsibility or competency. When Poythress made his offhand disclaimer, all hell broke loose. The jury was ordered out of the room. The sleepy-eyed judge and attorneys became electrified. Intense questioning followed, with a self-consciousness worthy of Dostoevski, until everyone finally understood that Poythress was only saying in public what was usually reserved for private talks, and that he did not mean to suggest he was not expert on the case or the subject matter.

The same thing would happen if an expert were to proffer that his or her findings both should be believed and should not be believed. After these ratiocinations had hit the fan, inevitably the expert would move on to conclude that what was meant was "best professional judgment," and that unfortunate language had been used. Our excessive introspection about such legal-psychological concerns is best done alone, behind closed doors, and we should wash our hands afterward.

The Heisenberg principle. When physical chemistry researchers attempt to pinpoint an electron in space, they are confronted with a dilemma called the Heisenberg principle. The act of observing and exactly locating the electron interferes with its natural spinning movement. To know with precision means stopping the electron, which creates an effect of its own. Chemistry has resolved this problem by settling for an approximate position estimate.

In psychological assessment we can see a parallel effect. Arnold Buss (1980) has labeled this public self-awareness. The normally fluent person who stumbles and stutters in front of a judgmental audience demonstrates this principle. So does the person walking down a city sidewalk who modifies gaze and gait if others watch attentively. Every parent who sees a child in cute, unselfconscious play knows this effect as the child poses and postures before the camera.

This awareness of others' attention often creates problems and occasionally has disastrous effects. For example, in Kurt Vonnegut's 1959 novel *The Sirens of Titan*, the messenger Salo, a three-legged, three-eyed, tangerine-skinned machine, the most handsome, healthy, and clean-minded of his species, had been chosen by the planners of his planet Tralfamadore to carry a sealed message from one end of the universe to the other. Against explicit orders, he opens this message prepared by the wisest elders of his world. With agonizing self-consciousness, he discovers the message says only "Greetings." He promptly takes himself apart and throws his components in all directions.

Not everyone disassembles himself on the sands of Titan in moments of sudden self-consciousness. Still, becoming suddenly aware of aspects of the presentation of self does have the potential for dramatic effects. The act of assessing individual clients often yields atypical behaviors and produces the equivalent of the experimenter effect. In her book *Individualizing Psychological Assessment*, Constance Fischer (1985) has expanded the understanding of such assessments. One of her foundations for a new vision is to attend to the meaning of the situation for the client. She argues: "Assessment, even of the traditional sort, always affects the client—who inevitably finds the experience meaningful in one way or another. . . . We recognize that people participate in what happens to them; they shape as well as are shaped by their worlds" (p. 47).

The problem, of course, is that we usually have no baseline. Without a historical context we have trouble digging out the Heisenberg principle. Is this the way the person was an hour ago? Was the hospital ward the same last week? Did any major changes occur because we were there? The best answers may well be "yes" and "I don't know." We say "I don't know" far too seldom in our scientific work. We do know that a ward or cellblock, like a mental health center or a cocktail party, can be transformed by a newcomer.

The limitations of single point in time assessments are substantial. We have only one porthole to gaze through, and we never know what information we are missing. Without multiple observations, it is often unrealistic to believe that reliable answers are forthcoming.

The best answer for the one-time assessor of institutional settings often is "I don't know." Yet sometimes we do know. Consider a hospital ward I inspected as part of a class action against the hospital administrators. The complaint described 120 elderly, disturbed women, fouled with their own wastes, lying in locked rooms all day, with no furniture, toothbrushes, or programs and only four staff members. The hospital administration had become litigaphobic (Brodsky, 1983; Breslin, Hall, & Brodsky, 1985) and was determined to abort this suit.

The news that I was to inspect the building had a noticeable effect. When I arrived the building was immaculate—newly air conditioned and painted and brightly furnished. All the residents were in clean dresses, and each had an aide or volunteer helping her color in coloring books. No smell was present. Seven senior hospital administrators followed me around, cooing with pride. I was first startled and then amused. Heisenberg was alive and well and hiding in a sprawling state hospital.

NOISE IN THE SYSTEM

One limitation on data interpretation is "noise in the system," which Loewen (1982) has especially applied to problems in sex discrimination suits. Loewen describes how misunderstanding of questionnaires and population migrations (so populations differ from census data) fit this category. In institutions, the potential for other static is considerable. When a major incident has occurred, such as a strike by the staff, a killing, or the closing of a housing unit, the reactive emotion may be temporary and not a good indication of long-term institutional effects. Similarly, the J-curve of unfulfilled expectations, when a group of inmates realizes that hopes that had been raised will be thwarted, leads to transient, uncharacteristic problems.

Similar noise arises from more positive sources. A change of administration, a new and creative kitchen supervisor, the opening of a recreation yard causes passing but impressive changes in how the institution feels to its residents. Like other static, such effects are short term, and it is the continuing baseline about which an assessor must be concerned.

Interpreting Prison Data: Case Studies

I shall approach the next aspect of data interpretation through prison case studies. A first step is defining purpose. A projective process frequently is implicit in task definition within the overall limits of the class action complaint. Our own conceptual frames of reference sharply delimit what we hear and do. Consider a prison suit against a northern state in which I was involved.

One expert in cognitive-legal development had assessed this state's prison system. He had testified, before I was called to the stand, that the effectiveness of the entire system and surely all existing and proposed treatment programs could best be understood in terms of the inmates' cognitive-legal development. Apparently he was a compelling witness, and opposing counsel asked me if his assertion was true.

The good witness's answer to such a question would have been that this was not within my particular area of expertise and I could not speak knowledgeably on the topic. Instead I took the opportunity to address how a worldview, as Watzlawick (1978) has formulated the concept, of the workings of systems and people comes from many beginning points. The whole sphere of human experience may be divided into an infinite number of slices. Looking at each slice, we see a full circle. Cognitive-legal development is only one such slice. Operant approaches would be another, as would hierarchy of motives, homeostasis, and so on.

Few of our worldviews are directly accessible to us. Thus, as I describe these institutional assessments, this limitation on awareness of assumptions applies to me as well. The next case study I shall consider is of the prison system in a large southwestern state, which has been either sued or under court order for overcrowding for more than ten years.

My inspections were intended to assess the effect of population density on the inmates. An underlying assumption was that close confinement and crowding in both dormitories and cells constitute a clear psychological health hazard. However, inmates are seen as differentially vulnerable to such hazards. Furthermore, other institutional factors, such as inmate environmental control and out-of-cell time, are assumed to be potential ameliorating influences.

The data were gathered in two prisons. No prison visit is complete without a walk-through inspection, despite the major limitations on knowledge gained from the walk through. Thus I made a personal inspection of the living quarters and the institution as a whole, briefly interviewing inmates in their cells and staff on duty. I examined available data on psychological effects, such as medication patterns, suicide attempts, and assault records. Finally I drew a random sample of inmates for interviewing, taking every 40th prisoner from an alphabetical roster of all inmates: 30 men were interviewed.

When I interviewed the men, I used a standard introduction intended to encourage openness without explicitly evoking descriptions of pathology or other prisoner response sets. I told the prisoners:

> My name is Dr. Stan Brodsky and I am a psychologist from the University of Alabama. I am here to inspect the living units in this prison. When I came in, I walked through all the cell blocks. However, I know there is a difference between walking through and looking at cells and living in them. Your names have been taken at random alphabetically from a roster of prisoners. I would appreciate it if you would be willing to share with me what it is like living here in the cellblock and if it has had any effect on you. Although I will take notes on what you say, no names will be used in my report.

In this first of the assessed institutions the interviews indicated that 20% of the men preferred double-celling and found having a cell partner a positive emotional experience. Another 40% described double-celling as a substantial personal problem. The remaining 40% reported some difficulties with double-celling but said it was not a severe problem.

The men who reported no problem and who preferred a cell partner said they liked the company and enjoyed having a choice of cellmates. They made the following comments.

> I'd rather have a cellie. Someone to talk to. My cellie was with me at another prison. Here you have a choice and can get a cell partner.

> I got a home buddy with me. No anxiety, no problem, no threats. I would rather share a cell. It's all right with me. I like someone to talk to.

> I like having the cell partner. I need someone to talk to. It takes understanding toward one another.

> It's all right to have a cell partner. I'm happy with my cell partner. The space is not too cramped. Not really.

> I have been with a cellie for a while, and then without one and then with one. Together you help each other. it's a big load off your back.

My brother and I are cellies. We talk and relate real well. It's wonderful having him as a cellie. It makes time go by much easier.

The experiences and self-reports of the inmates for whom these double cells were a problem were so different that it sounds as if they were in a different institution. Their comments focused on the lack of privacy, the sense of crowding, and the resultant tension. They stated:

It's uncomfortable. You can't sleep at night because you don't know what he's done. Cells are too small, too. You can't sleep because the first rule in a place like that is you don't trust nobody.

Tense. My cellie is in the way. It's a hassle. We stay in the house most of the time.

It's a hell of a problem. My cellie before had 60 years. He was bringing punks in the house. My commissary was coming up missing. You get diseases from using the same stuff as your cellie. I've a skin rash on my penis. I want to be alone, to have a little privacy.

I've double-celled one and a half years and had eight cellies. A problem. Not enough room to house our stuff. Different work shifts. If I'm in a bad mood, not enough privacy. It interferes with my sleep.

I just can't get along with a cell partner. One, he told me to take my picture down, so I beat him up. The bosses laugh in my face and talk about me.

Such data and comments do lead to a consideration of what conclusions might be drawn about this institution. Is it likely that about three fifths of these men suffer no substantial adverse psychological consequences of the double-celling? I think so. Interviews of inmates at a similar maximum-security prison (a third institution that I will not discuss here) produced approximately the same incidence. We must note that not all the men reporting problems may have psychological sequelae; however, a majority surely do.

Are there important ameliorating influences at this institution? Yes. The maintenance of some open cells, the ready self-choice of cell partners, and the daily switching of over 50 cell assignments definitely helped. The more opportunity there is to choose one's cell partner and to get rid of a difficult one, the less stress is felt in double-celling. Furthermore, some aggressive men are single-celled. The extensive work and education programs are other ameliorating influences. I mention such influences because of the importance of balancing one's evaluation. If not everyone is equally affected, which is a safe bet in most aspects of reactions to institutional living, then differential effects must be addressed.

Let us consider a second institution in this same state. This prison, opened in 1982, is constructed of corrugated metal—the staff members good-naturedly call it a Reynolds Wrap prison. All inmates are housed in 16 dormitories with 66 beds each (33 double bunks). The dormitories are all essentially alike: long rooms with a center aisle 18 feet wide dividing rows of 15 to 18 double bunks, their heads against the walls. The ceilings are high, there is a locked storage chest at the foot of each bed, and about 3 feet separate the bunks. Two urinals and two toilets are present.

Every 20th man was chosen from an alphabetical roster. All 43 men selected were interviewed, using small groups of five or six men at a time, in 30- to 40-minute sessions. The interviews indicated that 46.5% of men interviewed had substantial psychological problems with living in the dormitories. These problems took the form of tension effects, bottled-up anger or frustration, insomnia, anxiety, depression, or anger control.

No problems or psychological reactions were found in 23.3% of the interviewed men. They asserted that it made no difference to them, that they liked the freedom to walk around, that things simply didn't bother them, that they tried to fit in, or that they actively and successfully avoided spending time in the dormitory. The third group of prisoners had some adjustment difficulties; 30.2% of the men interviewed fell into this category. Although these men complained of the lack of privacy or the noise, there were no indications of substantial adjustment disruptions.

This second prison illustrates that unpleasant living conditions are not necessarily associated with psychological harm. Three specific concerns were voiced by men in all three categories of psychological impact. They described these fundamental issues:

1. Toilet availability. The number of toilets was seen as inadequate, particularly since so many men in each dorm get up at the same time. As a result, men wait long periods for their turns at the toilets.

2. Noise levels. With this many men sharing the space, the noise from televisions, radios, fans, conversations, and door closing constitutes a substantial din. No place is available for quiet.

3. Space. Although the overall square footage appears adequate, much dormitory space is underutilized. The bunks are crowded

together on the sides, double-bunking is used, and only four seats are available for the entire dormitory population.

To recapitulate, just over 40% of these prisoners described the subjective experience of crowding as a problem. Just over 20% reported no difficulties, and the remaining men had mild to moderate difficulties. The three areas of concern identified were toilet availability, noise, and space.

To what use were the conclusions about these two institutions put? Their utilization was typical of such assessments. I prepared reports for an anticipated trial date, which was postponed and postponed again. Both sides worked with episodic success at negotiating an out-of-court settlement. The extensive preparation with the unclear outcome is a bit like the experience of Shel Silverstein's Melissa of Coconut Grove, who twists, turns, and tumbles in every way imaginable off the diving board, only to discover that an empty pool waits below.

Conclusion

It is useful to put these observations in perspective. Case law has been serving as an instrument of social change in the arena of institutional reform. Much like racial desegregation laws, class action outcomes have been slowly redefining our joint obligations to the powerless and disenfranchised. In the process, society is becoming reeducated. Psychological assessments are just one part of a giant, slowly moving apparatus. The assessments do play an educative role in aiding defendants, typically the state, to recognize problems in their correctional and mental health systems. Empirical and replicable assessments thus can be seen not only as tools in the adversarial process, but also as a common information base on which planning and decisions can be made. Granted they are inexact information sources, yet their imprecision represents a challenge thrown to us to move toward more reliable and useful means of understanding the effects of institutions on our citizens in their care.

REFERENCES

Beck, A. T. (1976). *Cognitive therapy and the emotional disorders*. New York: International Universities Press.

Berk, R. A., & Oppenheim, J. (1979). Doing good well: The use of quantitative social science data in advocacy proceedings. *Law and Policy Quarterly,*
1, 123–146.

Brehm, S., & Brehm, J. W. (1981). *Psychological reactance: A theory of freedom*
and control. New York: Academic Press.

Breslin, F., Hall, K., & Brodsky, S. L. (1985). *The development of a litigaphobia*
scale. Paper presented at the Southeastern Psychological Association
Convention, Atlanta.

Brodsky, S. L. (1982). Prison action suits: The aftermaths. In J. Gunn & D. P.
Farrington (Eds.), *Abnormal offenders, delinquency, and the criminal justice*
system. New York: Wiley.

Brodsky, S. L. (1983). A case report of the litigaphobic release from involuntary confinement. *Public Service Psychology, 2*(3), 11.

Brodsky, S. L., & Miller, K. S. (1981). Coercing change in prisons and men-
tal hospitals: The social scientist and the class action suit. In J. M. Joffe &
G. W. Albee (Eds.), *Prevention through political action and social change.*
Hanover, NH: University Press of New England.

Brodsky, S. L., & Perino, A. (1967). *The uninvolved prisoner.* Fort Leavenworth, KS: Council for Research and Evaluation, U.S. Disciplinary Barracks.

Buss, A. H. (1980). *Self-consciousness and social anxiety.* San Francisco: W. H.
Freeman.

Fischer, C. T. (1985). *Individualizing psychological assessment.* Monterey, CA:
Brooks/Cole.

Galanter, M. (1983). Reading the landscape of disputes: What we know and
don't (and think we know) about our allegedly contentious and litigious
society. *UCLA Law Review, 31*, 4–11.

Holzer, R. J. (1981). Class actions: Some practical observations from the
bench. *Chicago Bar Record, 62*, 176–182.

Jones, S. E. (1985). *Judge versus attorney-conducted voir dire: An empirical inves-*
tigation of veniremen self-disclosure. Unpublished doctoral dissertation,
University of Alabama.

Loewen, J. W. (1982). *Social science in the courtroom: Statistical techniques and*
research methods for winning class action suits. Lexington, MA: Lexington
Books.

Loftus, E. (1979). *Eyewitness testimony.* Cambridge, MA: Harvard University
Press.

Mehrabian, A. (1981). *Silent messages: Implicit communication of emotions and*
attitudes (2nd ed). Belmont, CA: Wadsworth.

Poythress, N. G., Jr. (1982). Concerning reform in expert testimony: An
open letter from a practicing psychologist. *Law and Human Behavior, 6*, 39–
43.

Rhode, D. L. (1982). Class conflicts in class actions. *Stanford Law Review, 34,* 1183–1262.

Snyder, M., & Swann, W. B., Jr. (1978). Behavioral confirmation in social action: From social perception to social reality. *Journal of Experimental Social Psychology, 14,* 148–162.

Suggs, D., & Sales, B. D. (1981). Juror self-disclosure in the voir dire: A social science analysis. *Indiana Law Journal, 56,* 245–271.

Vonnegut, K. (1959). *The sirens of Titan.* New York: Dell.

Watzlawick, P. (1978). *The language of change.* New York: Basic Books.

Zimring, F. E., & Hawkins, G. J. (1973). *Deterrence: The legal threat in crime control.* Chicago: University of Chicago Press.

The Law as an Instrument of Socialization and Social Structure

Gary B. Melton
University of Nebraska–Lincoln
Michael J. Saks
Boston College

Introduction

*T*he other papers in this Symposium have primarily addressed the direct relationship between law and behavior. Thus, Nader examined changes in the law and the legal system as a reflection of changes in the behavior of the users of law. Other authors have considered the efficacy of law in altering individual and group behavior through rewards or through fear of aversive consequences. Although these issues are important, there is questionable utility in confining ourselves to a stimulus-response approach in attempting to determine whether and how the law affects behavior.

In this paper, we do not conceptualize the law as a carrot or a stick motivating citizens to comply with the will of the legislature and other state authorities. Indeed, as discussed elsewhere in this Symposium (Melton), the remedies available for noncompliance often may be so limited that they render the law a tiger that, if not toothless, is realistically more growl than bite.[1] Even if the law is ineffective as a deterrent (which is not to suggest that it necessarily is), it

---

1. Of course, the crucial variables in determining whether deterrence occurs should be *perceived* certainty and severity of punishment (see Gibbs, this volume). Although it would be surprising to find no correlation between perceived and actual probability of punishment for noncompliance, obviously perceptions and reality need not be congruent. This observation underscores the importance of the issues discussed in this chapter. The *symbolic* authority of the law may play an important role in determining whether a threat of punishment is perceived and, therefore, whether deterrence occurs.

still may have important indirect effects on the behavior of both individuals and the community as a whole.

We will focus on two additional types of effects that may mediate
whether the law affects behavior in the short term and may underlie
the enduring role of law in transmitting core social values across
generations. We will first examine the role of law in stitching
together the social fabric, in establishing the *structures* for implementation of the values expressed in the law. Thus, even if the contingencies ostensibly established in law (e.g., imprisonment for
misconduct) are ineffective, the law ultimately still may affect behavior by altering social structures and the opportunities and environmental demands for particular forms of behavior. The *social*
contingencies affected by law may be effective in altering or maintaining behavior even if the *legal* contingencies themselves are not.

Second, we will discuss the socializing effects of law. The law may
function as moral educator. Rather than *changing* the norms of the
community, it may serve primarily to *announce* social norms, to provide cues for moral behavior. As such, the law may be a major con-
tributor to social stasis.

A brief and homely illustration will make clear these three paths
of legal influence on behavior. Consider the choice of which side of
the road cars should drive on. This is an issue without inherent moral content. Which side of the road the state chooses is of no importance. But that the state choose one is a necessity. And that compliance be widespread is a necessity as well. How does the law
achieve this compliance? First—but least—the law is prepared to
impose sanctions on drivers who violate the announced norm. Imposing such sanctions is rarely necessary, however. The announcement of an official norm that, like this one, facilitates the action of
the public, offers immediate and obvious rewards to those who will
comply. Because large numbers of people are complying, it becomes
difficult for others to violate the norm. Behavior is channeled into
the normative pattern by the flow of everyone else's behavior and
by the design of some highways that make norm violation a virtual
impossibility. This is an example of the second general path by
which the law influences behavior: a structuring of the social world
(the flow of other people) and the physical world (the roads themselves) so as to promote compliance without direct application of
carrot or stick. And third, a person being socialized into such a
world becomes so accustomed to cars' driving on a certain side of
the road that the serious possibility of driving on the other side does
not even occur to most people. The norm defines the world of the

road. The choice becomes so "intuitively obvious," the behavior so habitual, that a person is far more likely simply to comply with the norm than to think about violating or questioning it. The norm becomes "second nature" to citizens, so much a part of their schemas that it is all but lost from awareness. Thus Americans who visit British driving territory, either as drivers or as pedestrians, find themselves dangerously disoriented. Their habits of walking and driving do not fit the British world into which they have wandered and which is now rushing past them at high speed. Many readers know this experience firsthand.

Thus the law may so structure society and through the announcement of a norm may so socialize the members of a society that punishment becomes all but superfluous as a means of bringing about compliance with the announced norm.

The Law as an Instrument of Social Structure

Initially, we will explore and elaborate upon some of the ways the law may structure society so as to make some behavior more likely and other behavior less likely. An early experiment by Mowrer ("reported" through films, cited in Daniel, 1942, and elsewhere) provides an illustration of the general phenomenon, and we offer it not as evidence but as analogy. In his demonstration, Mowrer placed several rats in a cage with a feed hopper and a bar to press. His interest was in the social relations that would develop among the rats as he varied features of their physical environment, notably the locations of the bar and the hopper and the temporal relation between presses of the bar and the delivery of food in the hopper. Such simple manipulations created drastically different "societies." One configuration produced cooperative turn taking, another a class structure of drones and aristocrats, another a society of rugged individualists.

There are several different aspects of the law as a designer of the behavioral architecture of our world. The first we shall examine is what might be called the downstream effects of direct sanctions.

DOWNSTREAM EFFECTS OF DIRECT SANCTIONS

The direct creation of contingencies of reward and punishment not only affects the behavior immediately concerned but also may set up a chain of behavior that conditions other behavior, which in turn conditions still other behavior. This is, in essence, the system theorist's dictum that you cannot change just one thing (Saks & Miller, 1979). Let us look at some examples of both the inadvertent and the deliberate use of this domino effect of law.

Criminal law is the usual place to start. The law imposes criminal sanctions in order to reduce the probability of certain behavior under some theory of general or special deterrence. Some commentators and researchers have pointed out that these sanctions often carry unintended side effects that may work at cross-purposes to the legislature's goal.

In one study, Hart (1978) used a cross-lagged panel design to study the effects of punishment in 50 military companies (about 200 soldiers per company). He found that punishment at Time 1 led to *increased* misbehavior at Time 2 rather than to the intended decreased behavior. The punishment apparently interacted with intergroup processes operating among black soldiers and white officers. When punishment was seen as racially motivated, it was likely to have the effect of increasing the very behavior it sought to deter.

In a less direct example, consider the attempt to control illicit drugs through increased criminal sanctions and greater investment in investigation and enforcement. If the police, like those in Campbell and Ross's (1968) study of speeding, feel the new penalties excessive, they might enforce them less fully than before. Juries may find the penalty more onerous than their intuitive sense of justice can tolerate and respond by acquitting defendants they would otherwise have convicted. In eighteenth-century England, 320 crimes carried a penalty of death. Juries often nullified those laws by refusing to convict (Rembar, 1980). Other commentators have noted the economic spiral created by increased expenditures on drug law enforcement. As more resources are put into enforcement and the enforcement is more successful in removing drugs from the marketplace, the demand for drugs grows, the price goes higher, and it becomes more attractive to enter the business of importing and distributing. The higher profitability will ensure that the drugs keep flowing. If the government responds by investing even more resources in stemming the flow of drugs, it ensures that the drug business becomes more profitable even as—or really because—it grows more risky. The goal of rational law enforcement is never to enforce more and more—to the point where enforcement produces more harm than the evil under attack—but to find the optimal point where both the costs (broadly defined) of the proscribed conduct and the costs of enforcement are damaging the society the least (e.g., Nagel & Neef, 1977).

These are but a few examples where penalties go up and punishment goes down. These seemingly paradoxical effects occur because the sanctions are conceived in a relative vacuum but must operate in the context of a legal *system*. If the law builds up its system piece by piece, each in isolation from the others, it loses control over itself. No social system, of course, is going to be prefabricated and erected all at once. But renovations are more likely to succeed to the degree that they are made in awareness of how they will fit in with the existing structure.

The tax laws are perhaps the most deliberate and knowing attempt by the government to promote some behavior by creating incentives for engaging in it. Consider the charitable deduction. The federal tax laws seek to promote altruism, or at least charitable giving, by rewarding people with a deduction for a portion of the amount donated. So much for the direct reward. What are some of the downstream consequences? Some scholars (Needham, 1971; Tax Institute, 1972) have noted that the amount of the reward (or deduction, as the Internal Revenue Service calls it) is a function of the taxpayer's marginal tax rate. Thus wealthier taxpayers, who are in higher tax brackets, get larger absolute and relative rewards for their deductions than taxpayers with lower marginal tax rates. And this in turn means that the charities preferred by the well-to-do (more likely to be educational, scientific, and cultural) will be better financed than those of less affluent taxpayers (more likely to be religious organizations). This superior financing occurs, first, because the incentive is greater for the wealthier taxpayer with the higher marginal tax rate, and second because the loss to the Treasury owing to the deduction is made up by the payments of other taxpayers. The effect is to create a not entirely obvious flow of money from the poorer taxpayers to charities favored by the richer taxpayers. Those better subsidized causes are then better enabled to carry on their own business of structuring the social world in their own way. Obviously this stream of structure, behavior, and money continues, but we will forgo further exploration.

As a final example of this kind of downstream effect of law, let us consider the law of torts. The purposes of tort law, as explicated by the scholars of the law and economics movement (e.g., Calabresi, 1970; Kronman & Posner, 1979), is—essentially and to oversimplify—efficient cost spreading and behavior modification. Moreover, many of the doctrines that have developed within tort law can be explained as attempts to accomplish these goals. This contrasts with the general public's vision of tort law as a kind of punishment for such civil wrongdoing as crashing your car into someone else's or amputating the wrong leg. What the law of torts seems to be trying to do is to spread the cost of society's accidents fairly widely, yet within predictable limits, and at the same time to create costs and rewards for certain behavior and thereby to shape the probability of future behavior. Tort doctrines can be seen to a large extent as an attempt to serve these two goals simultaneously. The legal economists who have studied tort law from their vantage point have been rather good at looking at its downstream effects.

Consider an example from medical malpractice. A surgeon is sued because a sponge is left inside a patient. It turns out that the job of counting sponges and other instruments is the responsibility of the surgical nurses. Surgeons are busy with other matters. As a result, counting instruments is an important task placed firmly on the shoulders of the nurses. The surgeon relies on their count. And indeed, if the surgeon spent much time worrying about the accuracy of sponge counts, it could only work to the detriment of the patient.

Suppose it is clear that a surgeon relied on the count made by the nurses and their assurance that all sponges were accounted for. But the nurses erred. If the patient with the sponge sues the doctor the patient will very likely win. In terms of attribution of blame, this seems an unjust result. The negligence was that of the nurses. The defendant surgeon fulfilled his or her responsibilities well. But in cost-spreading terms it can be seen as the most just result available. Normally one might think to sue the hospital, as the employer of the nurses, which hires, trains, and supervises them. The nurses' error becomes the hospital's responsibility. This is the doctrine of *respondeat superior:* employers pay for the torts of their employees. But owing to the (now defunct) doctrine of charitable immunity, the hospital was immune from suit. If the doctor were held not liable because she or he was not negligent, the only defendant left to sue would be the nurses, and they do not have enough money to compensate the patient. The doctor, on the other hand, is in the best position to absorb and spread the cost of the injury. The surgeon can treat such eventualities as part of the cost of doing business and increase fees a bit among all patients (or better yet, purchase insurance) as a way to spread cost.

Now let us look at the behavioral implications of two different legal rules for accomplishing this same result. In *Guilbeau v. Saint Paul Fire and Marine Insurance Company* (1975), just such a case, the

Louisiana Supreme Court ruled that leaving in sponges was "negligence per se," in effect strict liability: anytime instruments are left inside a patient the surgeon will pay. That is, the nurses' errors are automatically to be charged to the doctor. What is the effect of this on the doctor's behavior? Probably and ideally, none. There is nothing the surgeon can do to improve the behavior of the nurses without neglecting more pressing matters. So the rule in Louisiana appears to achieve the spreading of compensation costs without affecting behavior.

In an analogous Texas case, *Sparger v. Worley Hospital, Inc.* (1977), the court applied the "borrowed servant" doctrine, making the doctor liable only if she or he in fact controlled the nurses' conduct. This makes the existence of borrowed nurses a factual question for a jury to decide. Sometimes a surgeon will be seen as taking charge, other times as leaving the nurses' responsibilities to their employer. In *Sparger*, the jury found that because the surgeon specifically asked the nurses about the accuracy of the sponge count, he was supervising and was therefore liable for their errors. Whereas the Louisiana rule affects cost spreading but not surgeons' behavior, this Texas rule creates a *disincentive* for being prudent. It does so by making the extra-careful surgeon, who double-checks the nurses' actions, more likely to incur liability. The behavior-modifying effects of the Texas rule, if any, would be to encourage *less* careful medical practice by surgeons.

We have been speaking, so far, of the downstream effects of legal actions that have as their object more immediate aims. The illustrations presented show that the goals in view may be defeated by a legal doctrine, may be magnified by later effects of the rule, or may at the least be some among a wider set of effects the rule will have. A doctrine chosen is an option from among a number of "solutions" to the legal policy problem at hand. In all these situations the law, like a chess player, must look beyond the present move to see how the game is likely to go as a result of the strategies played. That social science might be able to offer the law some help in this enterprise has been recognized (or hoped for) since the early part of this century (Llewellyn, Pound, Holmes) and, in revised form, still is (Bok, 1983). How far the law should go in trying to understand its effect on the future before taking action is far less clear. As Ackerman (1984) has recently observed:

> What is required . . . is something I shall call a *structural* account—a statement of the facts that reveals the ways an activity might be feasibly

reorganized to avoid or ameliorate the inefficiencies and injustices it may be generating. If lawyers are successful in producing such an account, moreover, their very triumph will serve to push them deeper into the structural enterprise. For it will quickly become obvious that the regulation of one activity—say driving a car—will have an important impact on the way other activities—walking, breathing, and the like—are organized. Should lawyers not, then, try to understand these important "second-order effects" by imbedding the initial description into a more comprehensive structural account?

This quest for ever-broader empirical understanding must, of course, be kept under reasonable control in practical law-craft, lest it delay necessary decisions in a continually expanding and pointlessly expensive fact-finding spiral. [For the traditional lawyer, the broader understanding is considered unnecessary.] If a series of particular decisions yields untoward results, there will be time enough to consider the problem whenever "any visible inconvenience doth appear."

From an activist perspective, this cavalier attitude toward the future does not merely generate avoidable hardship; its self-confident assertion of future reactive prowess is often unjustified. . . . [M]any systemic "inconveniences" may never appear in a way that is "visible" to reactive decision-makers because the injured parties lack the money, energy, and organizational incentives to force their grievances onto the reactive agenda. The refusal to interpret particular facts within their social and economic context seems guaranteed, in the end, to achieve only one objective: to blind the reactive lawyer to the very existence of the systemic failures that motivate activist concerns. (pp. 29–31)

THE LAW AS SOCIAL ARCHITECT

Let us turn now to the kinds of legal structure creation that Lon Fuller (1968) might have found most interesting. This is the deliberate creation of structures that are intended to facilitate the business of human existence in a society. Here we are less concerned about the law's attempt to influence behavior through the direct application of stick or carrot, or that application's sequalae, than about the effects on behavior of the social institutions and relations that the law has the power to erect. These legally erected social structures bring about behavior in a variety of ways. The structures may foster relationships that carry with them social contingencies on which behavior may be conditioned. They may set up models that people depend on to decide how certain goals are to be pursued, and the existence of these models may make that behavioral path to the goal much more likely than unmodeled alternatives. Or the structures may simply make alternative behavior impossible.

The Constitution, for example, is essentially a structure-creating instrument. It divides different kinds of power among particular branches of government in particular ways. In a social psychologist's terms, it places reward power primarily with the legislature, coercive power primarily with the executive, and expert power primarily with the judiciary. That is, it allocates the power of the purse, the power of the sword, and the power to say what the law is. The consequences of these structural choices are the stuff of constitutional theory and political analysis. This is not merely a matter of who will do what, but of the effective diffusion of power and the balancing and checking of each other's power. The Constitution is characterized by "various moves to break up and counterpoise governmental and decision authority" (Ely, 1980, p. 80).

Even in contemplating the relations between citizen and citizen, the founders can be seen to have eschewed confidence in a ruler of goodwill—that is, one with the right attitudes or the disposition to act in desired ways. They were instead disposed to place their trust in structures that would tend to ensure the desired social behavior. One such example is provided by James Madison in *Federalist* 51:

> It is of great importance in a republic not only to guard the society against the oppression of its rulers, but to guard one part of the society against the injustice of the other part. . . . If a majority will be united by a common interest, the rights of the minority will be insecure. There are but two methods of providing against this evil: the one by creating a will in the community independent of the majority . . . the other by comprehending in the society so many separate descriptions of citizens as will render an unjust combination of a majority of the whole very improbable, if not impracticable. The first method prevails in all governments possessing an hereditary or self-appointed authority. This, at best, is but a precarious security; because a power independent of the society may as well espouse the unjust views of the major, as the rightful interests of the minor party, and may possibly be turned against both parties. The second method will be exemplified in the federal republic of the United States.

That is, in a society so structured that power cannot be consolidated, in a society that is structurally pluralistic, tyranny will be less likely to develop. Thus, a reading of the *Federalist Papers* suggests that the founding parents were engaged in self-conscious creation of social structure through the law.

The law is, of course, a major vehicle for bringing about social change through the restructuring of social and economic relationships, whether one prefers to look back to the American Revolution, around us to socialist revolutions, or forward to impending Kelsonian experiments (Ashford, 1984; Kelso & Hetter, 1968) and beyond. The new order is a vision of new social arrangements translated into behavior by law. But some social-change theorists have suggested that most social change is attributable to technological change. This is to say, social change will follow more surely from technological change than from anything else humans deliberately do. If so, then the law's effect on many other aspects of our lives is mediated by the law's effect on technology. And this tends to make the law's effect on behavior indirect and nonobvious. An unusually strong and practical statement of this view is provided by Etzioni and Remp's (1972) notion of "technological shortcuts to social change." Whereas socialization requires learning, usually over a long period, behavior influence through social architecture often can be fast and automatic (see Krasner & Ullman, 1973; Skinner, 1953). Brodsky's and Bonnie's discussions in this volume include examples, notably affecting public health, that demonstrate how structure affects behavior. The following illustrations seek to clarify the notion further, highlighting the law's sometimes nonobvious role.

One of the familiar conflicts of life in agrarian England was the problem of animals' escaping from the close and wandering onto cultivated lands to eat or trample the crops. To regulate this problem the common law developed a rule whereby owners were held strictly liable for the damage done by their animals. Thus the onus was on the herder to fence in the animals, rather than on the farmer to fence animals out. In a small green, rocky and wooded country, this was a workable strategy and a reasonable allocation of a burden on the animal owner to build fences in order to avoid liability.

The transplanting of this common law rule to the Great Plains of the New World was not so workable, and it certainly was not simple or uncontroversial. The range wars of the nineteenth century between farmers and ranchers took place in an environment quite different from that of Britain. Fencing material was scarce, lands were vast. If the common law rule of fencing in was maintained, cattle ranchers could not take advantage of the open plains. The range wars of the plains were also legal battles between fencing in and fencing out. The great dilemma was that both farming and ranching were valued activities. But because fencing material was scarce and expensive, the legal rule might put out of business altogether whichever side had the burden of putting up fences. In *Delaney v. Errickson* (1880), a Nebraska trial court applied the common law rule and held for the plaintiff landowner. But the Nebraska Supreme Court, citing the circumstances and customs of the times and making much of legislative silence on liability for trespass onto unenclosed lands, reversed—dramatically choosing one industry over another. This was the situation on the plains of the West, where fencing out became the rule, while in the farmlands of the East the law favored the rule of fencing in livestock.

Although legal, political, and physical battles took place to try to resolve this conflict, the eventual solution came from a different quarter entirely. The conflict abated when a technological invention made fencing cheap and easy: the invention of barbed wire (Webb, 1931). Although it might have seemed at first blush that the solution to this problem must come from the law of trespass, it turned out that other laws played a larger part, namely those creating incentives for and protecting inventions, those governing the creation of businesses, and those facilitating transportation. These laws made possible a technological solution to the problem. This is an example of an indirect legal solution that worked by creating conditions that would eventually lead to an unexpected end to a serious conflict.

A similar example of the structure-creating power of law, which in turn influences behavior, is the invention, manufacture, and marketing of the automobile. A number of commentators point to the car as initiating the most dramatic social change of this century, doing more to change who we are and how we live than any other single development.

Imagine a legislator at the turn of the century whose constituents ask how the law might help bring about the following changes: reduce the family to a kernel of its former self, reduce the control parents have of their children, increase premarital sexual activity, cause cities to bulge and flow outward, breaking into segments increasingly alienated from each other, and—while we're at it—send 54,000 people a year to cemeteries and another 2,000,000 to hospitals (*Statistical Abstract of the United States*, 1984), pollute the air, and stimulate the growth of emergency medicine, insurance, and personal injury litigation and, in turn, the flowering of medical malpractice litigation.

Assuming a turn-of-the-century legislator was persuaded to seek such changes, how might they be accomplished? The most effective way, apparently, would have been not by the usual method of trying to mandate such changes directly through law, but instead by using the law to promote the advent of the automobile. The law's greatest impact on behavior may be mediated through technology and through the social structures and contingencies that technology in turn erects. The anticipation of technological and behavioral consequences called for here (see Burke, 1978) may border on crystal-ball gazing. Unlike a chessboard, the social system is open; the future is a course that has not been previously traversed, and the variables are both profound in their effects and numerous. And, indeed, it is doubtful the law does particularly well even with a narrower set of options on a much more familiar playing surface: a court.

The law sometimes tries to structure itself, and even then it often fails to anticipate all the important behavioral consequences. Let us take an example with which we are more closely associated than we might wish. The legislature wishes to reduce the cost to the legal system of trials and decides that one easy method is to reduce the size of juries. This seems like a straightforward enough way of reducing cost. A group of six jurors certainly can render a decision more cheaply than a jury of twelve. And since there are fewer of them, they might even get the job done a little faster.

An overlooked aspect of size reduction is that as sample sizes get smaller, the standard error of their verdicts gets larger. Lawyers sense this by feeling that the results to be reached are less predictable than they were previously. Although this makes them more uneasy about going to trial, and therefore more motivated to settle, the lack of clarity about a result makes the settlement discussions less successful. For example, the unpredictability of civil jury awards means that what formerly was the "value of a case" now has a larger standard error, with the range of expected awards including both lower awards (which gives greater hope to the defense) and higher awards (giving greater hope to the plaintiff).

And, in fact, what data we have indicates that when lawyers are looking ahead to smaller juries, they are less likely to settle their cases than when they are scheduled for trial before larger juries. If fewer cases settle than before, more go to trial. And if more go to trial, the cost to the legal system goes up, not down. What was planned as a modest saving may have turned into unanticipated increased cost (Saks, 1977; Zeisel, 1971).

Of course, the law structures more than itself. The law often is called upon to regulate the conduct of all sorts of activities and to protect the general public's health, safety, and welfare. The law, for example, can allocate the right to perform certain services for the public and the rewards that come with the exclusive right to perform such services. Again, by creating certain structures, the law may bring about behavior—some of it intended, some of it unforeseen, and some of it exactly contrary to what was intended. Recent studies and commentary on professional regulation suggest that this is one set of allocative rules that may inadvertently work against its own goals.

From the public's viewpoint, the basic idea of licensing professionals is that the state seeks to protect the public from being harmed by unqualified and incompetent practitioners. The state, or a professional group to whom the state delegates the licensing function, will create licensing standards presumed capable of separating the competent from the incompetent. Once an applicant passes licensing muster, it is presumed safe to turn the practitioner loose on the public.

A number of researchers and theorists have questioned whether the goal of providing quality services for the public is actually undermined by this particular exercise of the state's police power (e.g., Baron, 1983; Friedman, 1962; Hogan, 1983). The effects of licensing electricians are illustrative. The legislative theory, presumably, would be that the more demanding the licensing requirements, the better the electricians, and the better the electrical work. In one empirical study (Carroll & Gaston, 1981) the states were ranked according to the stringency of their licensing laws for electricians. The researchers next obtained data on the rate of death by electrocution among homeowners and correlated the ranks on this variable with the ranks on the licensing variable. What they found was that the more stringent the licensing laws, the more likely homeowners were to be electrocuted.

The findings may be explained as follows: the higher the standards, the fewer electricians become licensed. The fewer who become licensed, the fewer practicing, advertising electricians there are. Those few reap the benefits of scarcity. But for the consumer this scarcity means electricians may be unobtainable, either because their fees are prohibitive or because they are unavailable at any price. As a result, many unskilled homeowners attempt their own electrical work and are killed in the process.

The criticisims of licensing professionals have drawn more attention than criticisms of licensing other workers. In addition to creating an artificial scarcity, the objections raised include the following. Licensing, it is argued, reduces innovation and progress by reducing competition and reduces the consumer's active choice making by removing choice from the marketplace. The state seems to have given its imprimatur to those licensed, and in everyday practice the profession is the only judge of its own abilities. The available data tend to confirm these fears.

Historically, at least, licensing reduced the amount of diversity in medicine. What had been a profusion of health-care fields in the age of Jacksonian democracy was, until quite recently, reduced to the victory of the allopathic school. From the allopath's viewpoint, of course, the one true approach prevailed—with the help of wise legislators—over the false competitors. But legislative alternatives did exist. One might have been to legislate more medical evaluation research and information dissemination, thereby allowing science and informed consumers to separate the effective from the ineffective, the desirable from the undesirable. Without the protection of licensing statutes, essentially creating a monopoly on medical practice, medicine might have been forced by competition to begin evaluation research earlier and identify iatrogenic treatments sooner. The first controlled clinical trial took place in 1952 (Cochrane, 1972), and Bunker and Mosteller (1977) tell us that a large portion of standard medical treatments have been found by subsequent controlled studies to be either ineffective or iatrogenic.

LEGAL AND SOCIAL EVOLUTION

This implies something broader than that we might improve professional services through alternative statutes. It raises the possibility that a substantial proportion of the variation in innovation, science, and quality of practice between societies is shaped by the structures the law helps create. This echoes the almost scientific law advocated by numerous utilitarians, instrumentalists, and legal realists. They saw the law as a tool for bringing about behavior desired on other value grounds. The law need have no inherent moral content. The focus is on the law's effects. If the chosen legal rules "work," they can be retained. Otherwise they can be modified or replaced by rules that will do the job better. Llewellyn (1931) wrote of "the conception of law as a means to social ends and not as an end in itself; so that any part needs constantly to be examined for its purpose, and for its effect, and to be judged in the light of both and of their relation to each other." But the legal rules that evolve need not be so deliberately and rationally crafted as all this to be still essentially instrumental. Marvin Harris's (1974, 1979) work on cultural materialism suggests the possibility of a relationship between legal norms and social structure that is more subtle, more mysterious, and yet no less instrumental.

Harris observes that religious, legal, and other norms vary profoundly—indeed, bizarrely—across cultures. Many anthropologists have turned to sociobiology, to Marxism, to mysticism, and even to analytic psychology for possible explanations. But the cultural materialists propose that the explanation for these "riddles of culture" is to be found in an ecological analysis of the conditions of existence for a given culture. Even the most bizarre customs, Harris argues, can be explained by reference to the necessities of survival in the material world. Survival in a given environment may be accomplished by many sociocultural solutions, but each is limited by some minimal conditions. That is, some cultures' "solutions" to the problems of survival may not work, and those cultures must change their customs or die out. The cultural norms need not in themselves be the solutions but may facilitate the solution. A concrete example will make this clearer.

What is the basis of the Hindu obligation of cow worship? On the surface, to Western eyes, this appears self-defeating. Starving Hindus will continue to scrape at their near-barren fields rather than slaughter the cow standing in the shade of the only tree in sight. Such behavior, Westerners are tempted to suggest, displays the primitive superstitions of the Hindus and even borders on madness.

By contrast, the explanation suggested by cultural materialism is this. An examination of the human and animal ecology of the Indian subcontinent reveals that human life is dependent upon cow life. Cows feed people directly by providing milk and indirectly by being the only source of fertilizer for the fields. Cow dung is also the main source of fuel for heating and cooking. Cows are the only nonhuman labor available for plowing and for transportation. And so on. To slaughter a cow to end today's hunger is to ensure tomorrow's starvation. The religious precept of cow worship—a law we may call it—is a cultural device for increasing the probability of long-term survival. The path to survival is to forgo the short-term gains of eating the cow and instead to hang on for the long-term gains of using the cow for many of life's other necessities.

How is this survival strategy to be passed on to succeeding generations? It might work to describe to each new generation the ecology of the Indian subcontinent and explain why, therefore, they must keep their cows alive. But the older members of the culture probably are not themselves aware that their respect for cows is built on this need for material survival. Assuming the materialist interpretation is true, they need not know the explanation in order to benefit from the rule. Indeed, the religious and moral and emotional basis of that rule may make it *more* effective than the underlying explanation could. A rule that successfully promotes survival may accomplish its purpose more easily and more surely in its morally peremptory form.

On the other hand, if such rules do evolve out of material needs, might it not pay to be aware of that fact, so that rules whose effectiveness has been rendered obsolete by time do not become harmful vestigial norms? If circumstances change, the strategies for survival must change as well. The slow cultural evolution that may prevail in the traditional cultures anthropologists study may work there. But can it work in complex, rapidly changing technological societies? We may need legal systems that can more closely track the world's changes and revise legal rules without undue deference to ancestral precedents. Justice Cardozo (1921), in his classic work *The Nature of the Judicial Process,* approvingly quotes from the opinion in an old Connecticut case: "That court best serves the law which recognizes that the rules which grew up in a remote generation may, in the fullness of experience, be found to serve another generation badly, and which discards the old rule when it finds that another rule of law represents what should be" (p. 151). And indeed our legal system apparently has evolved, with the rest of our culture, to add to, refine, and rewrite rules with unprecedented vigor. Grant Gilmore has referred to the past 40 to 50 years, less charitably, as an "orgy of statute making."

Does such enlightened pragmatism mean that any rules that serve the same structural purposes will work equally well? Perhaps not. It might be that these new rules are more effective still if they have apparent moral force, if they connect with a society's existing values and symbols in such a way that they not only are structurally appropriate but also appear to be moral imperatives.

Kohlberg has commented that the Constitution is a document that reasons at stage 5, while most adult Americans operate at stage 4 or lower. Might it be that constitutional government, the adversary process, tort and contract doctrines, and other forms of law are ecologically and structurally sensible but announced in ways that are not comprehensible to many people? Could this defect account for some of the interminable problems of legal socialization? Can even the most structurally sensible laws work, in Llewellyn's terms, if no one but a lawyer knows about them, and if even most lawyers find them not meaningful in cognitive moral terms and not impelling in motivational terms? Even so administrative a matter as driving on the right side of the road may be a more effective norm if people regard the choice with some elemental moral fervor: "It is *our* way; it is the *right* way!"

The problem of effective law, then, presents a double challenge: First, to figure out the most functional rule for the context, in all its economic, social-ecological, structural complexity. And second, to discover how to announce the norm in ways that can be comprehended by people at all levels of moral cognizance and perhaps even to invest the rule with an intuitively comprehensible, elemental, moral force.

The Law as Socializer

SOCIALIZATION AND COMPARATIVE LAW

Having examined ways the law has enduring effects through its establishment or support of structures for reinforcement within the community, we shall now look at the law as a socializing force. Law teaches the moral and social norms of the community and, in a sense, announces, reiterates, and indeed ritualizes the myths and themes of the culture. Although these functions have been de-emphasized in modern Western jurisprudence and political theory, they are nonetheless there.

Geertz's (1980) conclusion to his analysis of the "theater state" of Bali is a telling statement of the significance of symbolism in political life:

> That master noun of modern political discourse, *state*, has at least three etymological themes diversely condensed within it: status, in the sense of station, standing, rank, condition—*estate* ("The glories of our blood and state"); pomp, in the sense of splendor, display, dignity, presence—*stateliness* ("In pomp ride forth; for pomp becomes the great / And Majesty derives a grace from state"); and governance, in the sense of regnancy, regime, dominion, mastery—*statecraft* ("It may pass for a maxim in state that the administration cannot be placed in

too few hands, nor the legislature in too many"). And it is characteristic of that discourse, and of its modernness, that the third of these meanings, the last to arise (in Italy in the 1540's; it was not even available to Machiavelli), should have so come to dominate the term as to obscure our understanding of the multiplex nature of high authority. Impressed with command, we see little else. (p. 121)

In Geertz's view the state—and the law within it—functions as a parody of itself. The underlying theory of the state is imitated in its rituals. The law functions, then, as a symbolic representation of the ideals of the state, and it purports to teach the citizenry these principles, to serve as a model of natural social order.

East Asian legal systems. In much of the world, such a concept of law is paramount. For example, most East Asian legal systems, including those in communist states, still are built on ancient Confucian principles of government and justice (see generally Cohen, Edwards, & Chang Chen, 1980; Kim, 1981; Moser, 1982).

> [The law] is a part of Confucius' general conception of the state: ideally a cooperative commonwealth, in which the ruler and his officials are dedicated to the welfare of the people, and the people in turn render loyalty and willing obedience to those above them. The most potent force for causing the people to be good, Confucius repeated over and over, was proper example set for them by the rulers. The people should be motivated by *li*, to do that which they ought; if they are intimidated by fear of punishment they will merely strive to avoid the punishment, but will not be made good. To render justice is all very well, but the important thing, Confucius said, is to bring about a condition in which there will be no lawsuits. (Creel, 1980, p. 39)

Li and its counterpart, *fa*, are roughly analogous to the dual terms for law present in most major language systems, although not in English. *Li* refers to customary law and *fa* to declared law (analogous, e.g., to *ius* and *lex* in Latin and to *pravo* and *zakon* in Russian). However, *li* means more than that. Sometimes translated "propriety," it refers to behavior consistent with the natural ordering of people and, indeed, the universe. In that context society dwarfs the individual, and people stand in awe before their social and political superiors. The legal system exists only to exemplify the cosmic balance and, if necessary, to restore it when disturbed by those who have failed to act in consonance with the natural social order. Lawyers and formal legal arguments in such a value system are essentially superfluous. Rather, judges in East Asian courts tend to act as superior moral teachers, lecturing disputants about traditional Confucian ideals (e.g., respect for parents and husbands) and directly mediating disputes to restore harmonious feelings (Moser, 1982). (Put into such a philosophical and historical context, the much-touted paucity of lawyers in Japan [cf. Bok, 1983], which was heavily influenced by Chinese law, is not surprising and is an inapposite example for those who wish to reform the American legal system.)

Marxist legal systems. The law's symbolic and educational purposes are also preeminent in Marxist legal philosophy. Although the fundamental assumptions about why these purposes are paramount obviously differ from those in Confucian legal philosophy, the results are remarkably parallel. With the assumption that the law, with the state, should and will ultimately wither away, law as an autonomous institution (cf. Weber, 1925/1954) and lawyering as a profession are relatively insignificant in the Soviet system. As Berman (1963) has noted, the result of the "mystical concept" of the ultimate decay of the state under communism is that "the main purpose of official law is to shape and develop that unofficial law-consciousness [cf. Petrazhitskii, 1904–1910/1955], so that people will actually think and feel what the state, through official law, prescribes. When the state has fully educated all people to internalize the legal system, then that legal system will no longer be needed" (p. 75). The purpose of the law, then, is to help create the "new Soviet person" (Berman, 1977); the law is perceived as purely instrumental rather than analytic. In other words, the law is not viewed as an autonomous system of reasoning (Collins, 1982). Consistent with this view, the Soviet Union has developed a remarkable system of lay or predominantly lay legal organizations (i.e., People's Volunteer Militia; Comrades' Courts; People's Courts), operating even on the streets or in the factories, to educate and reeducate people in communist morality, primarily through the use of shame and reprimand (Berman, 1963; Hildebrand, 1972).

Perhaps because of their European heritage, formal courts in the Soviet Union are professionalized and have much in common with Western liberal legal systems that are based on an ideology of the rule and autonomy of law. Nonetheless, even higher-level Soviet courts have a primary mission of education. The Russian (RSFSR) statute on court organization is illustrative:

Article 3. Tasks of courts. By all its activity a court shall educate citizens in the spirit of loyalty to the Motherland and to the cause of communism, and in the strict and undeviating execution of Soviet laws, of an attitude of care toward socialist ownership, of observation of labor discipline, of an honorable attitude toward state and social duty, and of respect for the rights, honor, and dignity of citizens and for rules of socialist community living.

In applying measures of criminal punishment a court not only chastises criminals but also has as its purpose their correction and reeducation. (Translated in Berman & Quigley, 1969)

AMERICAN SOCIALIZATION

Political socialization. Such legal purposes may seem both literally and figuratively foreign to Americans socialized into liberal ideals. The blatant subordination of individual interests to the state found in both Confucian and Marxist legal systems seems, at first glance, to be unjust and perhaps even a bit quaint. However, it is worth noting that statutes in American jurisdictions frequently provide as overtly for political and legal indoctrination and moral education, albeit in institutions other than the legal system. Consider, for example, Nebraska's compulsory school attendance law (Nebraska Revised Statutes, 1971/1981):

An informed, loyal, just, and patriotic citizenry is necessary to a strong, stable, just, and prosperous America. Such a citizenry necessitates that every member thereof be fully acquainted with the nation's history, that he be in full accord with our form of government, and fully aware of the liberties, opportunities, and advantages of which we are possessed and the sacrifices and struggles of those through whose efforts these benefits were gained. Since youth is the time most susceptible to the acceptance of principles and doctrines that will influence men throughout their lives, it is one of the first duties of our educational system to so conduct its activities, choose its textbooks, and arrange its curriculum in such a way that the love of liberty, justice, democracy, and America will be instilled in the heart and mind of the youth of the state.

The statute also requires each school board to appoint a committee on Americanism to "examine, inspect, and approve all textbooks used in the teaching of American history and civil government" and to "assure themselves as to the character of all teachers employed, and their knowledge and acceptance of the American form of government." Elementary schools are obligated to ensure that "every pupil shall memorize the Star Spangled Banner and America," and high schools are mandated to teach "the duties of citizenship" and "the benefits and advantages of our form of government and the dangers and fallacies of Nazism, Communism, and similar ideologies."

The law as teacher. In keeping with the consciously neutral character of the courts in Western jurisprudence (Weber, 1925/1954), one is unlikely to find such purposes expressly articulated in the statutes organizing the legal system in American jurisdictions. Nonetheless, even if a positivistic separation of law and morals were desirable, the conclusion seems to us inescapable that a major purpose of the law and the legal system is to function as moral and perhaps political educator. It is important to note here that we are talking not about deterrence of immoral behavior, but instead about what Andenaes (1966, 1975, 1977) has termed *general preventive effects* of legal action. As Gibbs (this volume) emphasized, deterrence is based on fear of legal sanctions. Nonetheless, to the extent that the law affects behavior, the process may be based more frequently on the cues the law provides about socially and morally appropriate behavior and the resulting internalization of legal norms (note the parallel with Berman's, 1977, description of Soviet law, as described previously).

In arguing that law and morals are properly separate, Holmes (1897) contended that law was nothing more than the prediction of when the force of the state would be applied. "If you want to know the law and nothing else," Holmes wrote, "you must look at it as a bad man, who cares only for the material consequences which such knowledge enables him to predict, not as a good one, who finds his reasons for conduct, whether inside the law or outside of it, in the vaguer sanctions of conscience" (p. 459). However, in our view, Pound's retort to Holmes is more persuasive:

> If . . . [one] is the bad man of whom Mr. Justice Holmes speaks, who has no care for the straight path but wishes to know what path he may take up with impunity, he will no doubt think of a legal precept as a threat. But the ordinary man who does not "wash the idea in cynical acid" has more commonly thought of it as a rule of conduct, a guide telling him what he ought to do at the crisis of action. This is the oldest idea of a law. It goes back to the codified ethical custom of the earlier stages of legal development. (Pound, 1959, p. 130)

It is a cliché of deterrence theory (Andenaes, 1977; Gibbs, this volume) that for every law there are essentially three groups of people: good actors, who would obey the law even without the threat of punishment; potential bad actors, who are deterred from breaking the law by the threat of punishment; and actual bad actors (criminals), who are undeterred by the threat of punishment. Like Justice Holmes, deterrence theorists have focused on the second group (potential criminals). However, being more optimistic about the human condition, we would argue, like Dean Pound, that for most potential offenses the first group is of more interest. Does the law provide an adequate guidepost for those who would obey it if they could? More acutely, does the law offer adequate direction to those who would use it to ascertain morally or socially correct behavior?

These questions are both normative—pertaining to the relation between law and morals (see e.g., Fuller, 1968; Hart, 1961; Holmes, 1897; Pound, 1926)—and empirical—pertaining to the actual effects of law. In regard to the latter, Andenaes (1977) has postulated four educative effects of law. First, the law may act as a "moral eye-opener." It may sensitize citizens to the harmful social consequences of prohibited acts. The law may operate to prick the conscience and create or maintain moral inhibitions and social norms. As Andenaes (1977) points out, such an effect would be superior to "mere deterrence" because it "may work even when a person need not fear detection and punishment" (p. 51).

The second possible effect is related to, but less subtle than, the moral eye-opening effect, which depends upon the individual's evaluation of the morality of prohibited conduct. The law may also offer authoritative statements of morality: "Do this" or "Don't do that." Thus, legal commands may have direct educative effects, even if the citizen does not reason about them, as long as one has achieved a level of moral decision making in which obedience to the law has acquired a value in itself apart from avoidance of punishment (see Kohlberg, 1976, stage 3). As Fuller (1968) has pointed out, the law may in such a way keep alive moral opprobrium for *mala in se* that otherwise would survive because of the short-term social advantages involved (what Platt, 1973, terms "social traps"; see Peachey & Lerner, 1981). Consider, for example, the "reciprocity between those who seek advantages and those who control access to them" (Fuller, 1968, p. 28); for example, the would-be contractor and the purchasing agent, both of whom stand to gain from "under the table" deals. Beyond their deterrent effect, legal rules serve to structure such relationships for the ultimate social good.

Third, the law may indirectly educate through neutralization and punishment of bad examples. By incapacitating or deterring actual or would-be criminals, the law avoids the modeling of bad conduct and desensitization to it among good actors ("if everybody's doing it, it can't be too bad"). It is noteworthy that even a few examples of bad conduct may substantially alter the cognitive availability (cf. Tversky & Kahneman, 1973) of such behavior and lead, illogically, to the belief that "everybody's doing it."

Fourth, and also indirectly, the law may provide a framework for moral education. Andenaes (1977) unfortunately seems to approve of parents' using the legal system as a sort of moral bogeyman: "Many parents probably use references to police and prison as means of communicating to children the absolute necessity of 'going straight'" (p. 56). Nonetheless, he is undoubtedly correct that parental injunctions are likely to have diminished effects if children see people around them violating moral and social norms without adverse consequences. Such a modeling effect may be especially pronounced for young children, who evaluate the morality of an action by its consequences (Kohlberg, 1976; Piaget, 1932/1965). Andenaes may also be correct in hypothesizing a second-order deterrence effect. That is, the motivation of parents and teachers to provide children with moral instruction may be increased by their own fear of legal sanctions against themselves for neglect or, ultimately, against the children for misconduct.

The law as a system of behavioral cues. Perhaps most generally, the nature of law, apart from its underlying ideology, is such that a primary function is to provide cues for behavior the society approves of, or at least to provide inhibiting cues to suppress behavior the society disapproves of. Indeed, the essence of declared law is its precedential value (Pospisil, 1971). A legal decision not only resolves a particular dispute, it also offers information about state-approved behavior. Law consists, then, of both the direct behavior of the authorities and the principles derived from it.

The universality of legal systems suggests the adaptive value of these cues (cf. Harris, 1979; see also Nader, this volume). Law serves a cultural purpose by directly or implicitly announcing the themes of the culture—what the culture is about and therefore the overriding principles of behavior. The significance of these declarations is vividly illustrated by the emotion surrounding the debate about abortion, Baby Doe cases, and capital punishment. Advocates on both sides of each of these issues claim that to adopt their opponents' position would be to take a large step toward destruction of the culture through symbolic diminution of the central value of the sanctity of life.

IS THE LAW AN EFFECTIVE TEACHER?

By now it should be clear that the hortatory, socializing functions of law are important in Western legal systems, just as they are in East Asian and Marxist systems in which such functions are express. We have also indicated, albeit somewhat tangentially, the apparent congruence between such functions and cognitive behavioral theory. The arguments of Andenaes, Pound, and other jurisprudential scholars concerned with legal-moral pedagogy have rested on assumptions about modeling, expectancies, and behavioral cues. The psychologist of law should have much to say to Andenaes and like-minded theorists about the maximization of the law's educational effects and to fellow psychologists about the influence of macrolevel social cues on behavior.

Unfortunately, knowledge of this topic is still in its infancy. Elsewhere in this Symposium, the methodological problems in studying the effectiveness of deterrence (Gibbs) and indeed the impact of law generally (Melton) have been chronicled. These problems are even more severe when attempts are made to study the law's efficacy as a moral teacher. First, there is the jurisprudential chicken-and-egg problem. Which came first, changes in community attitudes or changes in the law? Second, if attitudes have changed as a result of the law, are they the product of deterrence (fear of punishment) or educative effects? Making the matter still more complicated is the fact that deterrent and educative effects are interwoven. Behavior that began in fear may become habituated and sustained by covert stimuli; or, as already noted, altering some key actors' behavior through legal contingencies may change the social structure enough to modify social contingencies. Third, most of the possible processes we have described are subtle, long-term, and in some cases indirect. Clearly, designing internally valid research in this area is no mean feat. Whether for that reason or others (see Melton, this volume), few have tried.

Nonetheless, several literatures offer some initial bases for speculation on the efficacy of the law as a socializing instrument. First, as we have already seen, comparative law and legal anthropology may provide some clues to the diverse functions and meaning of law cross-culturally. Second, there is a small directly apposite literature in which sociolegal scholars have attempted to separate deterrent and educational effects of changes in the law. These studies generally compare attitudes and values in a time series before and after a change in the law, or between people who know the law and those who do not. Third, some inferences about educative effects of law may be made from experiments comparing the effects of appeals to conscience with the effects of threats of prosecution. Fourth, the literatures on legal socialization and attitudes toward civil liberties tell us about both the process of law-related education and development and the effectiveness of the society in inculcating core legal and political values. These literatures on education about the law thus may give us clues to the circumstances in which the law itself functions as a teacher.

Directly apposite studies. The example that first comes to mind in considering the educative effects of law is the change in public attitudes and behavior regarding racial segregation. Although it would be foolish to claim that racism has been eliminated in this country, it would be equally foolish to argue that society is unchanged. Not only are segregated lunch counters absent, but it seems nearly impossible to find anyone today who claims to support racial segregation in public facilities. Certainly the forces at work in these changes are complex, but it seems intuitively clear that the actions of the federal courts in *Brown v. Board of Education* (1954) and its progeny compelled many people to reconsider their views on race relations. Several psychological processes might explain such attitudinal change: fear of legal sanctions (i.e., deterrence); the need to restore consistency between attitudes and behavior; conscious moral decision making, precipitated by the presentation of alternative social ordering; a primary value of obedience to the law; and so forth. On the other hand, it is clear that integrationist attitudes were painfully slow to develop in many communities.

The extent of the law's direct influence as a moral educator on race relations is difficult to document. Studies in the schools themselves generally failed to find reductions in prejudice, at least during the first year after desegregation (Stephan, 1978). Critics (e.g., Gerard, 1983) have indicated lack of surprise in these results, because it was naive to expect that the conditions assumed in the contact hypothesis would be present (but cf. Cook, 1984). It is interesting that the parties in this debate have not considered the question of the law's ineffectiveness (or at least partial ineffectiveness) in shaping community norms. On the other hand, the educative effects may still apply over the long term. For example, there is evidence for changes in community voting behavior two to three years after implementation of a desegregation order. After an initial period of protest, there is a tendency for election of black candidates and defeat of antibusing candidates (Rossell, 1978).

In the case of desegregation, advocates frequently expected that legal action to effect school desegregation would improve race relations more generally, primarily through increased interracial contact (i.e., a change in social structure; see Allport et al., 1953). It would also have been plausible, of course, to hypothesize positive generalizations on the basis of the legal imprimatur for racial integration (i.e., a moral eye-opening effect). In other instances, though, no such generalization is expected; rather, the intent is simply to alter a particular behavior. For example, drinking-and-driving laws fall into such a category. In that regard, a frequent finding has been substantial noncompliance when enforcement is reduced or never adequately introduced (see, e.g., Ross, 1973, 1982). This result is consistent with deterrence theory but largely inconsistent with a theory of moral education through law, because the declaration of the badness of the act remains on the books. Even in this case, though, there is the possibility that the behavior of generally law-abiding people is strengthened by legal prohibition—even unenforced prohibition—of drinking and driving (Andenaes, 1975, p. 359).

Nonetheless, there is little support for short-term attitudinal change in the few available studies of the effects of legal change on moral attitudes. Walker and Argyle (1964) tested the notion that repeal of even an ineffective criminal statute would change the public's estimation of the morality of the now-permissible behavior. They found that repeal of the crime of attempted suicide did not change attitudes among Britons who were aware of the change in the law. Changes in attitudes about other behavior (e.g., prostitution) were evoked by claims that most people shared a particular attitude. Similar statements of illegality generally did not elicit increased negative sentiment about the behavior; indeed, there was a slight tendency to be less censorious when vices were said to be criminal.

Appeals to conscience. Results of a second line of studies are more positive, though still mixed. The symbolic aspects of law appear to be like appeals to conscience. That is, they carry no penalty but often are intended to prick the conscience. Therefore, studies of the effects of such appeals appear to offer some lessons for scholars of jurisprudence.

In several experiments by behavioral community psychologists, behavioral prompts involving appeals to conscience have been found useful in reducing illicit behavior (see, e.g., Geller, Koltuniak, & Shilling, 1983; McNees, Egli, Marshall, Schnelle, & Risley, 1976; McNees, Kennon, Schnelle, Kirchner, & Thomas, 1980). Merely placing signs stating that "Shoplifting Is Not Uplifting" or "The Newspaper Carrier Must Pay for the Papers in This Rack" has been found to reduce theft substantially for as long as the signs are in place.

Interestingly, comparable studies in the legal system have suggested that, at least in some circumstances, appeals to conscience may be more effective controls of behavior than punishment or threat of punishment. In one such study (Mecham, 1968), juvenile traffic offenders were randomly assigned to one of four dispositions: a fine, restraint from driving (presumably a license suspension), attendance at traffic school, or writing an essay on traffic safety. Contrary perhaps to intuition, the fine was the least effective in preventing recidivism and the essay was the most effective. Of the juveniles who were fined, 52% were cited for a traffic violation in the following year, but only about 15% of those who were required to write an essay became recidivists. There is a possible but implausible deterrence-based explanation for the findings; that is, the essay may have been the most noxious alternative subjectively. More likely, the essay reminded juveniles of the moral responsibilities associated with driving, but the fine was a sort of "cost of doing business" to stay a part of a peer group in which fast cars and fast driving were sources of esteem.

In an analogous, frequently cited experiment, Schwartz and Orleans (1967) found that although both appeals to conscience (e.g., reminders of civic responsibility) and threats of prosecution increased tax collections, the former were substantially more effective. The threats of sanctions seemed to induce reactance (cf. Brehm, 1966) in a minority of the prosecution-threat group, who *increased* their deductions noticeably. More recent data (Associated Press, 1984) indicate that tax noncompliance is common; about 20% of Americans interviewed admit cheating on their income taxes. Common rationales include beliefs that others are paying less than their fair share and that cheating is normative behavior in the American tax system. Essentially, many Americans perceive no real moral dilemma in deciding whether to underpay their taxes. Therefore, to increase compliance, the moral and social consequences of tax cheating would need to be emphasized.

Somewhat contradictory findings were obtained, however, in Tittle and Rowe's (1973) study of cheating in undergraduate sociology classes. Students in three sections were permitted to grade their own quizzes. Unknown to them, however, the instructor had already graded them all. Cheating was found to be rampant; only five of 107 participants refrained from cheating across the entire quarter. After return of the fourth of eight quizzes, students in the experimental sections were reminded, without effect, of their moral obligation to fulfill the trust that had been placed in them. After the return of the seventh quiz, students were informed that there had been complaints about cheating and that the instructor was obliged to spot-check for accuracy. Before grading of the last quiz, the instructor announced that a student had been found to have cheated and would be punished. The threat of apprehension and, even more, the declaration of enforcement significantly decreased cheating, especially among females and among students who were doing well in the course.

Although the research available is still rather skimpy, the studies of the attitudinal effects of law and the effects of appeals to conscience suggest that moral declarations often may be more effective than threats of punishment in eliciting changes in values and behavior. However, there are three major qualifiers to this conclusion. First, hortatory effects are likely to be most significant when the belief that "everybody's doing it [committing bad acts]" can be nullified by the authoritative statement of community norms. When experience teaches that the prevailing norm is in fact to behave badly, a statement of moral condemnation or social responsibility is likely to sound hollow. Tittle and Rowe's (1973) findings may have been more an unfortunate reflection of social acceptability of cheating, in the absence of punitive consequences, than an indicator of general ineffectiveness of appeals to conscience. Thus the efficacy of moral statements, especially those embedded in laws and rules, is based on the information they provide about consensual values and social contingencies. When experience provides a very different message, the efficacy of hortatory appeals is likely to diminish or even disappear accordingly. In short, if law is to be effective, reliance upon deterrence will necessarily increase when law and custom are markedly incongruent (Zimring & Hawkins, 1977).

Second, there are undoubtedly individual differences in both the internalization of moral norms and the assessment of risk. Holmes's (1897) cynical man, whom he believed to be representative of the public, bears a remarkable resemblance to the clinical psychopath, whose obedience or disobedience of law is likely to be based on a calculation of the immediate risks and benefits. More generally, educative effects of law would probably be most applicable to persons with highly internalized systems of values, who are especially likely to feel anticipatory guilt. These differences are based both on developmental factors in capacity for empathy and on the degree of use of inductive reasoning in parental discipline (Hoffman, 1976; Saltzstein, 1976).

Third, most of the hypothesized effects of law as a moral teacher depend upon knowledge of the law. For example, unpublicized repeal of an unenforced criminal statute could not be expected to provide an implicit imprimatur for previously condemned behavior (cf. Walker & Argyle, 1964). Nonetheless, the wide dissemination of a new court decision, regulation, or statute—even to the classes of people most directly affected—is the exception rather than the rule (see, e.g., Melton, 1981, 1983a; Wasby, 1976). Therefore, educative effects of law may often be contingent upon the establishment of structures for disseminating and implementing the law, as we discussed earlier.

Legal socialization. Thus far, we have looked primarily at the law's success in stimulating or suppressing particular behavior. The topic to which we now turn is a bit different. Rather than looking at attitudes about particular behavior, we will be examining more generally the effectiveness of the law in socializing an ideology about the law—that is, a system of legal beliefs and values. In this context, then, the focus will be upon the law's efficacy as a teacher about itself.

The topic of legal socialization is in fact quite broad. Fuller (1977), for example, has identified three definitions of *socialization*, each from a different jurisprudential perspective. First, socialization may be defined as "the process whereby a person comes to understand and accept the norms of conduct that a society imposes upon its members" (p. 33). From this perspective, socialization involves learning social norms, which may be taken to be something akin to social consciousness or the group will, which underlies the law. Second, socialization may be taken to mean "the process whereby a person becomes willing to accept and observe the constraints of state-made law" (p. 35). This process is substantially more complicated than it appears at first glance, because the rules of law often will not apply unambiguously to particular fact situations. Thus, even when the goal of socialization is to foster observance of law, one must "encourage more than a mere willingness to go by the book" (p. 37). The rule of law requires collaboration, not written rules alone. Third, socialization may be conceptualized as "the process whereby a person comes to perceive, respect, and participate in the creation of the reciprocal expectations that arise out of human interaction" (p. 37). Such customary relationships are given explicit recognition in a number of areas of law, including such diverse areas as commercial law, international law, and the law of search and seizure. In short, in the formulations of Fuller and a number of other jurisprudential scholars, socialization into the law is no less than socialization itself.

However, in our discussion we will focus on socialization to the core concepts in American jurisprudence of respect for personal autonomy and privacy. It is through such a process that the law sustains the basic values and operating principles of our society. There are now substantial bodies of research on both the process and the outcome of socialization to an appreciation of civil liberties and tolerance for expression of divergent points of view. Survey research across several decades (e.g., Erskine & Siegel, 1975; McClosky & Brill, 1983; Montero, 1975; Prothro & Grigg, 1960) Stouffer, 1955; Wilson, 1975; Zellman, 1975) has given us much information about adults' attitudes toward civil liberties and the social and personality factors affecting libertarian values. Also, largely through the efforts of Tapp and her colleagues to apply cognitive-developmental theories of moral development to the law (see, e.g., Tapp & Kohlberg, 1977; Tapp & Levine, 1974; Tapp & Melton, 1983; see also Melton, 1980), there is considerable research and theory on the development of such concepts, attitudes, and values.

Unfortunately, the most general conclusion that can be drawn from these two bodies of research is, as McClosky and Brill (1983, p. 4) noted, that "what makes political freedom so extraordinary is precisely that it gives evidence of being, if anything, 'unnatural.'" The social-psychological literature on group conformity (e.g., Asch, 1952) and obedience to authority (e.g., Milgram, 1974) gives little reason for optimism about either tolerance of minority views or perception of a sense of entitlement to express such views. Public opinion polls about civil liberties confirm this suspicion. To a classic liberal, it is chilling to read McClosky and Brill's (1983) 500-page report of the attitudes of a stratified random sample of American adults surveyed in the late seventies. To cite just a few of the findings, only 49% of the public disagreed with the use of a referendum to decide whether to ban expression of certain opinions, and only 23% disagreed with a requirement of loyalty oaths for all public employees. Seventy-seven percent favored monitoring classes of professors suspected of "spreading false ideas." Only 48% expressed agreement with a statement that "The employment of radicals by newspapers and TV is their right as Americans." Half of the sample advocated maintaining a police record of persons participating in protest demonstrations, and only 18% favored providing police protection to extreme groups during their public rallies. The majority of respondents did not endorse atheists' right to satirize religion. Two-thirds advocated denial of bail to persons accused of serious crimes, and only 40% said they believed the privilege against self-incrimination should be available when the charge is serious.

When the nature of civil liberties is examined closely, it is not surprising that the majority of Americans have not achieved a level of legal reasoning in which they are able or willing to apply to concrete situations the libertarian principles they say they espouse. Such concepts are simply difficult to teach. Most of the key concepts embedded in core American values are highly abstract (e.g., privacy, liberty, due process). Thus, like principled moral reasoning (Kohlberg, 1976), principled legal reasoning requires a level of cognitive development not usually achieved before adolescence (Melton, 1980; Tapp & Levine, 1974), if at all.

Even if this limitation were not present, however, the concepts still would be difficult to teach, in that indoctrination in libertarian values raises an inherent paradox. Consider the following case. In keeping with their statutory duty, the local school board decides to be careful to ensure that the instruction is in keeping with American values. The board learns that some of the books in the school library contain messages that are inconsistent with such values. For example, some books advocate racial separatism; others argue for jailing political protestors. If the board permits the books to stay, it will be tacitly supporting the spread of ideas inconsistent with democratic and libertarian ideals. On the other hand, if it removes the books, it will be modeling repressive behavior. Incidentally, in dealing with this problem (*Board of Education, Island Trees Union Free School District No. 26 v. Pico*, 1982), the Supreme Court decided, five to four, that school boards violate the first amendment when they remove books from the libraries of junior and senior high schools because the boards find the books politically objectionable. There were seven opinions issued in *Island Trees*. The difficulty of the problem is illustrated by the contorted logic adopted by the plurality: school boards may not censor books once they have been placed in the library, but they may be able to exercise judgments of political value in deciding which books to add to the library.

Island Trees also illustrates another reason why libertarian attitudes are not modal in a society that claims such values as its core: expression of divergent ideas is often perceived as dangerous. The *Island Trees* school board perceived enough threat in students' having easy access to Eldridge Cleaver's books to warrant taking the issue to the Supreme Court. Unfortunately, such an atmosphere of defensiveness is likely to be present in most of the settings where children find themselves. It is hard to imagine many school principals even informing children that they have the right to political expression in the schools (*Tinker v. Des Moines Independent School District*, 1969), much less actually providing a forum for such expression.

We suspect that the modal view is reflected in the dissent of Justice Black, reputedly a staunch libertarian, from his brethren's fostering "a new revolutionary era of permissiveness" (*Tinker*, 1969, p. 518) by acknowledging children's right to make a political statement by wearing black armbands to school:

> Change has been said to be truly the law of life but sometimes the old and the tried and true are worth holding. The schools of this Nation have undoubtedly contributed to giving us tranquility and to making us a more law-abiding people. Uncontrolled and uncontrollable liberty is an enemy to domestic peace. We cannot close our eyes to the fact that some of the country's greatest problems are crimes committed by the youth, too many of school age. School discipline, like parental discipline, is an integral and important part of training our children to be good citizens—to be better citizens. . . . Turned loose with lawsuits for damages and injunctions against their teachers as they are here, it is nothing but wishful thinking to imagine that young, immature students will not soon believe it is their right to control the schools rather than the right of the States that collect the taxes to hire the teachers for the benefit of the pupils. This case, therefore, . . . subjects the public schools in the country to the whims and caprices of their loudest-mouthed, but maybe not their brightest, students. . . . I . . . wish . . . wholly to disclaim any purpose on my part to hold that the Federal Constitution compels the teachers, parents, and elected school officials to surrender control of the American

public school system to public school students. (*Tinker*, 1969, pp. 524–526)

In an environment in which the very personhood of children is doubted (cf. Melton, 1983b), how can we expect that they will learn to tolerate diversity and to respect personal privacy and autonomy? For those children from disadvantaged backgrounds, how can we expect that they will acquire a sense of entitlement when virtually everything in their experience tells them that rights are subject to the whim of authority, that at most they are revocable privileges (cf. Coles, 1977)? It is hardly surprising then that the groups most in need of the protection of civil rights are the groups least likely to perceive themselves as having such rights (see, e.g., Melton, 1980; Note, 1973; Williams & Hall, 1972).

Indeed, although the antilibertarianism of the general public has already been noted, it is equally important to realize that there are substantial and consistent differences between the general public and community leaders in attitudes toward civil liberties. McClosky and Brill (1983) found a mean difference of 12.6 percentage points between the two samples in their answers to 29 questions about support for freedom of expression. When the community-leader sample was narrowed to include only legal elites, the difference was much more striking (a mean difference of 25.6 percentage points). The strongest correlate with libertarianism is educational level (McClosky & Brill, 1983; Montero, 1975; Prothro & Grigg, 1960; Wilson, 1975; Zellman, 1975). In general, people who express support for civil liberties tend to be unusually "worldly." The modal libertarian is young, lives in a metropolitan area, works in a professional occupation, tends toward "humanism" in religious beliefs, enjoys complexity, and feels confident of his or her own ability to generate interesting ideas.

In short, as a psychological matter, civil liberties are real only to the relatively small segment of our society who experience diversity in social roles and who work in the marketplace of ideas—who in fact are entitled. In making this observation, we do not intend to imply that civil liberties should be rejected on egalitarian grounds; obviously, such a position would harm the very groups most in need of the protection of law. Nor do we wish to imply that disadvantaged groups are somehow morally inferior because they do not possess a well-developed rights consciousness. However, we do intend to make clear that, in fact, the core values of our legal system—values we acknowledge as important guarantees of respect for persons (Rawls, 1971)—have not been successfully inculcated in the American mass public. That these values have been sustained for two centuries speaks to the power of the ideas themselves or, perhaps more directly, the structures the founders developed for protection of individual liberty and privacy.

Indeed, the proverbial question of half-empty or half-full is raised. Perhaps the fact that the inherently difficult concepts embedded in the Constitution, especially the Bill of Rights, have survived speaks to the success of the law as a major force in social stasis, the preservation of societal values. On the other hand, it is clear that much more could be done to educate the public in the application of civil liberties. There is a well-developed body of theory on the principles of rights education (see Tapp & Levine, 1974; Tapp & Melton, 1983), but there has been little research to test the efficacy of these principles in the real world. Psychologists could play a valuable role in refining these principles and examining the social systems that inhibit their application.

Toward a Psychology of Jurisprudence

In the introduction to this Symposium, the naïveté and questionable utility of psychologists' emphasis on the trial process was noted. Consistent with that view, both of us have devoted much of our scholarly energy to analysis of psychological assumptions in legal doctrines. With this paper (and indeed this volume), though, we hope to turn the attention of psycholegal scholars to an area of study that is still largely novel: the role and meaning of law in everyday experience and behavior. Thus, we have made some initial suggestions on the influence of law in shaping social institutions, structuring human interaction, and inculcating the social and moral norms of the community. In essence, we are arguing for a psychology of jurisprudence that would increase our understanding of (a) the forces that shape the law and legal reasoning (see e.g., the analyses by Melton, 1984a, 1984b, and Perry & Melton, 1984, of the largely unacknowledged influence of social constructs on judicial decisions about children and families): (b) the psychological meaning of law; (c) how that meaning is acquired; and (d) the ways the law shapes the behavior of individuals, groups, and communities.

In conclusion, therefore, we wish to call the attention of psycholegal scholars to the work of Leonid Petrazhitskii (1904–1910 / 1955), a turn-of-the-century Polish-Russian legal scholar who proposed a now-neglected psychological theory of jurisprudence. Petrazhitskii's work not only is remarkable for its unusual approach, it is also notable because some of his ideas bear an uncanny resemblance to modern social-psychological theories of emotion and socialization. Indeed, he developed a theory of motivation before he presented his theory of law (see Babb, 1938). A full explication of Petrazhitskii's theory is beyond the scope of this discussion (for such an analysis, see Babb, 1937, 1938, and Langrod & Vaughan, 1970), but we do wish to point out a few of his ideas that are especially pertinent.

The unique starting point in Petrazhitskii's theory was his assumption that the reality of the law lay not in the black letters of the statutes and case law or even in social customs, but in mental processes—a consciousness of law. He conceptualized law as a complex *imperative-attributive* motivational system. In Petrazhitskii's view, law was distinguished from ethics by the addition of attributions. That is, the relevant cognitions involved not simply duties but corresponding endowments of rights. "Law, in conformity with its imperative-attributive nature, is characterized by bilateral motivational action: side by side with passive ethical motivation (the consciousness of a duty) there is active ethical motivation (the consciousness of being empowered and endowed), and the result is individual and mass conduct correspondingly coordinated" (Petrazhitskii, 1904–1910/1955, p. 121). Petrazhitskii believed that consciousness of a legal rule leads in most people to a motivational pressure to act (or to refrain from acting) in order to fulfill a duty or vindicate a right. This ethical motivation is often strengthened by *auxiliary* motivation associated with reward and punishment. The combined operation of ethical and auxiliary motivation is such that Petrazhitskii believed that it commonly results in a pattern of social behavior and organization.

In addition to the law's motivational component, Petrazhitskii also perceived a second psychological aspect of law, its educative function:

> The very acts evoked by the law in countless numbers do not pass out of the picture without leaving a trace in the character of those who perform them. The repetition of certain acts develops corresponding habits—positive habits of doing, and negative habits of abstaining—which in turn influence the development of character, instilling certain traits and weakening others. Moreover, as it performs its complicated psychic symphony on different strings of the human soul—forcing

some impulsive propensities to operate and exercising them, while refusing to admit others or stifling their action (as brutal, malicious, or in general anti-social)—the law leads inevitably to the development and strengthening of some propensities and to the weakening and destruction of others. Rational law represents a complex and mighty school which aims at socializing the national character and adjusting it to rational coexistence. Unsuccessful law may spread demoralization and poison the national spirit—or at least counteract the healthy psychic process and retard the development and flowering of the valuable elements of individual and mass character. (Petrazhitskii, 1904–1910/1955, p. 301)

In this educative process, there is a continual interplay between intuitive and positive law. Motivation becomes expressed in custom and eventually finds its way into positive law and the accompanying system of rewards and punishments. On the other hand, as suggested above, positive law ultimately becomes internalized:

As human character grows better, less and less motivational pressure of the punitive-remunerative class is required in order to attain socially rational conduct. Punishments and rewards are lessened, and the collective responsibility of the whole group for violations–the intensifying motivational pressure—is replaced by individual responsibility. (Petrazhitskii, 1904–1910/1955, pp. 328–329)

Indicative of this general principle are Petrazhitskii's ideas about legal socialization:

If in the home the attitude to the child is that everything is permitted to the child with regard to others, and the child's demands of every kind are carried out unquestioningly, the result is an anomalous legal mind which may be characterized as a hypertrophy of the active legal mentality: the subject becomes possessed of a propensity to ascribe to himself with reference to others innumerable unreasoning and inordinate legal powers and legal claims, while at the same time acknowledging no rights in behalf of others. The abnormally developed legal mind elevates the child into a sort of being privileged among mortals. If, on the contrary, the child is neglected as regards the law—if no rights of any kind (not even the most modest) are acknowledged in his behalf and no active law sphere of any sort is assigned to him—the reverse psychic anomaly then ensues: underdevelopment of the active law mentality. (Petrazhitskii, 1904–1910/1955, p. 71)

The Law as an Instrument of Socialization and Social Structure

One may quarrel that Petrazhitskii's view of the law is overinclusive and perhaps insufficiently attentive to the special aspects of legal reasoning, and some aspects of his psychology are difficult to operationalize. However, the theory's focus on the *experience* of law—whether in the mind of a jurist or of a lay citizen—makes it worthy of attention. As Petrazhitskii (1904–1910/1955) pointed out, *"The number of everyday cases and problems of conduct contemplated and determined by official regulation, as compared with the immense quantity thereof anticipated by law . . . is infinitesimal"* (p. 71; emphasis in the original). If a rights consciousness is to develop more pervasively, there is a need for what Tapp and Levine (1974) call *legal continuity*, a recognition of the multitude of everyday experiences in which legal principles are applicable. More careful attention needs to be given to the circumstances that evoke (or perhaps should evoke, but do not) a consciousness of law. We need to begin to try to understand how people experience legal obligations, protections, and entitlements. Psycholegal studies should consider the subjective meaning of law as well as its instrumentality (see Melton, this volume).

Although the visions of the open society vary among the political theorists who are identified with the concept (e.g., Bergson, 1935; Germino, 1982; Germino & von Beyme, 1974; Popper, 1950; Voegelin, 1974), they have in common an emphasis on openness to new experiences and tolerance of diverse ideas. Psycholegal scholars have an opportunity to contribute to an understanding of both the social structures and the socialization practices that are likely to promote a jurisprudence consistent with such a concept of social good.

REFERENCES

Ackerman, B. A. (1984). *Reconstructing American law.* Cambridge, MA: Harvard University Press.

Allport, F. H., et al. (1953). The effects of segregation and the consequences of desegregation: A social science statement. *Minnesota Law Review, 37,* 429–440.

Andenaes, J. (1966). The general preventive effects of punishment. *University of Pennsylvania Law Review, 114,* 949–983.

Andenaes, J. (1975). General prevention revisited: Research and policy implications. *Journal of Criminal Law, Criminology and Police Science, 66,* 338–365.

Andenaes, J. (1977). The moral or educative influence of criminal law. In J. L. Tapp & F. J. Levine (Eds.), *Law, justice, and the individual in society: Psychological and legal issues* (pp. 50–59). New York: Holt, Rinehart & Winston.

Asch, S. (1952). *Social psychology,* New York: Prentice-Hall.

Ashford, R. H. (1984, September). *Evaluating the potential use of a consumer stock ownership plan for financing the capital requirements of public utilities.* Paper presented to the Fourth NARUC Biennial Regulatory Information Conference, Ohio State University.

Associated Press. (1984, December 1). 1 in 5 admit cheating on taxes. *Lincoln Star,* p. 2.

Babb, H. W. (1937). Petrazhitskii: Science of legal policy and theory of law. *Boston University Law Review, 17,* 793–829.

Babb, H. W. (1938). Petrazhitskii: Theory of law. *Boston University Law Review, 18,* 511–575.

Baron, C. H. (1983). Licensure of health care professionals: The consumer's case for abolition. *American Journal of Law and Medicine, 9,* 335–356.

Bergson, H. (1935). *The two sources of morality and religion* (R. Andra & C. Brereton, Trans.). New York: Henry Holt.

Berman, H. J. (1963). *Justice in the U.S.S.R.: An interpretation of Soviet law* (revised ed.). Cambridge, MA: Harvard University Press.

Berman, H. J. (1977). The use of law to guide people to virtue: A comparison of Soviet and U.S. perspectives. In J. L. Tapp & F. J. Levine (Eds.), *Law, justice, and the individual in society: Psychological and legal issues* (pp. 75–84). New York: Holt, Rinehart & Winston.

Berman, H. J., & Quigley, J. B., Jr. (Trans. & Eds.). (1969). *Basic laws on the structure of the Soviet state.* Cambridge, MA: Harvard University Press.

Board of Education, Island Trees Union School District No. 26 v. Pico, 457 U.S. 853 (1982).

Bok, D. C. (1983). A flawed system of law practice and training. *Journal of Legal Education, 33,* 570–585.

Brehm, J. W. (1966). *A theory of psychological reactance.* New York: Academic Press.

Brown v. Board of Education, 374 U.S. 483 (1954).

Bunker, J. P., & Mostetler, F. (1977). *Costs, risks, and benefits of surgery.* New York: Oxford University Press.

Burke, J. (1978). *Connections.* Boston: Little, Brown.

Calabresi, G. (1970). *The costs of accidents: A legal and economic analysis.* New Haven: Yale University Press.

Campbell, D. T., & Ross, H. L. (1968). The Connecticut crackdown on speeding: Time-series data in quasi-experimental analysis. *Law & Society Review, 3,* 33–53.

Cardozo, B. N. (1921). *The nature of the judicial process.* New Haven: Yale University Press.

Carroll, S. L., & Gaston, R. J. (1981): Occupational restrictions and the quality of service received: some evidence. *Southern Economic Journal, 47,* 959–976.

Cochrane, A. L. (1972). *Effectiveness and efficiency.* London: Nuffield Provincial Hospital Trust.

Cohen, J. A., Edwards, R. R., & Chang Chen, F. (Eds.). (1980). *Essays on China's legal tradition.* Princeton, NJ: Princeton University Press.

Coles, R. (1977). *Privileged ones (Children in crisis,* vol. 5). Boston: Little, Brown.

Collins, H. (1982). *Marxism and law.* New York: Oxford University Press.

Cook, S. W. (1984). The 1954 social science statement and school desegregation: A reply to Gerard. *American Psychologist, 39,* 819–832.

Creel, H. G. (1980). Legal institutions and procedures during the Chou dynasty. In J. A. Cohen, R. R. Edwards, & F. Chang Chen (Eds.), *Essays on China's legal tradition* (pp. 26–55). Princeton, NJ: Princeton University Press.

Daniel, W. J. (1942). Cooperative problem solving in rats. *Journal of Comparative and Physiological Psychology, 34,* 361–368.

Delaney v. Errickson, 10 Neb. 492, 6 N.W. 600, 35 Am. Rep. 487 (1880).

Ely, J. H. (1980). *Democracy and distrust: A theory of judicial review,* Cambridge, MA: Harvard University Press.

Erskine, H., & Siegel, R. L. (1975). Civil liberties and the American public. *Journal of Social Issues, 31*(2), 13–29.

Etzioni, A., & Remp, R. (1972). Technological "shortcuts" to social change. *Science, 175,* 31–38.

Friedman, M. (1962). *Capitalism and freedom.* Chicago: University of Chicago Press.

Fuller, L. L. (1968). *Anatomy of the law.* New York: Praeger.

Fuller, L. L. (1977). Some presuppositions shaping the concept of "socialization." In J. L. Tapp & F. J. Levine (Eds.), *Law, justice, and the individual in society: Psychological and legal issues* (pp. 33–40). New York: Holt, Rinehart & Winston.

Geertz, C. (1980). *Negara: The theatre state in nineteenth-century Bali.* Princeton, NJ: Princeton University Press.

Geller, E. S., Koltuniak, T. A., & Shilling, J. S. (1983). Response avoidance prompting: A cost-effective strategy for theft deterrence. *Behavioral Counseling and Community Interventions, 3*(1), 28–42.

Gerard, H. B. (1983). School desegregation: The social science role. *American Psychologist, 38,* 869–877.

Germino, D. (1982). *Political philosophy and the open society.* Baton Rouge: Louisiana State University Press.

Germino, D., & von Beyme, K. (Eds.). (1974). *The open society in theory and practice.* The Hague: Martinus Nijhoff.

Guilbeau v. Saint Paul Fire and Marine Insurance Company, 325 So.2d 395 (La. 1975).

Harris, M. (1974). *Cows, pigs, wars, and witches.* New York: Random House.

Harris, M. (1979). *Cultural materialism: The struggle for a science of culture.* New York: Random House.

Hart, H. L. A. (1961). *The concept of law.* Oxford: Oxford University Press.

Hart, R. J. (1978). Crime and punishment in the army. *Journal of Personality Psychology, 36,* 1456–1471.

Hildebrand, J. L. (1972). *The sociology of Soviet law.* Buffalo: William S. Hein.

Hoffman, M. L. (1976). Empathy, role-taking, guilt, and development of altruistic motives. In T. Lickona (Ed.), *Moral development and behavior: Theory, research, and social issues* (pp. 124–143). New York: Holt, Rinehart & Winston.

Hogan, D. (1983). The effectiveness of licensing: History, evidence and recommendations. *Law & Human Behavior, 7,* 117–138.

Holmes, O. W. (1897). The path of the law. *Harvard Law Review, 10,* 457–478.

Kelso, L. O., & Hetter, P. (1968). *Two-factor theory: The economics of reality.* Westport, CT: Greenfield Press.

Kim, H. I. (1981). *Fundamental legal concepts of China and the West.* Port Washington, NY: Kennikat Press.

Kohlberg, L. (1976). Moral stages and moralization: The cognitive-developmental approach. In T. Lickona (Ed.), *Moral development and behavior: Theory, research, and social issues* (pp. 31–53). New York: Holt, Rinehart, & Winston.

Krasner, L., & Ullmann, L. P. (1973). *Behavior, influence, and personality: The social matrix of human action.* New York: Holt, Rinehart & Winston.

Kronman, A., & Posner, R. (1979). *The economics of contract law.* Boston: Little, Brown.

Langrod, G. S., & Vaughan, M. (1970). The Polish psychological theory of law. In W. J. Wagner (Ed.), *Polish law throughout the ages* (pp. 299–362). Stanford, CA: Hoover Institution Press.

Llewellyn, K. (1931). Some realism about realism. *Harvard Law Review, 44,* 1222–1264.

McCloskey, H., & Brill, A. (1983). *Dimensions of tolerance: What Americans believe about civil liberties.* New York: Russell Sage Foundation.

McNees, M. P., Egli, D. S., Marshall, R. S., Schnelle, J. F., & Risley, T. R. (1976). Shoplifting prevention: Providing information through signs. *Journal of Applied Behavior Analysis, 9,* 399–405.

McNees, M. P., Kennon, M., Schnelle, J. F., Kirchner, R. E., & Thomas, M.

M. (1980). An experimental analysis of a program to reduce retail theft. *American Journal of Community Psychology, 8,* 379–385.

Mecham, G. D. (1968). Proceed with caution: Which penalties slow down the juvenile traffic offender? *Crime and Delinquency, 14,* 142–150.

Melton, G. B. (1980). Children's concepts of their rights. *Journal of Clinical Child Psychology, 9,* 186–190.

Melton, G. B. (1981). Effects of a state law permitting minors to consent to psychotherapy. *Professional Psychology, 12,* 647–654.

Melton, G. B. (1983a). Community psychology and rural legal systems. In A. W. Childs & G. B. Melton (Eds.), *Rural psychology* (pp. 359–380). New York: Plenum.

Melton, G. B. (1983b). Toward "personhood" for adolescents: Autonomy and privacy as values in public policy. *American Psychologist, 38,* 99–103.

Melton, G. B. (1984a). Developmental psychology and the law: The state of the art. *Journal of Family Law, 22,* 445–482.

Melton, G. B. (1984b). Family and mental hospital as myths: Civil commitment of minors. In N. D. Reppucci, L. A. Weithorn, E. P. Mulvey, & J. Monahan (Eds.), *Children, mental health, and the law* (pp. 151–167). Beverly Hills, CA: Sage.

Milgram, S. (1974). *Obedience to authority.* New York: Harper & Row.

Montero, D. (1975). Support for civil liberties among a cohort of high school graduates and college students. *Journal of Social Issues, 31*(2), 123–136.

Moser, M. J. (1982). *Law and social change in a Chinese community: A case study from rural Taiwan.* Dobbs Ferry, NY: Oceana.

Nagel, S. S., & Neef, M. G. (1977). *Legal policy analysis.* Lexington, MA: Lexington Books.

Neb. Rev. Stat. § 79–213. (Reissue 1981). (Last amended 1971).

Needham, R. A. (Ed.). (1971). *Tax aspects of charitable giving and receiving.* New York: Practicing Law Institute.

Note. (1973). Legal knowledge of Michigan citizens. *Michigan Law Review, 71,* 1463–1466.

Peachey, D. E., & Lerner, M. J. (1981). Law as a social trap: Problems and possibilities for the future. In M. J. Lerner & S. C. Lerner (Eds.), *The justice motive in human behavior: Adapting to times of scarcity and change* (pp. 439–461). New York: Plenum.

Perry, G. S., & Melton, G. B. (1984). Precedential value of judicial notice of social facts: *Parham* as an example. *Journal of Family Law, 22,* 663–676.

Petrazhitskii, L. J. (1955). *Law and morality* (H. W. Babb, Trans.). Cambridge, MA: Harvard University Press. (Original work published 1904–1910)

Piaget, J. (1965). *The moral judgment of the child.* New York: Free Press. (Original work published 1932)

Platt, J. (1973). Social traps. *American Psychologist, 28,* 641–651.

Popper, K. R. (1950). *The open society and its enemies.* London: Routledge & Kegan Paul.

Pospisil, L. (1971). *Anthropology of law: A comparative theory.* New York: Harper & Row.

Pound, R. (1926). *Law and morals* (2nd ed.). Chapel Hill: University of North Carolina Press.

Pound, R. (1959). *Jurisprudence* (Vol. 2). Saint Paul, MN: West.

Prothro, T. W., & Grigg, C. W. (1960). Fundamental principles of democracy: Bases of agreement and disagreement. *Journal of Politics, 22,* 276–294.

Rawls, J. (1971). *A theory of justice.* Cambridge, MA: Harvard University Press.

Rembar, C. (1980). *The law of the land.* New York: Simon & Schuster.

Ross, H. L. (1973). Law, science, and accidents: The British Road Safety Act of 1967. *Journal of Legal Studies, 2,* 1–78.

Ross, H. L. (1982). *Deterring the drinking driver: Legal policy and social control.* Lexington, MA: Lexington Books.

Rossell, C. H. (1978). School desegregation and community social change. *Law and Contemporary Problems, 42,* 133–183.

Saks, M. J. (1977). *Jury verdicts.* Lexington, MA: Lexington Books.

Saks, M. J., & Miller, M. L. (1979). A systems approach to discretion in the legal process. In L. E. Abt & I. R. Stuart (Eds.), *Social psychology and discretionary law.* New York: Van Nostrand Reinhold.

Saltzstein, H. D. (1976). Social influence and moral development: A perspective on the role of parents and peers. In T. Lickona (Ed.), *Moral development and behavior: Theory, research, and social issues* (pp. 253–265). New York: Holt, Rinehart & Winston.

Schwartz, R. D., & Orleans, S. (1967). On legal sanctions. *University of Chicago Law Review, 34,* 274–300.

Skinner, B. F. (1953). *Science and human behavior.* New York: Macmillan.

Sparger v. Worley Hospital, Inc., 547 S.W.2d 582 (Tax. 1977).

Stephan, W. G. (1978). School desegregation: An evaluation of predictions made in *Brown v. Board of Education. Psychological Bulletin, 85,* 217–238.

Stouffer, S. (1955). *Communism, conformity, and civil liberties.* New York: Doubleday.

Tapp, J. L., & Kohlberg, L. (1977). Developing senses of law and legal justice. In J. L. Tapp & F. J. Levine (Eds.), *Law, justice, and the individual in society* (pp. 89–105). New York: Holt, Rinehart & Winston.

Tapp, J. L., & Levine, F. L. (1974). Legal socialization: Strategies for an ethical legality. *Stanford Law Review, 27,* 1–72.

Tapp, J. L., & Melton, G. B. (1983). Preparing children for decision making: Implications of legal socialization research. In G. B. Melton, G. P.

Koocher, & M. J. Saks (Eds.), *Children's competence to consent* (pp. 215–233). New York: Plenum.

Tax Institute of America. (1972). *Tax impacts on philanthropy*. Princeton, NJ: Tax Institute of America.

Tinker v. Des Moines Independent School District, 393 U.S. 503 (1969).

Tittle, C. R., & Rowe, A. R. (1973). Moral appeal, sanction, threat, and deviance: An experimental test. *Social problems, 20,* 488–498.

Tversky, A., & Kahneman, D. (1973). Availability: A heuristic for judging frequency and probability. *Cognitive Psychology, 5,* 207–232.

Voegelin, E. (1974). *The ecumenic age.* Baton Rouge: Louisiana State University Press.

Walker, N., & Argyle, M. (1964). Does the law affect moral judgments? *British Journal of Criminology, 4,* 570–581.

Wasby, S. L. (1976). *Small town police and the Supreme Court: Hearing the word.* Lexington, MA: Lexington Books.

Webb, X. (1931). *The Great Plains.* Boston: Ginn.

Weber, M. (1954). *Law in economy and society* (M. Rheinstein, Ed.; E. Shils & M. Rheinstein, Trans.). Cambridge, MA: Harvard University Press. (Original work published 1925)

Williams, M., & Hall, J. (1972). Knowledge of the law in Texas: Socioeconomic and ethnic differences. *Law and Society Review, 7,* 99–118.

Wilson, W. C. (1975). Belief in freedom of speech and press. *Journal of Social Issues, 31*(2), 69–76.

Zeisel, H. (1971). . . . And then there were none: The diminution of the federal jury. *University of Chicago Law Review, 41,* 281–295.

Zellman, G. L. (1975). Antidemocratic beliefs: A survey and some explanations. *Journal of Social Issues, 31*(2), 31–54.

Zimring, F., & Hawkins, G. (1977). The legal threat as an instrument of social change. In J. L. Tapp & F. J. Levine (Eds.), *Law, justice, and the individual in society: Psychological and legal issues* (pp. 60–68). New York: Holt, Rinehart & Winston.

Subject Index

Author Index